SPEAK · TRUTH · TO · POWER

COMMANDER
STEVEN HAINES
ROYAL NAVY

THE DEVELOPMENT OF BRITISH
DEFENCE POLICY

To my Auntie Margaret – A force of nature that is sadly missed in our family

The Development of British Defence Policy
Blair, Brown and Beyond

Edited by

DAVID BROWN
Royal Military Academy Sandhurst, UK

ASHGATE

Published by
Ashgate Publishing Limited
Wey Court East
Union Road
Farnham
Surrey, GU9 7PT
England

Ashgate Publishing Company
Suite 420
101 Cherry Street
Burlington
VT 05401-4405
USA

www.ashgate.com

British Library Cataloguing in Publication Data
The development of British defence policy : Blair, Brown
   and beyond.
   1. Great Britain--Military policy. 2. Great Britain--
   Foreign relations--1997- 3. National security--Great
   Britain. 4. Great Britain--Politics and government--
   1997-2007. 5. Great Britain--Politics and government--
   2007- 6. Labour Party (Great Britain)
   I. Brown, David.
   355'.033'041-dc22

Library of Congress Cataloging-in-Publication Data
Brown, David, 1974-
   The development of British defence policy : Blair, Brown, and beyond / by David Brown.
      p. cm.
   Includes bibliographical references and index.
   ISBN 978-0-7546-7489-4 (hbk) -- ISBN 978-1-4094-0849-9 (ebk)
   1. Great Britain--Military policy. 2. National security--Great Britain. 3. September 11 Ter-
rorist Attacks, 2001--Influence. 4. Blair, Tony, 1953- 5. Brown, Gordon, 1951- I. Title.
   UA647.B859 2010
   355'.033541--dc22

                                                                                    2010008470

ISBN 9780754674894 (hbk)
ISBN 9781409408499 (ebk)

Printed and bound in Great Britain by
TJ International Ltd, Padstow, Cornwall

Contents

List of Tables

List of Contributors

David Brown is a Senior Lecturer in Defence and International Affairs at the Royal Military Academy Sandhurst. His main research interests are in terrorism and counter-terrorist responses, EU internal security matters and US and UK foreign and security policy. His first monograph *The EU's Counter-Terrorism Strategy 1991–2007: Unsteady Foundations?* was published in 2010. In addition, he has written a number of articles and book chapters on such matters, including in *European Security* and *Contemporary Security Policy*, as well as co-editing *The Security Implications of EU Enlargement: Wider Europe, Weaker Europe?* (2007) and *The New World Order? Multipolarity in the Twenty-First Century* (2011).

Michael Codner is the Director of the Military Sciences Department at the Royal United Services Institute for Defence and Security Studies (RUSI). He researches and directs research across a range of subjects, including defence policy, strategic theory, military ethics and military acquisition policy and practice. He has written extensively on British defence policy and defence issues more widely. He was previously a Seaman Officer in the Royal Navy. His degrees are in philosophy and experimental psychology.

Stephen Deakin is a Senior Lecturer at the Royal Military Academy Sandhurst, having worked both for the Department of Defence and International Affairs and Communications and Applied Behavioural Sciences. His research interests include British Defence Policy and military ethics. He has published a number of book chapters on such subjects, with a particular focus on the teaching of ethics to military personnel, in publications such as *Ethics Education in the Military* (2008) and *Ethics Education for Irregular Warfare* (2009).

Anthony Forster is Honorary Professor of Politics in the School of Government and International Affairs, Durham University, as well as Pro Vice Chancellor (Learning and Teaching). He has written widely on defence and foreign policy issues, notably the European Union's Common Foreign and Security Policy, British defence and foreign policy, the impact of Euro-scepticism on British policy-making and civil military relations across Europe and, more specifically, the politics of the British armed forces. His publications include 'Breaking the Covenant: Governance of the British Army in the Twenty-first Century', *International Affairs* (2006) and *Out of Step: The Case for Change in British Armed Forces* (2007), co-written with Tim Edmunds.

Stuart Gordon is a Senior Lecturer in the Department of Defence and International Affairs at the Royal Military Academy Sandhurst. He co-authored the UK government's Helmand Road Map and was also the lead researcher of the Helmand Quick Impact Project Programme Evaluation. He is part of a research network, based in Tuft's University's Feinstein Centre, that explores the use of development assistance in conflict environments. He specialises in the politics of conflict and has written widely on various aspects of strategic studies – principally military strategy, UN peacekeeping and the securitisation of development assistance. During 2003, he was the Operations Director for the US/UK's Iraq Humanitarian Operations Centre in Baghdad with responsibility for restoring Iraq's public food distribution system.

Steven Haines is Head of the Security and Rule of Law Programme at the Geneva Centre for Security Policy, having formerly been Professor of Strategy and the Law of Military Operations within the University of London. He was on the Naval Staff in the Ministry of Defence in Whitehall during the Strategic Defence Review and was the naval member of the post-SDR Strategic Development Study, which led to the establishment of what is now the MoD's Development, Concepts and Doctrine Centre at Shrivenham. While an MoD staff officer he wrote Britain's military strategic doctrine, *British Defence Doctrine*, published in 2001. He has also written widely on an array of international security issues, particularly in the area of international law and the use of force.

Trevor C Salmon was both Professor of International Relations and Director of Teaching and Learning in the Department of Politics and International Relations at the University of Aberdeen, retiring in the summer of 2010. He previously worked at both St. Andrews and Limerick Universities. He has published several books on the European Community/Union, including a co-authored volume, with Alistair JK Shepherd, *Toward a European Army: A Military Power in the Making?* (2003), a major book on the foreign and security policy of the Irish Republic, *Unneutral Ireland*, and a number of articles on developments in Ireland, both North and South, as well as on wider European security matters.

Alistair JK Shepherd is a Lecturer in Contemporary European Security in the Department of International Politics, Aberystwyth University. His research interests are in the field of security studies, especially European internal and external security, the development of ESDP, NATO and Transatlantic relations and Europe's role in conflict management. His publications include: '"A milestone in the history of the EU" – Kosovo and the EU's International Role', *International Affairs* (May 2009); a co-edited volume, with David Brown, *The Security Dimensions of EU Enlargement: Wider Europe, Weaker Europe?* (2007); 'Irrelevant or Indispensable? ESDP, the "War on Terror" and the Fallout from Iraq' in *International Politics* (2006) and a co-authored volume, with Trevor C Salmon, *Toward a European Army: A Military Power in the Making?* (2003).

Martin A Smith is a Senior Lecturer in Defence and International Affairs at the Royal Military Academy Sandhurst. His main research interests are in the fields of international and European security. He is the author/editor of eight books including: (co-authored with Graham Timmins), *Building a Bigger Europe: EU and NATO Enlargement in Comparative Perspective* (2000); (co-authored with Paul Latawski), *The Kosovo Crisis and the Evolution of Post-Cold War European Security* (2003) and the single-authored *Russia and NATO Since 1991: From Cold War through Cold Peace to Partnership?* (2006). His articles have appeared *inter alia*, in *International Peacekeeping*, *European Security*, *West European Politics*, *The Journal of Strategic Studies* and *Contemporary Security Policy*.

James Sperling is a Professor of Political Science at the University of Akron. His research interests are in the wider field of security governance, both at the international, transatlantic, European and individual state levels. He has written extensively on all of these issues, most recently as co-author of *EU Security Governance* (2007), and co-editor of *Global Security Governance* (2007), *European Security Governance* (2009) and *National Security Cultures: Patterns of Global Governance* (2010). His articles have appeared *inter alia*, in *International Affairs*, *International Organisation* (with Emil J Kirchner and Hans Dorussen), *European Security* and *Contemporary Security Policy*.

Acknowledgements

Thanks go particularly to Martin Smith for his help, both in terms of critical comment but also motivational support. My thanks also to all the contributors to this volume, for both the quality and timeliness of their analysis, and to Kirstin and her team at Ashgate, particularly Adam, for their patience and consideration.

List of Abbreviations

ANA	Afghan National Army
ARRC	Allied Rapid Reaction Corps
BBC	British Broadcasting Corporation
C4ISTAR	Command, Control, Communications, Computers, Intelligence and Surveillance, Target Acquisition and Reconnaissance
CBRN	Chemical, Biological, Radiological and Nuclear
CCRF	Civil Contingency Reaction Force
CDS	Chief of Defence Staff
CGS	Chief of the General Staff
CIRA	Continuity Irish Republican Army
COPS	Political and Security Committee
COTS	Commercial Off the Shelf
CSI	Competitive Strategies Initiative
CSR	Comprehensive Spending Review
DCMO	Defence Crisis Management Organisation
DFI	Direct Foreign Investment
DFID	Department for International Development
DIME	Diplomatic, Informational, Military and Economic
DIS	Defence Industrial Strategy
DLO	Defence Logistics Organisation
DoD	Department of Defense
DRC	Democratic Republic of the Congo
DSP	Director of Service Prosecutions
DUP	Democratic Unionist Party
EBA	Effects Based Approach
EBO	Effects Based Operations
EC	European Community
ECHR	European Court of Human Rights
ECJ	European Court of Justice
EDA	European Defence Agency
EEC	European Economic Community
EHRC	Equality and Human Rights Commission
ELN	National Liberation Army

EMU	Economic and Monetary Union
ERRF	European Rapid Reaction Force
ESDI	European Security and Defence Identity
ESDP	European Security and Defence Policy
ESS	European Security Strategy
ETA	Euskadi Ta Askatasuna
EU	European Union
EUMS	European Union Military Staff
FARC	Revolutionary Armed Forces of Columbia
FAS	Future Army Structures
FCO	Foreign and Commonwealth Office
FCS	Future Combat System
FDI	Foreign Direct Investment
FI	Formal Investigation
FRES	Future Rapid Effects Systems
FYROM	Former Yugoslav Republic of Macedonia
GCPP	Global Conflict Prevention Pools
GDP	Gross Domestic Product
GFA	Good Friday Agreement
GIA	Groupe Armee Islamique
GOC	General Officer Commanding
HHG	Helsinki Headline Goals
HR	High Representative
ICC	International Criminal Court
IDA	International Development Act
IED	Improvised Explosive Devices
IFF	Identification Friend or Foe
IICD	Independent International Commission on Decommissioning
IMC	Independent Monitoring Commission
INLA	Irish National Liberation Army
IPPR	Institute for Public Policy Research
ISAF	International Security Assistance Force
ISD	In Service Date
ISI	Inter Services Intelligence
JASP	Joint Approach on Social Policy
JIT	Just In Time
JRRF	Joint Rapid Reaction Force
JSF	Joint Strike Fighters
JTAC	Joint Terrorism Analysis Centre

LGB   Lesbian, Gay, Bisexual

MoD   Ministry of Defence

NAFTA   North Atlantic Free Trade Area
NATO   North Atlantic Treaty Organisation
NCC   Network Centric Capability
NCW   Network Centric Warfare
NEC   Network Enabled Capability
NHS   National Health Service
NPT   Non Proliferation Treaty
NSS   National Security Strategy

OAF   Operation Allied Force
ODA   Overseas Development Administration
OECD   Organisation for Economic Co-operation and Development
OECD-DAC   Organisation for Economic Co-operation and Development,
               Development Assistance Committee
OHQ   Operational Headquarters
OSCE   Organisation for Security and Cooperation in Europe

PCRU   Post Conflict Reconstruction Unit
PFI   Private Finance Initiatives
PIRA   Provisional Irish Republican Army
PoW   Prisoner of War
PRT   Provincial Reconstruction Team
PSA   Public Service Agreements

R2P   Responsibility to Protect
RAF   Royal Air Force
RHC   Red Hand Commando
RIRA   Real Irish Republican Army
RMA   Revolution in Military Affairs
RMP   Royal Military Police
RUSI   Royal United Services Institute

SDLP   Social and Democratic Labour Party
SDR   Strategic Defence Review
SHAPE   Supreme Headquarters Allied Powers Europe
SSR   Security Sector Reform
SU   Stabilisation Unit

UK   United Kingdom
UN   United Nations

UNPROFOR	United Nations Protection Force
UOR	Urgent Operational Requirements
US	United States
UUP	Ulster Unionist Party
UVF	Ulster Volunteer Force
WEU	Western European Union
WMD	Weapons of Mass Destruction

Chapter 1

Introduction: New Labour and Defence

David Brown[1]

A new dawn has broken, has it not? (Blair, 1997)

As if to suggest not only their mastery of the political environment, but also the environment more generally, the sun broke over the Royal Festival Hall in a moment of characteristic choreography, heralding the return to government for the Labour Party for the first time in 18 years. New Labour, boosted by a political landslide in the 1997 General Election that left them with a majority of 179, seemed like a breath of fresh air, sweeping out a tired, demoralised and discredited Conservative Party that would be left licking their political wounds for the next 13 years. While armed with a well-publicised pledge card, which focused exclusively on domestic issues, such as a commitment to cut class sizes to 30 or under for the years five to seven, New Labour seemed somewhat unprepared for the specific strains of government. This was unsurprising, given that only Margaret Beckett, of the initial Labour government of 1997, had any real prior experience of government, having served in a series of junior ministerial roles for both Harold Wilson and James Callaghan; it should be borne in mind that the only governmental position Tony Blair has ever held was that of Prime Minister. Such inexperience was particularly notable in the field of defence and foreign affairs, with Kampfner pointing out that Blair had only made one serious exposition of his views on international affairs prior to entering government (Kampfner, 2004 3–5). As such, much of the early deliberations regarding foreign policy more widely was made by New Labour's first Foreign Secretary, Robin Cook, with its emphasis on morality and human rights at the centre of New Labour's international image (Wheeler and Dunne, 2004; Williams, 2002).

Cook was also to be a central figure in the development of New Labour's first – and, to date – only formal defence review, the 1998 Strategic Defence Review (SDR). Having been scarred by the experience of dealing with defence matters, notably the future of Britain's independent nuclear deterrent, during a succession of general elections in the 1980s, tactically the Labour Party sought to keep the electorate's attention on matters domestic, whether it be the protection of the

---

1 The views contained within this chapter reflect solely those of the author, and are not representative of the views of the Royal Military Academy Sandhurst, the British Army, the Ministry of Defence or the British government more widely.

National Health Service (NHS), being 'tough on crime and tough on the causes of crime' (Labour Party, 1997) or bringing an end to the 'boom and bust' years of Conservative government (Gordon Brown cited in Swaine, 2009). Questions regarding the management of Britain's defence were postponed to a future defence review, to be held once the Labour Party were safely in government; in this they were helped by the continuing internecine warfare over Europe that succeeded in highlighting the weaknesses of the Major administration and the adverse reaction to a series of Conservative defence reviews, notably 'Options for Change' and 'Frontline First', during the 1990s, which effectively robbed the Conservatives of one of their previously held ace cards.

The SDR was portrayed as a reaction against the perceived limitations of the Treasury led approach redolent of the preceding defence reviews, which had been primarily internal Whitehall affairs, predicated on taking advantage of the changed security environment of the perceived 'peace dividend' following the collapse of the Cold War. In its place, it was claimed, would be a more strategic approach to defence policy, based on a more explicitly stated foreign policy baseline, from which the projection of military force could be derived, subject to proposed limitations via the SDR's stated 'scales of effort' (Ministry of Defence, 1998). This expeditionary approach to the use of military force would be used both to advance the United Kingdom's (UK) strategic goals, as well as wider humanitarian concerns, as part of the newly declared 'ethical dimension' to foreign policy (Cook, 1997). Given that the SDR was based on the assumption that the UK was effectively safe from conventional attack for the duration of the review's framework, such an approach seemed, on the face of it, to make strategic and practical sense – 'we must prevent our enemies from tying up our forces in defence of the home base – otherwise they have won' (Hoon, 2001). In addition, as part of a concept that would become ever more prominent as the years progressed, the projection of force would serve as one tool within a wider, more 'comprehensive' approach to international affairs, alongside both the Foreign and Commonwealth Office (FCO) and the newly created Department for International Development (DFID). Robin Cook and Defence Secretary George, now Lord, Robertson were to be in the driving seat in terms of determining the contours of the review, aided by a wider process of consultation, both of noted experts from the fields of journalism, academia, business and the military, and of the wider public (Ministry of Defence, 1998a; McInnes, 1998).

In 2009, under a different Prime Minister – Gordon Brown having finally achieved his ambition to move permanently into Number 10 Downing Street in June 2007 – the government committed itself to a second Strategic Defence Review, to be completed whichever party is successful in the 2010 General Election. At the time of writing, the Labour government, under its sixth Defence Secretary, Bob Ainsworth, has already committed to outlining its initial assumptions regarding the future of defence policy in a Green Paper, to be in place prior to the election. Both of the other main political parties are also committed to holding a formal review immediately after the election, should they take power, and all are committed to ensuring that such reviews will, henceforth, take place on a more regular, scheduled basis, whether it be on a four to five year review process or in the immediate aftermath of a General Election (Interview, 2009). Yet, the political atmosphere – and, equally importantly, the economic environment – is significantly different to when its predecessor was promulgated. Malcolm Chalmers, in one of the first comprehensive assessments of the impact of the economic crisis on defence spending, has highlighted the possibility of between 10–15 per cent cuts in real terms in the existing defence budget – predicted to be £36.89bn by 2011 – between 2010–2016 (Chalmers, 2009, 1). Such figures are predicated on a number of unknown variables, such as the level of political protection offered to other government departments (both Labour and the Conservatives are committed to protecting the health budget, while the latter has also ring-fenced DFID's budgetary totals), the speed at which the total national debt interest can be serviced and the debt levels repaid and reduced and the longer term projected figures for UK economic growth (with its impact on the level of spending allocated to tackling unemployment and wider welfare concerns).

In addition, while the Labour Party was able to effectively silence defence as an electoral issue in 1997, there seems little chance of that happening again, with defence once again a central political issue in the run up to the 2010 General Election, featuring heavily in press coverage and popular debate. Propelled onto the front pages of Britain's national newspapers by a tragic torrent of bad news stories and accusations of mishandling, both of the allocation and management of defence spending, defence has once again regained its place as one of the premier political issues of the age. This has been particularly prevalent during Gordon Brown's premiership, where it has been intimated that decisions taken during his decade as Chancellor of the Exchequer have effectively come back to haunt him as Prime Minister (Cornish and Dorman, 2009a). Having finally – by the end of April 2009 – escaped from the shadow of the controversial deployment of UK troops to Iraq to concentrate more fully on the so-called 'good' war in Afghanistan, Brown has, at times, seemed almost helpless, despite his best efforts (Brown, 2009b–d), to stem the rising tide of concern regarding the overall purpose and likely outcome of the UK's military intervention. A toxic combination of allegations of Afghan corruption, notably in the 2009 election, the seemingly slow-time search for a suitable strategic vision for Afghanistan in the US (carried out in public thanks to a series of well-publicised leaks) and the tragic roll-call of British deaths and life-changing injuries in Afghanistan (at the time of writing, Britain had suffered 289 deaths (BBC, 2010)) has sapped further the British public's confidence in the military intervention.

Without the 'cover' of the Iraqi campaign to divert attention – although the political fallout from the 2003 intervention in Iraq may not yet be at an end, given that the Chilcot Inquiry only began its deliberations in the latter half of 2009 – scepticism over the UK's efforts in Afghanistan has continued to grow. This has been evident in an array of opinion polls questioning the necessity of continued UK involvement – with one conducted in mid-November 2009 noting a substantive 71 per cent of those interviewed wanting the UK to withdraw from Afghanistan within a year (Merrick and Brady, 2009). Another noted that 64 per cent did not believe that success was possible, even if General Stanley McChrystal, Commander of the International Security Assistance Force (ISAF) in Afghanistan, was to get his way completely in terms of the troop levels from the United States (US) and its partners in the North Atlantic Treaty Organisation (NATO). More worryingly still, only just over half of those interviewed – 54 per cent – were confident that they understood fully what 'success' would look like in Afghanistan (BBC, 2009), a fairly damning indictment of both the UK – and the wider international community's – failure to convincingly and conclusively get their message across with regard to the underlying rationale for the UK's continued presence in Afghanistan.

This is not the only aspect of the wider defence debate that has coloured political discourse in recent times. In addition, there has been the high profile campaign to repair the so-called 'Military Covenant', an Army specific document that serves as the focal point for both the nation and its political elite's moral, if not legally binding, obligations to ensure that service men and women are treated in a suitably respectful and acceptable manner, both on operations and at home (British Army, 2000). In operational terms, the focus has been on the need for a more speedy and effective provision of appropriate defence equipment, as highlighted by the pungent conclusions of the 2009 Gray Report into the so-called 'Smart Procurement' process (Gray, 2009). At home, campaigns have been undertaken to highlight the state of military accommodation, the provision of appropriate health care facilities and their relative pay levels compared to other public services, whether it be traffic wardens (Dannatt, 2008) or Ministry of Defence civil servants (Barker, 2009). Public outrage has been further fuelled by national campaigns by charity groups, such as 'Help for Heroes' and the Royal British Legion.

While media attention has become ever more focused on defence matters, academia has taken much longer to effectively catch up. By definition slower moving, focusing on more reasoned analysis, rather than immediate comment, it is clear that – with a few notable exceptions (Cornish and Dorman, 2009a–b; Dorman, 2006; Robinson, 2005a–b) – academia has not devoted sufficient attention to the wider development of British defence policy under the New Labour government as a whole. There have been campaign specific assessments, most notably of Iraq (North, 2009; Steele, 2007; Stewart, 2007; Synnott, 2008) and Afghanistan (Tootal, 2009), but also what Dorman terms the 'successful war' in Sierra Leone (Dorman, 2009). However, what has been lacking throughout this period has been a comprehensive assessment of how defence policy has been shaped, developed and undertaken by the successive governments of Tony Blair and Gordon Brown. In fact, the last over-arching assessment of defence issues more generally – as opposed to highlighting specific aspects in article length treatments, such as the 2004 Future Army Structures (FAS) process (Dorman, 2006), or more ideologically inspired attacks on the underlying thrust of the Blair approach particularly (Robinson, 2005a–b) – was Stuart Croft et al.'s assessment of the initial SDR, undertaken in the first flush of the New Labour government (Croft et al., 2000). Given the central importance of defence in terms of assessing the effectiveness of the government more generally – the first responsibility of the state being to protect its people – and its foreign policy more specifically, as well as the impact that the conduct and consequences of both Iraq (primarily for Blair) and Afghanistan (for Brown) will have on their respective legacies, such an omission must be rectified. This volume, which takes a more holistic approach, in terms of both timescale and themes assessed, seeks to do just that.

Chronology and Chapters

Given that each chapter explores a different aspect of defence policy under New Labour, it is worth briefly outlining the key milestones in its development, to give some wider shape to the subsequent discussions. 1998 not only saw the production of the SDR, which still provides the general underlying framework for developing defence policy in the UK, but also saw two additional developments that are of particular interest to this volume. Firstly, significantly bolstering Blair's eventual legacy, was the signing of the Belfast Agreement (known colloquially as the Good Friday Agreement – GFA), which took the peace negotiations in Northern Ireland into a new, and ultimately more successful, phase, providing the structures – an Assembly, cross-community Executive – that would eventually bring some greater degree of stability to the Province, in the unlikely form of the Democratic Unionist Party (DUP)'s Dr Ian Paisley as First Minister and Sinn Féin's Martin McGuinness as his Deputy. Such internal developments had noted consequences for the conduct and reputation of the British Army, and the impact of this peace process on British defence policy is given due consideration by Trevor C Salmon, an analyst with a long-standing interest in the politics of the Province, with a particular emphasis on what lessons can be learned from the Army's experience in Northern Ireland for future operations. Secondly, as the year came to an end – on December 3 1998 – the UK and French governments signed an agreement at St Malo that would form the basis for wider European Union (EU) defence co-operation. The agreement called for the development of a Union 'capacity for autonomous action, backed up by credible military forces, the means to decide to use them and a readiness to do so, in order to respond to international crises' (Ministry of Defence, 1998b). It has subsequently been subsumed within the formal auspices of the EU, and has led to an array of acronyms – not least the European Rapid Reaction Force (ERRF) – operations and political debates, all of which is supported by its own rapidly expanding literature. One of the leading participants in the UK debate, Alistair JK Shepherd, considers the impact of such European developments, assessing whether a 'permanent European turn' has been taken in UK defence policy.

The wider development of EU specific policies and capabilities is only one half of the UK's wider Atlantic commitment, as was emphasised the following year, when the UK played a leading role in both the conception, execution and presentation of the NATO military campaign to bring an end to ethnic cleansing in Kosovo. A key element of the wider legal and political justification for such an operation, which was undertaken without specific United Nations (UN) approval, was Tony Blair's speech to the Economic Club of Chicago in 1999 (Blair, 1999). By proposing five 'tests' to be considered when assessing the legitimacy of the use of force within the wider international arena, Blair effectively outlined what has become known as the 'Doctrine of International Community' (a version of which was subsequently adopted by the UN in 2004 (UN, 2004)). Such an approach, as well as chiming with the earlier overt focus on an 'ethical dimension' to foreign policy, also contributed to a wider debate over the necessity and practicalities of over-riding state sovereignty in the name of wider humanitarian concerns, which now centres on the application of the internationally approved 'Responsibility to Protect' (R2P) concept. Steven Haines, a leading academic expert and practitioner in such legal debates, places this 'Doctrine' under the microscope and provides a critique of its seeming central importance to both national and international debates, particularly in relation to subsequent operations in the Middle East.

The controversial decision to join the US in its determination to permanently remove the threat posed by a Saddam led Iraq possessing Weapons of Mass Destruction (WMD) was considered to be part of the development of a wider 'war on terror' (although the relevance of Iraq to such a 'war' has been disputed, with many critics considering Iraq to be effectively a distraction from the main effort, to contain and combat the threat posed by a network of international Islamist terrorist groups, centred around Al Qaeda (see Clarke, 2004; Robinson, 2005b; Woodward, 2007)). The UK's response to a more prominent terrorist threat, institutionally with the 2002 New Chapter to the SDR and operationally in both Afghanistan and Iraq, is critiqued by this author. The chapter focuses primarily on the deconstruction of the underlying rationales and priorities of the New Chapter and asks what role, if any, the British military can play in combating international terrorism.

The 2003 invasion of Iraq also serves as the apex – and, some would argue, the nadir – of the so-called 'Special Relationship' between the US and UK in action (although there were any number of points within the chronological development of New Labour's defence policy, from Kosovo to Afghanistan to the more limited military operations to contain Saddam Hussein's regime during the Clinton era, where such a policy perspective could be raised). Despite the substantive opposition to such a military commitment, both within the UK – at all levels, from public anti-war demonstrations to Cabinet walk-outs – and within continental Europe particularly, Blair took the decision that this was another moment when the UK had to be prepared to 'pay the blood price' by standing shoulder to shoulder with the Bush administration. Drawing on his years of experience in examining political and institutional developments on both sides of the Atlantic, James Sperling explores the development of this relationship and the key importance of matters military to its continued centrality within the wider narrative of British defence and foreign policy.

The dual deployments to Afghanistan and Iraq would colour the remainder of the Blair premiership, with the conduct of smooth government marred by Cabinet resignations (first Robin Cook and then Clare Short), independent inquiries into the handling of intelligence material in presenting the case for intervention in Iraq, vitriolic bureaucratic battles with the British Broadcasting Corporation (BBC) over its reporting of Iraq (which culminated in the tragic death of Dr David Kelly in 2003) and attacks on both the UK and US governments for their ill-prepared approach to the need for state building in both theatres. The remainder of the Blair era would also see a number of internal reorganisations, as the MoD and the British Army attempted to continue the 'normal' business of defence management. In particular, in successive years, the MoD produced three White Papers, amending the controversial 'scales of effort' adopted in the initial SDR process, producing the legislative framework for a reorganisation of the Army through the Future Army Structures (FAS) process and attempting (not for the first or last time) to inject political momentum into the crucial issue of defence procurement, as part of the 2005 Defence Industrial Strategy (DIS). The impact that technological developments have had on both the progression and future posture of British defence policy will be a central concern of any prospective SDR, regardless of which party is in charge. Michael Codner has been a leading light in discussions regarding the technological dimension of defence policy, bringing years of practical and academic experience to bear on the debate. He explores the lessons learned from New Labour's management and harnessing of military technological development and looks forward to explore how such developments will impact on the future shape of both the 2010 SDR and defence policy more generally.

One of the final substantive decisions that Blair took before departing office in June 2007 concerned the future of the independent nuclear deterrent. Convinced that it was central to both the UK's continued security and also the wider relationship with the US, which had become one of the defining motifs of his premiership (although not necessarily in the way popularly claimed in the media, which centred on the inappropriate and insulting 'poodle' label – see D Brown, 2008), the decision was taken to replace the existing Trident system when it reached the end of its current operational cycle, estimated to be in 2024. Support for the wider principle of an independent nuclear deterrent has continued into the Brown government, although not necessarily in its current form (Brown, 2009a). In part, this argument has shifted subtly, to take into account the expressed rhetorical desire of US President Barack Obama to make pragmatic, although longer term, moves towards the ultimate goal of a non-nuclear international system (Obama, 2009; Foreign and Commonwealth Office, 2009). In his chapter, Martin A Smith utilises his long-standing research expertise in the politics of nuclear weapons, both at a national and international level, to good effect, to assess New Labour's handling of the question of the UK's continued independent nuclear deterrent, particularly in the post-11 September era.

New Labour entered its second phase of government on 27 June 2007, when the terms of the alleged 'Granita' bargain were finally met, with Gordon Brown moving unchallenged from the Treasury to Number 10 Downing Street. There are three chapters in this volume dealing with aspects of defence management and organisation that were prevalent throughout New Labour's time in office, but which have acquired particular prominence in the Brown era. Firstly, Anthony Forster, one of the UK's leading experts on the management of defence, explores both the scale of the problem and the efficacy of New Labour's solutions with regard to the maintenance of the 'Military Covenant', which has become one of the popular touchstone issues of the Brown administration. Stephen Deakin brings a new perspective to a debate that has primarily been carried out in the US (Scahill, 2007; Singer, 2005, 2007), but which is becoming of ever greater importance in the UK as well, namely the role of private financing and support for defence across the board, both in terms of the process of contracting out at home and the greater use and regulation of Private Military and Security Companies (PMC/PSC) in operational theatres. Building on his own wider research interests in the area of values and standards, Deakin poses the question of whether there is a moral objection – in terms of a distinct difference in ethos between private entities and the Armed Forces more generally – that needs to be given greater prominence in the current debate. As the FCO, in 2009, produced its own long-awaited conclusions regarding the requirement for regulation of such bodies within the national or international arenas, such matters are likely to colour the ensuing defence debate for some time to come.

Finally, drawing on extensive practical experience, both within the wider development community and on operations in both Iraq and Afghanistan, Stuart Gordon considers an additional dimension to this debate, namely the place for the military within a wider and more 'comprehensive' approach to policy-making more generally, both on the home front and in the field. His chapter pays particular attention to the relationship between the MoD and DFID, exploring and assessing the potential obstacles posed by differences in ethos, objective and approach, as well as considering how such matters can be made to work more effectively in the future. The expressed desire for a more 'joint' concept of policy-making to tackle intractable security problems has been seen in institutional form, both in the UK – the creation of a separate Security Minister in the form of Admiral the Lord West, the establishment of a National Security Committee and the production of a series of National Security Strategies along the lines mandated in the US – and wider, with the EU, as part of its 2008 examination of 'European Home Affairs in an open world', raising the possibility of 'greater co-ordination' of 'military, police, civil protection, development and rule of law devices' in order to provide 'comprehensive support' (Future Group, 2008, 6). As such, the development of these trends are likely to shape defence policy and co-ordination for some time to come, and therefore are worthy of examination, in order to provide a more comprehensive assessment of contemporary British defence policy.

Striking the Balance?

Given the size of the UK, its relative capabilities and resources, in military, economic and political terms, as well as the peculiar impact that both its geography and history have had on the development of contemporary policy, the UK has consistently sought to 'strike a balance' – in Baylis' terms (Baylis, 1989) – when developing its overall defence posture. This has been a theme throughout both the academic and practitioner debate regarding British Defence Policy, with the discourse sprinkled with images such as 'walking a tight-rope' throughout both the Cold War (Carver, 1992) and into the New Labour era. In fact, Tony Blair made this idea of balancer explicit, using the 'bridge' motif as a means to explain the UK's central role, linking up the US and EU. It has also been central to one of the few academic critiques of New Labour's defence policy, with Paul Robinson trenchantly arguing that New Labour had failed to strike any sort of reasonable balance, particularly in relation to the potentially competing demands of homeland defence and expeditionary power projection (Robinson, 2005a–b). Rather than make as stark a choice as Robinson has indicated, in terms of the narrowing of the 'national' interest to primarily the defence of the territorial integrity of the UK – ironically, an equally unbalanced policy option – the key has been to maintain some form of balance between the various choices presented before decision-makers, both uniformed and civilian. Such balancing is needed across a range of issues in contemporary defence policy:

- Between the potentially competing demands of the US 'Special Relationship', both through NATO and in less formal coalitions, and the developing defence identity within the EU. This balance will be the particular focus of the chapters by James Sperling and Alistair JK Shepherd.
- Between the demands of defending the UK homeland and of projecting military power into the wider international arena – the so-called 'home and away' debate. Such a theme will be explored particularly in the chapters by Haines, Brown and Salmon.
- Between treating the Armed Forces – notably the Army, which has been the focus of particular attention in the New Labour era – as a *sui generis* institution, different in ethos and approach to much of the wider public sector, and to considering it as part and parcel of a wider approach to management and governance. This will be the central focus of the chapters by Gordon, Deakin and Forster.
- Between the demands of manpower, both in terms of recruitment and retention, and in relation to the wider level of scale of treatment due to military personnel, and the need to ensure modern technology is being effectively harnessed to maximum effect. This issue is particularly important within the context of straitened economic circumstances and in terms of whether contemporary or future defence requirements are of greatest import in

terms of shaping wider defence procurement and organisation. This will be a feature both of Smith's chapter, examining the specific nuclear dimension to British Defence Policy, and Codner's more wide-ranging, future looking assessment of technology and defence.

How such balances are managed, where the priorities lay during the Blair and Brown eras – and indeed what changes are potentially going to be made under a putative Conservative government – will form the central assessment of the New Labour era in British Defence Policy.

Incidents and Individuals

The final theme to be considered in this volume is the relative contributions made by policy agents – in this case, the shifting premierships from Blair to Brown particularly, and, where appropriate the positions held by the Conservative Party – and events in determining the shape of defence policy. Taking each in turn, the volume will highlight areas of policy that were undoubtedly shaped by the particular personality traits and priorities of notably Tony Blair, as the dominant figure in British politics over much of the last decade. Such personality based politics does have the disadvantage of leaving the particular policy area overly dependent on the continued involvement of such a persona, and, in considering the totality of New Labour's time in government, the volume seeks to place in context that which was a New Labour policy and that which was more accurately considered an initiative undertaken primarily, if not exclusively, in the Blair era. It will also seek to further widen the nature of the debate to consider more comprehensively the stated views of David Cameron's Conservative Party, which have yet to really receive the academic interest worthy of – if polling trends are to be believed – a potential future government (Lee and Beech, 2009; Elliott and Hanning, 2007). In doing so, a clearer indication of both the legacy of New Labour, in both its incarnations, and the nascent outline of a putative Conservative administration will be delineated; as both are likely to cast considerable shadows over the developing SDR process, it is important to both accurately understand and appreciate the relative significance and importance placed on certain key aspects of the debate thus far, in order to determine their wider longevity.

Additionally, when asked to determine the largest obstacle to producing a coherent policy, most notably in the field of foreign affairs, Harold Macmillan is said to have remarked 'events, dear boy, events'. While perhaps rather too readily dismissing the possibility of wider strategic planning as a means to shape, rather than react to wider events, arguably, in contemporary international politics, the key evidence in defence of Macmillan's view would be the perceived impact of 11 September 2001 on defence, foreign and internal security policies around the world. If the most powerful state in the international system, the US, can be effectively blown off course from what it had originally intended to be the defining features of its foreign policy – as explained, for example, by then prospective National Security Advisor Condoleezza Rice in 2000 (Rice, 2000) – then a state of the size and resources of the UK is surely even more vulnerable to the shifting sands and changing circumstances of the wider international environment. Certainly, this is redolent of the rhetoric surrounding the events of 11 September 2001, which, given its international magnitude, was seen by many as a dividing line in wider international politics (Blair, 2001). Yet, with the advantage of time, which gives greater perspective, there is a need to more comprehensively consider the *actual* impact of such an event on the development of policy, in this case wider British defence policy.

Bibliography

Barker, A (2009), 'Brown Stands Up for MOD Bonuses', *The Financial Times* 13 November

Baylis, J (1989), *British Defence Policy: Striking the Right Balance* (Basingstoke: Palgrave Macmillan)

BBC (2009), 'UK "Not Convinced" by Afghan Goal' – http://news.bbc.co.uk/1/hi/uk/8348942.stm

BBC (2010), 'UK Fatalities in Afghanistan and Iraq' – http://news.bbc.co.uk/1/hi/uk/8260060.stm

Blair, T (1997), *Comments by the Prime Minister on the Occasion of the Labour Party's Election Victory on 2 May 1997* (London: Labour Party)

Blair, T (1999), *Speech by the Prime Minister to the Economic Club of Chicago on 24 April 1999* (London: HMSO)

Blair, T (2001), *Speech to the Labour Party Conference on 4 October 2001* (London: Labour Party)

Booth, J (2008), 'Army Troops Paid Less Than Traffic Wardens', *The Times* 5 June

British Army (2000), *Army Doctrine Publication Document Volume 5: Soldiering* (London: British Army)

Brown, D (2008), 'Britain: Cheerleader for the US in the "War on Terror"?' in Eder, F and Senn, M (eds) *Europe and Transatlantic Terrorism: Assessing Threats and Counter-measures* (Berlin: Nomos)

Brown, G (2009a), *Speech by the Prime Minister to the United Nations General Assembly on 23 September 2009* (London: HMSO)

Brown, G (2009b), *Afghanistan: National Security and Regional Stability – Speech by the Prime Minister to the International Institute for Strategic Studies on 4 September 2009* (London: HMSO)

Brown, G (2009c), *Speech by the Prime Minister on Afghanistan to the Royal College of Defence Studies on 6 November 2009* (London: HMSO)

Brown, G (2009d), *Speech by the Prime Minister to the Annual Lord Mayor's Banquet on 16 November 2009* (London: HMSO)

Carver, M (1992), *Tightrope Walking: British Defence Policy Since 1945* (London: Hutchinson)

Chalmers, M (2009), 'Preparing for the Lean Years', *RUSI Future Defence Review Working Paper* 1

Clarke, R (2004), *Against all Enemies: Inside America's War on Terror* (London: Simon and Schuster)

Cook, R (1997), *Speech by the Foreign Secretary on 12 May 1997* (London: FCO)

Cornish, P and Dorman, A (2009a), 'Blair's Wars and Brown's Budgets: From Strategic Defence Review to Strategic Decay in Less Than a Decade', *International Affairs* 85:2, 247–61

Cornish, P and Dorman, A (2009b), 'National Defence in the Age of Austerity', *International Affairs* 85:4, 733–53

Croft, S, Dorman, A, Rees, W and Uttley, M (2000), *Britain and Defence 1945–2000: A Policy Re-evaluation* (London: Longman)

Dannatt, R (2009), *Keynote address by the Chief of the General Staff, General Sir Richard Dannatt to the Royal United Services Institute Land Warfare Conference on 23 June 2009* (London: RUSI)

Dorman, A (2006), 'Reorganising the Infantry: Drivers of Change and What This Tells Us About the State of the Defence Debate', *British Journal of Politics and International Relations* 8:4, 489–502

Dorman, A (2009), *Blair's Successful War: British Military Intervention in Sierra Leone* (London: Ashgate)

Elliott, F and Hanning, J (2007), *Cameron: The Rise of the New Conservative* (London: Harper Press)

Foreign and Commonwealth Office (2009), *Lifting the Nuclear Shadow: Creating the Conditions for Abolishing Nuclear Weapons* (London: FCO)

Franco-British Summit (1998), *Joint Declaration on European Defence on 3–4 December 1998* (London: FCO)

Future Group (2008), *Freedom, Security, Privacy: European Home Affairs in an Open World. Report of the Informal High Level Advisory Group on the Future of European Home Affairs* (Brussels: Future Group)

Gray, B (2009), *Review of Acquisition for the Secretary of State for Defence: An Independent Report by Bernard Gray* (London: MoD)

Hennessy, P (2007), 'He Spoke of a New Dawn – And Clouds Rolled In', *The Daily Telegraph* 13 May

Hoon, G (2001), *11 September – A New Chapter for the Strategic Defence Review – Speech by the Defence Secretary on 5 December 2001* (London: MoD)

Kampfner, J (2004), *Blair's Wars* (London: Free Press)

Kilcullen, D (2009), *The Accidental Guerrilla: Fighting Small Wars in the Midst of a Big One* (London: C Hurst and Co)

Labour Party (1997), *The Labour Party's Manifesto 1997* (London: Labour Party)

Lee, S and Beech, M (eds) (2009), *The Conservatives Under David Cameron: Built to Last?* (Basingstoke: Palgrave Macmillan)

McChrystal, S (2009), *Commander's Initial Assessment – Initial United States Forces – Afghanistan on 26 June 2009* (Washington, DC)

McInnes, C (1998), 'Labour's Strategic Defence Review', *International Affairs* 74:4, 823–45

Merrick, J and Brady, B (2009), 'War in Afghanistan: Not in Our Name', *The Independent* 15 November

Ministry of Defence (1998), *The Strategic Defence Review: Modern Forces for a Modern World* (London: HMSO)

Ministry of Defence (2002), *The Strategic Defence Review: A New Chapter* (London: HMSO)

Ministry of Defence (2003), *Delivering Security in a Changing World: Defence White Paper* (London: HMSO)

Ministry of Defence (2004), *Future Capabilities*: *Defence White Paper* (London: HMSO)

Ministry of Defence (2005), *Defence Industrial Strategy: Defence White Paper* (London: HMSO)

North, R (2009), *Ministry of Defeat: The British War in Iraq 2003–2009* (London: Continuum Books)

Obama, B (2009), *Remarks by the President of the United States in Prague on 5 April 2009* (Washington, DC: Office of the White House)

Rice, C (2000), 'Campaign 2000: Promoting the National Interest', *Foreign Affairs*, January/February

Robinson, P (2005a), 'Are We Wasting Money on Defence?', *The Spectator* 9 July

Robinson, P (2005b), *Doing Less with Less: Making Britain More Secure* (London: Imprint Academic)

Scahill, J (2007), *Blackwater: The Rise of the World's Most Powerful Mercenary Army* (London: Nation Books)

Singer, PW (2005), 'Outsourcing War', *Foreign Affairs*, March/April, 84:2, 119–32

Singer, PW (2007), *Corporate Warriors: The Rise of the Privatised Military Industry* (Cornell: Cornell University Press)

Steele, J (2007), *Defeat: Why They Lost Iraq* (London: IB Tauris)

Stewart, R (2007), *Occupational Hazards: My Time Governing in Iraq* (London: Picador)

Swaine, J (2009), 'UK Recession: Gordon Brown Refuses to Admit Return to "Boom and Bust"', *The Daily Telegraph* 23 January

Synnott, H (2008), *Bad Days in Basra: My Turbulent Time as Britain's Man in Southern Iraq* (London: IB Tauris)

Tootal, S (2009), *Danger Close: Commanding 3 PARA in Afghanistan* (London: John Murray)

United Nations (2004), *A More Secure World: Our Shared Responsibility – Report of the High Level Panel on Threats, Challenges and Change* (New York: United Nations)

Wheeler, N and Dunne, T (2004), *Moral Britannia? Evaluating the Ethical Dimension in Labour's Foreign Policy* (London: Foreign Policy Centre)

Williams, P (2002), 'The Rise and Fall of the "Ethical Dimension": Presentation and Practice in New Labour's Foreign Policy', *Cambridge Review of International Affairs* 15:1, 53–63

Woodward, B (2007), *State of Denial: Bush at War Part III* (London: Pocket Books)

Chapter 2
Permanent Allies or Friends with Benefits? The Anglo-American Security Relationship

James Sperling

The British embrace of the transatlantic relationship had serviced both its long-standing interest in preventing the emergence of a continental hegemon and protecting the freedom of the seas, critical to a maritime and trading power. The close relationship with the US, particularly between 1945 and 1989, was central to achieving each goal. The military presence of the US in Europe countered the ambitions of the Soviet Union and guarded against a Franco-German dominated Europe, while the close alignment of British and American commercial and strategic interests outside of Europe allowed the UK to make an orderly withdrawal from empire, while continuing its global commercial ties and maintaining influence over extra-European developments, particularly in those geographic spaces abutting the Commonwealth.

Although these maritime and continental strategies were complementary – a continental balance in Europe had provided the opportunity for Britain's outsized global engagement – the developing process of European integration, particularly in the spheres of foreign and defence policies after the Maastricht (1992), Amsterdam (1997) and Nice (2002) Treaties, was perceived as a potential threat to the viability of NATO and the transatlantic relationship, the foundation of Britain's security strategy inside and outside Europe. The foreign policy legacy of Margaret Thatcher to the Conservative Party was an enduring scepticism of the European project in foreign and security affairs, a single-minded embrace of the 'special relationship' with the US and the zero-sum calculus that closer security integration in Europe would necessarily loosen the profitable and essential post-war bond with the US (Rees 1991, 146–7). New Labour claimed that the oppositional logic of the Conservative Party presented Britain with a false choice between Europe and NATO. Instead, New Labour maintained that Britain had to choose EU *and* NATO, Europe *and* America.

New Labour considered British leadership in crafting a politically and militarily capable Europe as an opportunity for assuming the pivotal role of mediating between a Europe and America experiencing geopolitical and diplomatic estrangement as the common bond forged by the Soviet threat slowly dissipated and then finally disappeared. New Labour proposed to place Britain 'at the heart of Europe', lending Britain an authoritative voice over the trajectory of the European project, perhaps acquiring sufficient leverage to pry apart the Franco-German axis at its core and ensuring that the transatlantic tie would remain intact. Arguably, New Labour's foreign policy did not significantly deviate from the traditional grand strategy of continental balance and global influence. Yet, it did view Europe through a more subtly refracted lens: full British participation in an EU possessing an autonomous defence capability would reinforce, rather than weaken, the transatlantic alliance, enhance rather than diminish London's influence in Washington – as well as in Berlin, Brussels and Paris – and protect, rather than harm, Britain's strategic interests inside and outside Europe. What New Labour did not seek, however, was any disruption of the Anglo-American defence and security relationship.

This Anglo-American relationship rests on three pillars. The first is a shared identity unique even within the wider transatlantic community; it provides an emotional resonance for the American and British foreign policy elites and electorates that sustains close relations between both states, even when interests diverge. Moreover, when conflicts do erupt, the common bonds forged by history and a shared culture erect a barrier to a permanent rupture or recurring distrust of the other's motives. The second pillar of the relationship is material: the US has been a primary destination for British capital and manufactures, while the UK has been a primary destination of US capital. In addition, the British and American defence industrial bases are increasingly intertwined. Common geostrategic orientations, particularly the shared assumption that the UK and US have a responsibility for global order and shared continental and maritime interests, constitute the third pillar of the relationship. However, two questions remain – does the combined force of these three pillars create a 'special relationship' between the US and the UK that is qualitatively different from American relations with its other major allies? What impact does the Anglo-American relationship have on the content and form of British defence policy?

The Idea of the 'Special Relationship'

The centrality of the Anglo-American relationship to the security interests of either party periodically undergoes intense scrutiny and scepticism, particularly after American presidential elections failing to return an incumbent or a change of government in Britain. The elections of Bill Clinton, George W Bush, and, most recently, Barack Obama to the White House raised concerns that the incoming administration would deprive Britain of its rank of *primus inter pares* within the NATO alliance or even promote France or Germany at Britain's expense. Barack Obama, for example, was considered the most reliably Anglophile of the American presidential candidates in early 2008, but, shortly after his election, pundits began to surmise that the new president's Kenyan heritage would preclude sharing his predecessor's 'affinity for Britain' (Borger 2008; McNamara 2008; Shipman 2009; Spillius 2009). When Tony Blair resigned as Prime Minister, similar fears were expressed that Gordon Brown, his successor, would engineer a distancing – or, to some, a normalisation – of Anglo-American relations (BBC News 2007;

Bremmer 2007). In each case, the imminent demise of the 'special relationship' was greatly exaggerated.

The recurrent doubts about the state of the 'special relationship' are compounded by questions over its very nature. Some claim that the 'special relationship' is 'almost entirely foreign to American ears' and is little more than a British 'cult ... rooted in national self-delusion' (McGuire 2009; Berry 2003). Similarly, others claim that the asymmetry in Anglo-American power resources has inexorably led Britain to play 'poodle' to the American top dog or reduced Britain to America's client rather than 'candid friend' (Abramsky 2008; BBC News 2007). Although Britons and Americans may question the persistence or existence of the 'special relationship', such doubts have not been shared by third party-observers. The French, in particular, have been particularly preoccupied with the potential for an extended Anglo-Saxon hegemony. French President Charles de Gaulle most famously viewed Britain as America's 'Trojan Horse' that would thwart Europe's re-emergence as an independent centre of power. More recently, an observer in *Le Figaro* claimed that the UK was America's 'only credible partner' (cited in Harris 2002).

Winston Churchill gave purchase to the descriptor 'special relationship' in 1946, but its terms of reference were relatively narrow, referring to the nuclear and defence cooperation that evolved over the course of the Second World War and carried over to meet the anticipated Soviet challenge to the immediate post-war status quo. After the mid-1960s, however, the 'special relationship' began to take on the character of a burdensome and ill-defined diplomatic prop and a sometimes embarrassing rhetorical ritual. Both Harold Wilson and Ted Heath made an effort to jettison the adjective 'special' and replace it with 'close' or 'natural' (Marsh and Baylis 2006, 180). That effort to downgrade the Anglo-American relationship, presumably to allay French fears towards facilitating British accession to the European Economic Community (EEC), left many Americans puzzled. Henry Kissinger, for example, expressed surprise and disappointment that Prime Minister Heath 'dealt with us with an unsentimentality totally at variance with the "special relationship"' (Kissinger 1982, 141), despite his earlier assessment in the mid-1960s that the 'special relationship' was an artefact of the Second World War and fast losing its relevance (Kissinger 1965, 79–81).

The 'special relationship' experienced a renaissance during the joint tenures of President Ronald Reagan and Prime Minister Margaret Thatcher, despite bruised feelings over the initially even-handed treatment of Argentina and the UK at the onset of the Falklands War (Freedman 2006). The precariousness of Britain's place in American strategic calculations was belied in the wake of German unification, when the Bush administration offered Germany the role of partner in leadership in reconstructing the European order, thereby implicitly demoting Britain (and France) in American foreign policy calculations. As it turned out, the American offer was premature and the challenges of the post-Cold War environment eventually underscored Britain's continuing utility and importance to the US.

The rhetoric and reality of the 'special relationship' persists today, although efforts have been made to re-brand the relationship. New Labour has toyed with alternative formulations, in equal measure to give credence to its initially buoyant European aspirations and to recalibrate the relationship on terms better attuned to presumed American sensibilities. Despite the different formulations tested and discarded – 'a close and enduring relationship', 'a strong relationship', 'an historic partnership of shared purpose', 'our most important bilateral relationship' and the less exclusive 'our special relationship' (Miliband 2007; Blair 2002; Brown 2007; Browne 2008; Brown 2009a) – the 60 year-old diplomatic cliché persists, as does the rhetorical discomfort with it on both sides of the Atlantic. British and American politicians nonetheless inevitably return to it in order to capture the unique quality of Anglo-American relations (Blair 2002; Brown 2007; Brown 2009b; Bagehot 2009, 65). And, whenever an American official relies upon a substitute formulation or suggests Britain is merely one of America's closest allies, attentive British foreign policy elites experience a crisis of confidence and fear that their role as the interlocutors between America and Europe, and the status attending it, is in jeopardy (Burns 2009; Borger 2008). Given this background, the persistence of the 'special relationship' as the official descriptor of the Anglo-American relationship requires explanation.

An uncommonly shared identity   Timothy Garton Ash made the simple observation that identities are 'voluntary but not arbitrary' (Garton Ash 2001, 1). The Anglo-American shared identity is rooted in a common historical memory, common philosophical and cultural foundations and the shaping of an American consciousness that has been perpetuated by the pre-Revolutionary and seemingly entrenched Anglo-Saxon ruling class, if not in ethnicity at least in habit of mind. American historical figures prior to the twentieth century were predominately of British ancestry, if not in fact at least in perception. The vast majority of the signatories to the Declaration of Independence and Constitution had British surnames, as is the case for the majority of American Presidents. As an ethnic group, Americans of British ancestry have had a disproportionate and long-lived influence on the trajectory of American foreign policy, particularly with respect to the close relationship with Britain on issues of war, peace, and global order. Moreover, the Anglo-American culture served as the template for the assimilation of immigrants culturally and linguistically (De Conde 1992, 191).

The historical memory of common struggles against existential threats to the American and British way of life, particularly in the twentieth century, provides an ongoing legacy binding the two nations together. America provided Britain material support prior to both the First World War and the Second World War, despite its legal status as a neutral in both conflicts, while large numbers of Americans became members of the Canadian or British armed forces prior to the American entry into either war. While the Great War united Britain and America, it was the joint effort to defeat Nazi Germany that still exerts a considerable emotional resonance on both sides of the Atlantic. In Gordon Brown's 2009 address to the US Congress, he evoked that joint experience when he noted that American and British soldiers were fighting 'side by side in the plains of

Afghanistan, the streets of Iraq, just as their forefathers fought side by side in the sands of Tunisia, the beaches of Normandy, and then on the bridges over the Rhine' (Brown 2009a). This common endeavour to harness force and justice in the international system was carried over into the entire post-war period of Anglo-American cooperation, ranging from the joint design of the Bretton Woods monetary system, preventing the proliferation of nuclear weapons, meeting the military threat posed by the Soviet Union, and now combating terrorism. The cultural and philosophical foundations of the Anglo-American relationship are broader and deeper. A confluence of philosophical traditions has produced a common aversion to speculative philosophy that finds favour in continental Europe and a uniquely 'Anglo-American' model of capitalism. High and low culture is more profoundly interpenetrated. Shakespeare and Dickens are essential elements of every American high school curriculum. Popular film and television have drawn on British history and myth to illustrate existential threats to America (e.g., *Sea Hawke* drew a clear parallel between the Spain of Phillip II and Nazi Germany), and only the British spy James Bond would enable American audiences to suspend disbelief that anyone other than an American could save the world from SPECTRE. Yet, has the confluence of historical memory, philosophical and cultural interpenetrations, a common language and a long-lived Anglo-Saxon ascendancy created a common Anglo-American security culture? The short answer is no. Yet, the American and British security cultures are more alike than different and facilitate greater ongoing cooperation, in terms of goals and instruments, than is the case with America's other major European or Asian allies.

Divergent national security cultures can pose significant barriers to security co-operation, just as convergent cultures can facilitate and reinforce it. National security cultures consist of four elements: the worldview of the external environment; the nature of national identity; and instrumental and interaction preferences. The worldview of the external environment refers to the elite consensus on the underling dynamic of the international system. The national identity identifies the extent to which foreign policy elites have embedded the national interest in a broader, collective 'we', defined against some 'other'. The instrumental preferences differentiate between states relying upon the coercive instruments of statecraft and those relying upon persuasion and normative frameworks. State interaction preferences fall along a continuum, marked at one end by unilateralism and at the other by 'reflexive multilateralism' within formal institutional structures (Sperling 2007; Krahmann 2007).

The American and British world-views share a common core, perhaps best captured by Robert Conquest's assertion that 'within the West, it is above all the English-speaking community which has, over the centuries, pioneered and maintained the middle way between anarchy and despotism' (Conquest cited in Garton Ash 2001, 10). There has been another convergence of sorts after 11 September and 7 July: a radicalised Islam threatens the British and American way of life and is the primary threat to regional stability in areas of common strategic interest. Both the US and UK share a similar position on the global role and responsibility that each state must and ought to play in the international system. New Labour, for example, wished to be a 'force for good' in the international system and defined the UK as a global player and a major power, while the US views itself as the global custodian of order spreading the benefits of democracy and capitalism. This similar world view is tempered by British scepticism and American faith in the transformative power of democracy, the probability of imposing it successfully and its appropriateness as a primary foreign policy goal – a scepticism temporarily suspended in the person of Tony Blair.

Elites on both sides of the Atlantic have appealed to shared values and civilization as a rationale for continuing or deepening security cooperation, even where national interests overlap only imperfectly. The imbricated American and British identities provide the foundation for the rarely contested assumption that security cooperation is a constant in Anglo-American relations. A countervailing dynamic is periodically present in times of crisis, when both countries revert to a narrower national and self-referential identity. Yet, the close bonds of culture and history provide automatic stabilisers, minimising difference and facilitating cooperation.

The circumstances of the post-1989 world generated a fundamental and nuanced reassessment of the relationship between security and defence policies, a process common to both American and British foreign policy elites. The Clinton administration strategy of democratic engagement conceptually separated security and defence, a development that reflected the challenges of the post-1989 international system and was evident in New Labour's notion of 'defence diplomacy'. While the Bush administration adopted a more vulgar understanding of security and defence policies in the wake of 11 September, effectively collapsing security and defence into virtually indistinguishable categories, the Blair government retained the distinction and underscored the importance of addressing the root causes of terrorism at home and abroad.

American and British interaction preferences overlap imperfectly, no doubt reflecting American predominance in the international system and Britain's inability to go it alone. The events of 11 September and the unilateralist proclivities of the neo-conservatives in the Bush administration created a significant deviation from the American preference for working within the multilateral institutions it authored, notably NATO. British rhetoric underscores the importance of operating within multilateral frameworks, but the enthusiasm for defence multilateralism, particularly within NATO, dominates (Ministry of Defence 2003). Yet, the American 'abandonment' of NATO in Iraq and Afghanistan in its prosecution of the 'global war on terrorism' revealed that the core British interaction preference in defence has been bilateral cooperation with the US at the expense of the EU and even NATO in the case of Iraq (House of Commons 2008; Sperling and Webber 2009).

What does this tell us about the Anglo-American security relationship? First, the shared identity between the 'English-speaking' peoples creates a common frame of reference, a common orientation towards national roles and purpose in the international system and not dissimilar assessments of the more appropriate or efficient methods for realising jointly pursued objectives. Although neither Britain nor America are 'reflexive multilateralists' as Germany claims to be, both see instrumental value in multilateral cooperation on defence and security policy within NATO. The Americans retain a slight bias towards unilateralism, while the British understand that their bilateral relationship with the US makes possible their robust global role. To the extent that culture and belief systems shape interests, the 'special relationship' can account for the persistence of defence cooperation and the shallowness of conflicts between these two countries. It also remains true that there are also material and strategic factors explaining the robustness of the 'special relationship'.

The Material Foundations of the Anglo-American Relationship

The interaction density of the US and UK economies across any number of dimensions – the relative British share of externally held US Treasury debt, the bilateral trade relationship, the level of mutual direct foreign investment and the growing interpenetration of their respective defence industrial bases – are both cause and effect of the 'special relationship'. Two questions naturally arise: What is Britain's standing relative to America's other trade and investment partners? What consequences does this have for defence and security policy?

US direct foreign investment abroad (US DFI) and foreign direct investment in the US (FDI US) are undertaken almost exclusively by individual economic agents, rather than by governments. Nonetheless, the nationally aggregated holdings of FDI in the US do suggest the relative level of interdependencies between national economies that encourage bilateral or multilateral cooperation on a range of economic issues, particularly the regulation of capital markets, non-tariff barriers to trade and macroeconomic policy. Europe accounts for the overwhelming share of US DFI and FDI US, exceeding the shares held by Mexico, Canada, Latin America, and the Asia-Pacific combined. The concentration of US DFI in Europe has steadily increased from just under 32 per cent (1966) to almost 56 per cent (2007) of total US DFI; Britain has been home to upwards of 17 per cent of US DFI (1991) and, in 2007, registers a larger share than any individual state or any region outside Europe other than Latin America (see Table 2.1). FDI in the US tells a not dissimilar story. The UK is the single largest investor in the US. Since the mid-1960s, the British share of FDI US has ranged from a high of just over 25 per cent (1986) to a low of just under 15 per cent (2001). Today it equals almost 20 per cent of all foreign investment in the US. The wider politics of such developments are also worthy of brief consideration. Government holdings of externally-held US Treasury debt presents a potential source of geopolitical leverage. The Chinese have recently emerged as the largest holders of externally-held Treasury debt, with elements within the Washington beltway reacting in a similar way to the Japanese holdings of US debt in the 1980s. Tellingly, British

Table 2.1   US Direct Foreign Investment (USDFI) and Foreign Direct Investment in United States (FDIUS), 1991–2007 (in per cent)

		2007	2005	2001	1996	1991
NAFTA	FDIUS	10.47	9.91	7.73	9.44	9.00
	USDFI	12.49	14.45	14.05	13.70	17.77
Europe	FDIUS	70.85	70.75	74.34	62.01	61.09
	USDFI	55.57	46.74	46.85	37.90	n/a
Netherlands	FDIUS	10.01	10.37	10.83	12.60	15.06
	USDFI	13.26	8.65	10.11	6.81	4.34
UK	FDIUS	19.63	18.58	14.71	20.33	23.88
	USDFI	14.29	15.62	15.63	16.92	17.06
Latin America	FDIUS	3.01	4.20	4.33	4.74	3.47
	USDFI	16.91	13.62	18.97	17.17	13.93
Asia-Pacific	FDIUS	15.28	14.44	13.34	23.00	25.26
	USDFI	16.26	17.82	15.57	17.55	15.44
Japan	FDIUS	11.14	11.83	11.15	19.42	22.70
	USDFI	3.64	3.71	3.81	4.35	5.43

Source: US Department of Commerce (2009a–c). Author's own calculations.

holdings never raised this kind of policy concern (Orszag 2007, 2–3; Morrison and Labonte 2008; Qiao 2009, 11; US Department of the Treasury 2008).

Trade in services also highlights the importance of the UK relative to the other EU members, but also underscores the EU's continuing role as America's most important source and consumer of services. The UK share of US service exports was second only to Japan and the equal to that of Canada in 1995, but, by 2005, the UK emerged as the most important US services export market. On the import side of the ledger, the UK has been the single most important supplier of services to the US market between 1995 and 2005, accounting for no less than 12 per cent and no more than 15 per cent of total US service imports. No other country, other than Japan, has accounted for more than 10 per cent of US service imports over that time period.

With respect to merchandise trade, the UK alternated with Germany as America's third most important Organisation for Economic Cooperation and Development (OECD) trading partner after Canada and Japan between 1960 and 1980 and remained in that position until 2000, when it fell behind Mexico. Despite the persistence of the UK as a major US trading partner, its relative share of US exports and imports declined precipitously between 1960 and 2006: the British share of US exports fell from just under 11 per cent to just over 4 per cent, while the British share of US imports fell from just over 10 per cent to just under 3 per cent. More generally, the EU share of US global trade has declined over time, as that of the Asia-Pacific and the North Atlantic Free Trade Area (NAFTA) have risen (OECD 2008) (see Table 2.2).

Table 2.2   US Global Imports and Exports, 1960–2007 (in per cent)

		2006–07	2001–05	1996–00	1990–95	1980–85^	1970–75^	1960–65^
Canadian	Imports from	21.76	23.11	22.44	21.21	33.23	34.44	29.67
	Exports to	16.19	17.83	17.83	19.00	33.98	33.83	29.50
Mexican	Imports from	12.31	13.62	11.72	8.54	1.07		
	Exports to	10.74	10.89	10.36	7.07	1.29		
EU*	Imports from	31.92	30.71	27.36	25.61	28.70	33.68	37.94
	Exports to	35.65	34.40	32.20	32.54	34.30	35.83	34.91
British	Imports from	4.35	4.72	5.38	5.33	8.98	8.12	10.77
	Exports to	2.90	3.32	3.78	3.78	8.76	8.12	10.41
German	Imports from	4.14	3.90	3.77	4.32	8.51	9.15	12.45
	Exports to	4.82	5.25	5.10	5.15	8.20	9.69	12.61
Japanese	Imports from	5.56	7.00	9.06	10.99	18.21	17.99	13.92
	Exports to	7.71	9.45	17.97	17.97	18.05	16.91	14.14
Chinese	Imports from	5.48	3.78	>2.00	>2.00			
	Exports to	16.00	12.23	5.01	5.01			

Note: ^ OECD share only; * EU 15 from 1960–1995; EU 25 from 1996–2007 as share of total OECD imports and exports.

Source: TradeStats Express (2008b–c; OECD, 2008). Author's own calculations.

This changing pattern of trade may be attributed partially to rising European foreign direct investment in the US, to the trade creation effects of the NAFTA agreement and the emergence of China as the world's low cost producer of manufactures. Yet, more revealing than these trade figures are the bilateral trade imbalances with America's major trading partners. Of its major trading partners, the US has run either a small surplus or deficit with the UK. In 2007, the UK accounted for just 1 per cent of the $700.99bn American trade deficit, while Japan and China accounted for 48 per cent, Canada and Mexico accounted for just under 20 per cent and the EU as a whole accounted for 15.5 per cent. Britain, while a not unimportant American trading partner, does lack any claim to a 'special' role in the American trade ledger, with the important exception of the defence sector.

The transatlantic trade in defence, particularly with respect to European imports of American weapons systems and services, does not differentiate the UK markedly from the other major signatories of the North Atlantic Treaty (see Table 2.3). Yet, American purchases of British and Italian defence goods are in double-digits whereas those of France and Germany are at or below 1 per cent. Additionally, the UK and Canada jointly supply almost 60 per cent of US defence imports. Within NATO, North America is the primary destination for British defence imports and source of exports.

Yet, the US has not experienced or countenanced the same level of national defence base interpenetration with any other country other than the UK. Between 2001 and 2007, the UK accounted for fully one-half of American defence DFI

Table 2.3   Arms Exports and Imports, 2007 (in per cent)

	France		Germany		Italy		UK		US	
	Exports	Imports	Exports	Imports	Exports	Imports	Exports	Imports	Exports	Imports
Canada	0.33	2.03	0.48	0.10	1.66		6.16	2.93	1.66	24.25
France			0.02	2.01	2.22	2.98	0.14	1.27	0.99	0.76
Germany	0.43	0.24			0.74	16.03	0.82	14.14	2.67	1.27
Italy	0.49	6.81	2.38	0.91			4.21	0.19	1.56	0.70
Netherlands	0.52	0.60	1.00	14.97	0.35	0.32	0.55	8.56	1.49	
Portugal	0.12		2.20		1.76		0.67			
Spain	1.61	6.53	3.85		5.12		1.34		1.95	0.92
Turkey	4.23		15.32		3.68		1.36		7.77	
UK	0.13	1.27	2.13	3.05	2.71	20.59			5.47	34.34
US	0.20	70.89	1.00	77.27	10.45	59.26	14.01	71.51		
NATO total	16.17	91.00	60.70	98.31	38.98	99.18	33.77	97.56	31.84	62.63
NATO ($bn)	$4.70	$22.85	$19.38	$6.13	$3.01	$4.70	$7.81	$4.60	$57.39	$2.31
Global ($bn)	$31.93	$25.11	$31.93	$6.23	$7.71	$4.74	$28.85	$4.72	$224.04	$3.69

Source: SIPRI (2009a–b). Author's own calculations.

($5.1bn), while the US captures three quarters of British defence DFI ($7.3bn). Moreover, American and British DFI have taken the form of acquisitions: over the same time period, the UK acquired 50 American and the US acquired 27 British defence firms (Chao and Nisblett 2007, 21). BAE Systems, the world's fourth largest defence firm, has made the transition from a supplier of military equipment and services to the American Department of Defense (it was ranked 93rd in 2000 and outside the top 100 in 1996) to capture the prized status of prime contractor, with defence contracts worth $4.7bn in 2006. It has also ranked in the top ten in total Federal contracts since 2000 and, in 2008, it won contracts worth $16.25bn (Department of Defense, various years; White House, various years).

The growing interpenetration of the American and British national defence industrial bases – and the technological interdependencies engendered by it – has produced defence cooperation on a variety of weapons systems and new technologies, including ballistic missile defence, armour, surface ship radar and radio interoperability (Rood 2007). Britain's BAE is the major partner of Lockheed Martin in the Joint Strike Fighter (JSF) and the only foreign firm that is a 'phase one' contractor, extending BAE and the British MoD the prerogative of influencing 'all aspects of the JSF programmes as it moves into a new phase' (National Audit Office 2007, 70–1; Ministry of Defence 2005). Nonetheless, it is understood that American cooperation with the UK on defence platforms and technology is an option rather than a necessity, while the same cannot be said for the UK (Ministry of Defence 2005).

The primary goals of British weapons acquisition policy and Anglo-American weapons cooperation are to ensure that British forces are 'interoperable with US command and control structures, match US operational tempo and provide capabilities that deliver the greatest impact when operating alongside the US' (Ministry of Defence 2005; House of Commons 2008; House of Commons 2007, 15). Not incidentally, the British armed forces remain preoccupied with ensuring that the UK could acquire the appropriate maritime capabilities that would enable the UK to 'project power across the globe in support of British interests' (Ministry of Defence 2005; Ministry of Defence 2003; Ministry of Defence 2004).

The stated British concern with guaranteeing UK interoperability with US forces has trumped any concern with interoperability within the context of the EU, despite a significant number of cooperative defence projects with its EU partners. The official goal of deepening US–UK weapons cooperation reflects not only the commercial and technological benefits accruing to British defence contractors in the American and British defence markets, but the calculation that it would allow the UK to function as a 'bridge between Europe and the US', thereby increasing the prospects for NATO interoperability more generally (Ministry of Defence 2005). It is not at all clear that Britain will serve as a bridge; it could instead construct a wall between Britain and its major European NATO allies if the latter put a premium on procurement independence and intra-European interoperability. US–UK weapons cooperation also reflected the realistic assessment that the UK could not support 'a complete cradle to grave (defence) industrial base' or seek procurement independence (Ministry of Defence 2005). This willing dependence on some US weapons systems carries the caveat that the UK must retain operational independence, a guarantee that the US has been willing to supply once again with respect to the JSF (House of Commons 2007).

The 2007 UK–US Defence Trade Cooperation Treaty underscores the virtually unique relationship between the two and is emblematic of the 'special relationship'.[1] The goal of the Treaty from both the US and UK perspectives was to enhance their ability to engage in joint military and counter-terrorism operations, guarantee the unimpeded re-supply of British troops in the field fighting alongside US forces, accelerate UK–US research and development of 'the next generation of interoperable defence technologies' and benefit jointly from leveraging their respective defence technology strengths (Rood 2007; House of Commons 2008; House of Commons 2007, 9). The Treaty, perhaps as importantly, underscores the viability and formal extension of the already existing 'trusted communities' in the Anglo-American security relationship – such as in the areas of intelligence, nuclear weapons and ballistic missile technology – to the defence-industrial base (Chao and Niblett 2006, 7). Yet, despite the advocacy of the Treaty by the Bush and Obama White Houses, the Senate has yet to ratify the treaty, despite the acknowledged economic and technological benefits of the Treaty and the significant diplomatic support and military contributions that

---

1   A similar Treaty was signed with Australia, another stalwart American ally in deed as well as rhetoric.

the UK has made to American and NATO-led operations inside and outside Europe (Bromund 2008, 2–3). There are a variety of reasons for this resistance, the most important of which are abiding American concerns over the third party transfer of strategic technologies – even to a close ally – and an unwillingness to relinquish aspects of American technological superiority in warfare.

Geostrategic Concord

A 1964 FCO paper captured a simple truth about the Anglo-American security relationship:

> As much the weaker partner, dependent on overseas trade and with world-wide responsibilities, we find American support for our overseas policies virtually indispensable, while they find our support for theirs useful and sometimes valuable (cited in Parsons 2002, 4).

This self-evident asymmetry in the relationship, in conjunction with the limited assistance Britain can provide to the US, would suggest a normal rather than 'special' security relationship. Overlapping geostrategic interests, a common willingness to defend those interests and Britain's readiness to meet those challenges on American terms have been put forward as central to understanding Britain's role as America's first ally. A close examination of American and British defence and security documents since 1996 reveals a remarkable consistency with respect to the sources, nature and agents of threat facing both states in the international system.

The Clinton administration published its second National Security Strategy (NSS) in 1999. A well-demarcated set of threats were identified: the acquisition of nuclear weapons by Iran, Iraq, North Korea and other rogue states; the proliferation of nuclear weapons owing to the continuing problem of securing nuclear materials and sites in the Russian Federation; missile technology proliferation, particularly its acquisition by Iran and North Korea; and terrorism, including specific references to Al Qaeda. The administration also recognised the growing importance of threats best addressed with the 'soft' elements of power: cyber-vandalism and information warfare; the proliferation of dangerous technologies; unsecure supplies of energy; environmental and health threats (irreparable damage to regional ecosystems or epidemics); and the flow of narcotics into the US. The UK's 1998 SDR identified a similar but less specific set of threats: the acquisition of nuclear weapons by Iraq, international terrorism (although unspecified with respect to Islam or a geographic source), drug trafficking, an insecure supply of energy and threats to the environment and information infrastructure (Ministry of Defence 1998; McInnes 1998, 827–9). Unlike the Clinton administration, the UK also was preoccupied with the threats to British security posed by continuing Balkan instability, the problem of transnational organised crime and the threat to regional and global stability arising from an unrestricted competition for scarce resources (see Table 2.4).

The post-11 September security environment broadened the threat environment for the US. The Bush administration issued two NSS, the first in 2002, the second in 2006. In both security statements, the administration focused upon Islamic terrorist groups and their acquisition of chemical, biological, radiological and nuclear (CBRN) devices, and upon the acquisition of nuclear, chemical and biological weapons by the three states constituting the 'Axis of Evil' – Iran, Iraq and North Korea. While the Clinton administration shared these concerns, the 2002 National Security Strategy was clearly preoccupied with the threat posed by 'radical Islam'. The inflammatory rhetoric of post-11 September was given near-doctrinal status in the 2006 version; it described the 'war on terror' as a fight 'against terrorists and against their murderous ideology' and claimed that Al Qaeda sought 'a totalitarian empire that denies all political and religious freedom' (White House 2006, 1–9). The administration noted in more measured tones America's continuing vulnerability to a wide spectrum of threats, ranging from porous boundaries to unsecured key infrastructures (Office of Homeland Security 2002, 7–10). Compared to the Clinton administration, there was a considerable narrowing of the security agenda in the 2006 iteration, with the terrorist threat clearly emerging as the *idée fixe* of the Bush administration.

The New Chapter updated the SDR to account for the threat posed by international terrorism, but avoided the alarmist rhetoric found in its American counterpart. The analysis underscored the growing threat posed by the acquisition of CBRN weapons by state and non-state actors. The 2003 Defence White Paper was similarly concerned with these categories of threats, but also underscored the potential instability attending growing demographic pressures that could easily become translated into inter or intra-state conflicts, impinging on British security interests. The White Paper also identified sources of instability or conflict arising from the dislocations occasioned by climate change, the emergence of additional failed states or attacks on critical national infrastructures. The divergences between the US and UK in their assessment of threat can be viewed as largely marginal in nature: American security statements identified specific states and terrorist groups, whereas the British statements made primarily generic references to general categories of threat. Differences of substance, however, emerged in the immediate aftermath of 11 September. The American threat perception and security agenda was driven almost exclusively by a concern with meeting the challenge of terrorism, whereas the UK retained a broader definition of security independent of terrorism and viewed diplomacy and economic assistance, in addition to military force, as the most efficient instruments to meet them.

These divergences in threat assessment, such as they were, largely evaporated with the publication of the American and British National Security Strategies, in 2006 and 2008 respectively, and the 2009 UK Strategy for Countering International Terrorism (see Table 2.4). There was concordance with respect to the continuing threat of nuclear proliferation in North Korea and Iran, to the proliferation of chemical and biological weapons as well as ballistic missile technology, to the specific terrorist threat posed by Al Qaeda and to the growing threat posed by natural pandemics to national security and global stability. Although the British redirected their attention to the terrorist threat in the New Chapter and 2003 White

The Development of British Defence Policy

Paper, they did not minimise the continuing importance of other categories of threats drawn from the 'new' security agenda. This preoccupation with potential sources of regional instability and conflict remained in the 2008 National Security Strategy, an analysis consistent with the threat assessment found in the EU's European Security Strategy (Kirchner and Sperling, 2007).

Table 2.4   Threat Perception: US and UK Defence and Security Documents, 1998–2009

	NSS (1999)	SDR (1998)	NSS (2002)	SDR-NC (2002)	WP (2003)	NSS (2006)	UK-NSS (2008)	SCIT (2009)
Nuclear proliferation	+		+		+	+	+	+
• FSU	+		+					
• Iran	+		+			+	+	
• Iraq	+	+	+					
• North Korea	+		+			+	+	
• Rogue states	+		+			+		
• Terrorists			+			+		
Biological weapons proliferation			+	+	+	+	+	+
Chemical weapons proliferation	+		+	+	+	+	+	+
Missile technology proliferation	+		+			+	+	
• Iran	+						+	
• North Korea	+		+					
Terrorism	+	+	+	+		+	+	+
• Islam/Al Qaeda	+		+			+	+	+
Instability within Europe		+		+	+			+
Drugs	+	+	+					
Organised crime		+						
Disease (HIV/AIDS)	+		+			+		
Demographic pressures				+	+			
Energy Supply	+	+	+					
Competition for scarce resources		+			+			
Environment	+	+			+			
Failed states	+				+			
Infrastructure	+	+	+		+			+
Imbalance of power		+						
Poor governance						+	+	

Sources: White House 1999, 2002 and 2006; Ministry of Defence 1998, 2002 and 2003; Cabinet Office 2008; Home Office 2009.

Despite the relative concord on the strategic threats posed to national security, these various strategy documents belied the global preoccupations of the US and the more regionally limited concerns of the UK, despite claims that Britain has global interests on a par with those of the US (Brown 2009c; O'Sullivan 2001, 18) (see Table 2.5). The US and UK have overlapping regional preoccupations in South Asia and the Gulf Region. The British have been most preoccupied with strategic developments in the Balkans, Africa and the Mediterranean, while the Americans are oriented towards Latin America and Central and Northeast Asia. This disparity in geostrategic preoccupation is replicated in the assessment of individual states as sources of instability: China and the Russian Federation are considered a threat to American security by virtue of their potential emergence as peer competitors, a concern that does not factor into British assessments of threat (Reid 2006; Cabinet Office 2008, 47; Department of Defense 2005a, 5 and 2005b). The US and UK share a concern with the evolution of Iran, Iraq, and Afghanistan for virtually

Table 2.5   Sources of Threat: US and UK Security and Defence Documents, 1998–2009

	NSS (1999)	SDR (1998)	NSS (2002)	SDR-NC (2002)	WP (2003)	NSS (2006)	UK-NSS (2008)	SCIT (2009)
States								
Afghanistan			+	+	+		+	+
DR Congo					+			
North Korea	+			+		+	+	
FSU/NIS	+							
Russian Federation				+		+		
India–Pakistan	+			+			+	
Iran	+			+		+	+	
Iraq	+			+	+	+	+	+
Syria						+		
China	+			+		+		
Regions								
Balkans	+		+		+			+
Africa			+		+		+	
East Asia							+	
South Asia	+		+	+	+		+	+
Korean peninsula	+					+		
Mediterranean		+	+		+			+
Gulf	+	+	+		+			
South America	+			+				
Central Asia	+			+				

Sources: White House 1999, 2002 and 2006; Ministry of Defence 1998, 2002 and 2003; Cabinet Office 2008; Home Office 2009.

identical reasons, owing to the centrality of the Gulf region to assessments of national security and interest.

The institutional preferences of the two actors, as well as the pattern of bilateral relationships, serve as a final dimension of comparison. The unilateralist impulse of the Bush administration exaggerated the American willingness to act independently of its allies. While no American or British government has been willing to renounce the right to act unilaterally if necessary, they both recognise the instrumental utility and necessity of multilateral or bilateral action (see Table 2.6). Yet, the interaction preferences of the US and UK revealed a fundamental difference brought to the surface in the run-up to the invasion of Iraq, notably over the UK's dedication to working within the UN framework. This preference reflects the British calculation that only the UN can establish an effective basis for action in international law, promote the necessary international consensus permitting effective action, provide a broad basis for countering terrorism abroad and implement development and assistance strategies to mitigate the underlying sources of terrorism in failed and failing states (Ministry of Defence 2002; Ministry of Defence 2003b, 3). The FCO and MoD both share this preference, although Prime Minister Blair excluded a UN mandate as necessary in his 1999 Chicago Speech outlining the criteria for humanitarian military interventions. According to Oliver Daddow, Blair did not solicit the input of the Foreign Office in drafting that speech precisely to avoid adding a UN mandate as a sixth criterion for action (Daddow 2009, 56). Nonetheless, he did press Bush to obtain one in the run-up to the Iraq invasion. Although the US identifies a number of important bilateral relationships consistent with its global reach and treaty obligations, the UK has repeatedly identified the US as its most important bilateral partner, 'central to our national security, including through its engagement

Table 2.6   Interaction Patterns: US and UK Defence and Security Documents, 1998–2008

	NSS (1999)	SDR (1998)	SDR-NC (2002)	NSS (2002)	WP (2003)	NSS (2006)	UK-NSS (2008)
Regional Security Institutions							
• NATO	+	+	+	+	+	+	+
• EU/ESDP/WEU		+	+		+		+
• UN		+	+		+		+
Bilateral Security Relationships							
• US			+		+		+
• Japan	+					+.	
• Russian Federation	+			+		+	
• South Korea	+			+		+	
• China				+		+	+

Sources: White House 1999, 2002 and 2006; Ministry of Defence 1998, 2002 and 2003; Cabinet Office 2008.

in NATO' (Cabinet Office 2008, 8). Another significant divergence, noted above, is the opposed roles that China plays in each state's strategic calculations.

The UK has drawn a careful distinction between the relative roles of NATO and the EU. In the area of military defence, the UK expects its 'armed forces to operate in most cases as part of NATO or in [US-led] coalitions', while security cooperation within the EU or UN frameworks is restricted to the tasks of post-conflict stabilisation (Cabinet Office 2008, 9). Although the UK views the EU as performing an important security role for the UK, it did not enjoy the same level of attention that the St Malo Agreement would have implied after 11 September. Arguably, the UK has endeavoured to ensure not only a linkage between the EU and NATO, but also to ensure the subordination of the former to the latter. British security documents inevitably arrive at the same conclusion: the UK can only act with the US to realise its most important strategic objectives outside Europe (Scotland 2001). This recognition explains the British desire to retain its nuclear deterrent as a mechanism for not only guaranteeing its security in the face of an existential threat to its survival but also serves as the keystone supporting the edifice of Anglo-American security and defence cooperation (Browne 2008; Ministry of Defence 1998; Ministry of Defence 2006; Bacon 2008). This same calculation explains Britain's willingness to accommodate the American position on the (un)desirability of deploying a ballistic missile defence system in Europe, the enthusiasm for acquiring network centric warfare capabilities, the imperative of restructuring its armed forces to ensure interoperability with US forces and more generally the acquisition of force projection capabilities enabling the UK to conduct military operations across the entire spectrum of duration and intensity (Ministry of Defence 2002, 14; Cabinet Office 2008, 44; House of Commons 2003, 31–5; Ministry of Defence 2004, 14). The importance of the bilateral relationship for the UK is also reflected in the explicit privileging of interoperability with US forces and a secondary concern with interoperability with its 'European and other allies' (Ministry of Defence 2003, 19).

Conclusion

Mutually reinforcing historical legacies have sustained the 'special relationship' between the US and UK. The legacy of empire left two marks on the British defence and security orientation: the foreign policy elite not only reflexively adopts a global perspective, despite Britain's lack of global reach, but retains a heightened sense of obligation for the maintenance of global order. American hegemony after the Second World War, and the responsibilities it engendered, required the US to create global order and to assume responsibility for it. A second legacy uniting the two is the common cause made against Nazi Germany in the Second World War. Not only did it lend Anglo-American relations an emotional resonance unique among the war-time allies, but it laid the foundation for the extraordinary post-war levels of military cooperation in the areas of nuclear technology and intelligence sharing, among others. Moreover, America and Britain jointly designed the key institutional frameworks of the post-war order, notably the Bretton Woods monetary system and NATO. These legacies persist and have been replicated over time – in defence terms, the British willingness to expend blood and treasure alongside the US in the Balkans, Iraq and Afghanistan evokes the wartime alliance and underscores its continuing vitality, while the wider arrangements are noted in the framework proposals presented at the November 2008 and April 2009 G20 meetings for the institutional redesign of the international banking and financial governance systems. A global strategic orientation, reinforced by shared assessments of the critical geostrategic or geoeconomic regions of the world, facilitates defence cooperation and contributes to the 'naturalness' of the Anglo-American partnership, despite the undeniable asymmetry of power at its core.

These legacies, as powerful and dynamic as they may be, cannot solely explain the contemporary persistence of the 'special relationship', particularly given significant and fundamental policy differences over the Bush administration's reliance upon torture, rendition and 'black site' prisons in the 'global war on terror' (Danner 2009), America's uncritical support of Israel, American scepticism of climate change and hostility to the Kyoto Treaty, and the unwillingness to recognise the jurisdiction of International Criminal Court (ICC) in cases involving American citizens. Yet, both parties have a strategic interest in protecting the 'special relationship'.

The UK preference for NATO rather than the EU and a fully autonomous ESDP is undeniable, as is the privileging of interoperability with the US rather than with its European allies. This preference reflects not only the commercial and technological benefits of close Anglo-American defence cooperation, but three strategic considerations. First, there is the lesson of Suez, which has not faded from memory: Britain is unable to achieve its foreign policy goals outside Europe without the support of the United States, a lesson reinforced during the Falklands War. Second, a close relationship with the US within NATO and bilaterally provides Britain an opportunity (rather than the ability) to influence US foreign policy in times of crises. Tony Blair, for example, has been credited with persuading George W. Bush to seek a UN Security Council Resolution prior to the invasion of Iraq. And third, the close relationship and trust between the two is the precondition for the British aspiration to function as a 'global hub' or even to perform the more modest role of interlocutor between the continental European powers and the US, a role that guarantees the continued American military and strategic engagement in Europe and allows the UK to participate constructively in the EU's institutional evolution, particularly in the area of defence and foreign policy.

The preponderance of American power tends to obscure the tangible strategic benefits of the Anglo-American alliance. The US retains an interest in the transatlantic alliance, minimally to prevent the emergence of another pole of power that could challenge American interests or limit American freedom of action in regions of the world of critical strategic interest, particularly in the eastern Mediterranean, North Africa and the Persian Gulf. An American-led NATO still pays benefits:

it has extended the transatlantic security community to the borders of the former Soviet Union, it continues to provide a forum for addressing common security and defence concerns inside and outside Europe and it provides a pool of military personnel and materiel to support the American-led global order. Britain's fidelity to NATO and the US provides an insurmountable barrier to the construction of an EU that could emerge as an autonomous and potentially uncooperative military actor. Britain also serves as the poster-boy for the transformation of European armed forces to tackle the most likely military challenges of the twenty-first century. British efforts to preserve and enhance interoperability with US forces produce two benefits, one immediate and the other putative. It has produced an ally that is capable of making a significant contribution to out of area missions and an opening for greater cooperation between the EU and NATO in establishing common capabilities requirements and interoperability standards. Britain has also aided or enabled the US in undertaking out of area operations with or without NATO. The decision to invade Iraq would have been extraordinarily difficult diplomatically without the imprimatur of the Blair government. The British contributions to the two most important out of area conflicts since 11 September – Iraq and Afghanistan – have exceed those of America's other important NATO and non-NATO allies with respect to total forces committed and exposure to the risk of combat.

In the late nineteenth century, at the height of the British empire, Joseph Chamberlain claimed that 'friendship and unbroken amity between Great Britain and the United States is the best guarantee for the peace and civilization of the world' (Chamberlain 1897, 7). In the early twenty-first century, Prime Minister Gordon Brown was able to claim that 'there is no partnership in recent history that has served the world better than the special relationship between Britain and the United States' (Brown 2009c). The confluence of amity and purpose, interests and common endeavour, suggests that the Anglo-American relationship is the exception to Palmerston's rule that 'nations have no permanent friends or allies, they only have permanent interests'. Arguably, American and Britain are permanent allies and friends who provide one another mutual benefits.

Bibliography

Abramsky, S (2008), 'The Anglo-American Misalliance', *World Policy Journal* 25, 72–79

Bacon, R (2008), 'Nuclear Treaty Still Going Strong at 50', *Defence Policy and Business*, 4 September

Bagehot (2009), 'How Gordon Brown and Barack Obama Can and Cannot Help Each Other', *The Economist*, 8621

Battle, J (2002), *Government's Policy Towards the USA – Comments by the Foreign Office Minister on 18 February* (London: HMSO)

BBC News (2007), 'US and UK "No Longer Inseparable"' – http://news.bbc. co.uk/go/pr/fr/-/1/hi/uk_politics/6898587.stm

Berry, N (2003), 'The Curse of the Special Relationship', *Arab News*, 10 March.

Blair, T (2002), *The UK and the USA: Engaged on a Range of Global Issues – Speech by the Prime Minister on the 18 February* (London: HMSO)

Borger, J (2008), 'UK's Special Relationship with US Needs to be Recalibrated, Obama Tells Ex-pats in Britain', *The Guardian*, 27 May

Bremmer, I (2007), 'With Blair Gone, US–UK Relations May be a Little Less "Special"', *The Times*, 27 July

Bromund, T (2008), 'The Defence Trade Cooperation Treaties with the United Kingdom and Australia Advance the American Interest', *Webmemo No. 2090* (Washington, DC: Heritage Foundation)

Brown, G (2007), *Press Conference with the President of the United States George W Bush at Camp David on 31 July* (London: HMSO)

Brown, G (2008a), *Speech by the Prime Minister to the Council on Foreign Relations on 14 November* (London: HMSO)

Brown, G (2008b), *Press Conference with the President of the United States George W Bush on 17 June* (London: HMSO)

Brown, G (2009a), *Speech by the Prime Minister to US Congress on 4 March* (London: HMSO)

Brown, G (2009b), *Prime Ministerial Press Conference with President of the United States Barack Obama on 5 March* (London: HMSO)

Brown, G (2009c), 'The Special Relationship is Going Global', *The Times*, 1 March

Browne, D (2008), *Iraq, Afghanistan and Beyond: The UK–US Partnership in a Changing World – Speech by the Defence Secretary on 10 July* (London: HMSO)

Burns, J (2009), 'Britain's Prime Minister Hopes to Bolster U.S. Ties', *New York Times*, 4 March

Cabinet Office (2008), *The National Security Strategy of the United Kingdom: Security in an Interdependent World* (London: HMSO)

Chamberlin, J (1897), *Foreign and Colonial Speeches* (London: Routledge and Sons)

Chao, P and Niblett, R (2006), *Trusted Partners: Sharing Technology within the US-UK Security Relationship* (Washington, DC: CSIS)

Daddow, O (2009), '"Tony's War"? Blair, Kosovo and the Interventionist Impulse in British Foreign Policy', *International Affairs*, 85/3, 547–60

Danner, M (2009), 'The Red Cross Torture Report: What it Means', *New York Review of Books*, 51/7, 48–56

De Conde, A (1992), *Ethnicity, Race and American Foreign Policy: A History* (Boston: Northeastern University Press)

Foreign and Commonwealth Office (2006), *The Future of the United Kingdom's Nuclear Deterrent* (London: HMSO)

Freedman, L (2006), 'The Special Relationship, Then and Now', *Foreign Affairs*, 85/3, 61–74

Garton Ash, T (2001), 'Is Britain European?', *International Affairs*, 77/1, 1–13

Harris, R (2002), 'The State of the Special Relationship', *Policy Review*, 113 – http://www.hoover.org/publications/policyreview/3460326.html

Home Office (2009), *The United Kingdom's Strategy for Countering International Terrorism* (London: HMSO)

House of Commons (2003), *A New Chapter to the Strategic Defence Review: Sixth Report of Defence Select Committee Volume 1 on 7 May* (London: HMSO)

House of Commons (2007), *UK/US Defence Trade Cooperation Treaty: Third Report of the Defence Select Committee on 11 December* (London: HMSO)

House of Commons (2008), *UK/US Defence Trade Cooperation Treaty: Government Response to the Defence Select Committee's Third Report on 3 March* (London: HMSO)

House of Commons (2009), *Ministry of Defence Annual Report and Accounts 2007–2008, Volume 2 – Fifth Report of the Defence Select Committee on 30 March* (London: HMSO)

Kirchner, E and Sperling, J (2007), *EU Security Governance* (Manchester: Manchester University Press)

Kissinger, H (1965), *The Troubled Partnership: A Re-Appraisal of the Atlantic Alliance* (New York: McGraw Hill)

Kissinger, H (1982), *Years of Upheaval* (New York: Little, Brown & Company)

Krahmann, E (2007), 'United Kingdom: Punching Above its Weight', in Kirchner, E and Sperling, J (eds), *Global Security Governance: Competing Perceptions of security in the 21st Century* (Abingdon: Routledge)

Marsh, S and Baylis, J (2006), 'The Anglo-American "Special Relationship": The Lazarus of International Relations', *Diplomacy and Statecraft*, 17, 173–211

McGuire, S (2009), 'An Island, Lost at Sea', *Newsweek*, 23 February

McInnes, C (1998), 'Labour's Strategic Defence Review', *International Affairs*, 74/4, 823–45

McNamara, S (2008), 'Is the Special Relationship Still Special?', *The Journal of International Security Affairs*, 14

Miliband, D (2007), *Interview with the Foreign Secretary on National Public Radio in New York on 28 September* (London: HMSO)

Ministry of Defence (1998), *Strategic Defence Review: Modern Forces for the Modern World* (London: HMSO)

Ministry of Defence (2001), *Performance Report 2000/2001* (London: HMSO)

Ministry of Defence (2002), *The Strategic Defence Review: A New Chapter* (London: HMSO)

Ministry of Defence (2003), *Delivering Security in a Changing World: Supporting Essays* (London: HMSO)

Ministry of Defence (2004), *Future Capabilities: Defence White Paper* (London: HMSO)

Ministry of Defence (2005), *Defence Industrial Strategy: Defence White Paper* (London: HMSO)

Ministry of Defence (2008), *Annual Report and Accounts 2007–2008: Volume 2* (London: HMSO)

Morrison, W and Labonte, M (2008), *China's Holdings of US Securities: Implications for the US Economy* (Washington, DC: Congressional Research Office)

National Audit Office (2007) *Ministry of Defence. Major Projects Report 2007 Project Summary Sheets* (London: National Audit Office)

Office of Homeland Security (2002), *National Strategy for Homeland Security* (Washington, DC: White House)

Organisation for Economic Cooperation and Development (2008), *OECD Stat: Trade in Value by Partner Countries* (New York: OECD)

Orszag, P (2007), *Foreign Holdings of US Government Securities and the US Current Account Deficit – Testimony of the Director of the Congressional Budget Office before the Committee of the Budget US House of Representatives on 26 June* (Washington, DC: CBO)

O'Sullivan, J (2001), 'How "Special"? For How Long? Between Washington and London: US–UK Relations', *National Review*, 18/1, 18–20

Parsons, M (2007), 'The Special Relationship 1945–1990: Myth or Reality?' – http://www.cairn.info/revue-etudes-anglaises-2002-4-page-456.html

Qiao, Y (2009), 'How Asia Can Protect Itself from a Dollar Default', *Financial Times*, 1 April

Rees, W (1991), 'The Anglo-American Security Relationship', in Croft, S (ed.), *British Security Policy: The Thatcher Years and the End of the Cold War* (London: HarperCollins Academic)

Reid, J (2006), *Speech by the Secretary of State for Defence, at the 42nd Munich Conference on Security Policy on 4 April* (London: HMSO)

Reynolds, P (2007), 'The subtle shift in British foreign policy', *BBC News*, 15 July

Rood, J (2007), *The US-UK Defence Trade Cooperation Treaty: Entering a New Era of Transatlantic Defence Cooperation. Speech by the Under Secretary for Arms Control and International Security on 26 September* (Washington, DC: State Department)

Scotland of Asthal, Baroness P (2002), *Comments by the UK Attorney General on UK–US Relations on 18 February* (London: HMSO)

Shipman, T (2009), 'Barack Obama Plans to Make US Relationship with Britain Less Special than Before', *The Daily Telegraph*, 17 January

SIPRI (2009a), *SIPRI Trend Indicators of Arms Imports, 1990–2007* – http://armstrade.sipri.org/arms_trade/values.php

SIPRI (2009b), *SIPRI Trend Indicators of Arms Exports, 1990–2007* – http://armstrade.sipri.org/arms_trade/values.php

Sperling, J (2007), 'Regional or Global Security Cooperation: The Vertices of Conflict and Interstices of Cooperation', in Kirchner, E and Sperling, J (eds),

Global Security Governance: Competing Perceptions of Security in the 21st Century (Abingdon: Routledge)

Sperling, J and Webber, M (2009), 'NATO – From Kosovo to Kabul', *International Affairs*, 85/3

Spillius, A (2009), 'Hilary Clinton Lauds "Special Relationship" During Meeting with David Miliband', *The Daily Telegraph*, 4 February

TradeStats Express (2008a), *Global Patterns of Merchandise Trade: Exports* – http://tse.export.gov/NTDHome.aspx

TradeStats Express (2008b), *Global Patterns of Merchandise Trade: Imports* – http://tse.export.gov/NTDHome.aspx

US Department of Commerce Bureau of Economic Analysis (2008a), *International Investment Position: US Direct Investment Abroad* (Washington, DC: CPO)

US Department of Commerce Bureau of Economic Analysis (2008b), *International Investment Position: U.S. Foreign Direct Investment Position Abroad on a Historical-Cost Basis: Country Detail* (Washington, DC: CPO)

US Department of Commerce Bureau of Economic Analysis (2008c), *International Investment Position: Foreign Direct Investment in the United States* (Washington, DC: CPO)

US Department of Defense (various years), *Index of 100 Parent Companies Which Received the Largest Dollar Volume of Prime Contract Awards, Fiscal Year 200x* – http://gcfa.org/PDFs/Deptofdefence-Top100ParentCompanies200x.pdf

US Department of the Treasury Office of International Affairs (2008), *Treasury International Capital System: Major Holders of US Treasury Securities* (Washington, DC: CPO)

White House (various years), *Top 100 Recipients of Federal Contracts for FY 200x* – http://www.usaspending.gov/fpds/tables.php?tabtype=t2&subtype=t&year=200x&[romtmav+0

White House (1999), *A National Security Strategy for a New Century* (Washington, DC: White House)

White House (2002), *The National Security Strategy of the United States of America* (Washington, DC: White House)

White House (2006), *The National Security Strategy of the United States of America* (Washington, DC: White House)

Chapter 3

Blair, Brown and Brussels: The European Turn in British Defence Policy

Alistair JK Shepherd

Under Tony Blair, the long standing taboo of associating the EU with defence policy was broken. In December 1998, the Franco-British St Malo Declaration called for autonomous and credible military forces for the EU. This signalled a major shift in the UK's position on the EU's involvement in defence policy. While not abandoning NATO or the US, Blair's desire to be 'at the heart of Europe' led to one of the most significant shifts in the UK's defence policy in recent times – a turn towards the EU.

This chapter examines the motivations, objectives and implications of the UK's evolving defence and security relationship with the EU under Tony Blair and Gordon Brown. It explores the continuities and changes in UK government attitudes to the EU's ESDP from New Labour's election in May 1997, through the impact of 11 September, to the Brown Premiership. The chapter first sets out the European context of the UK's security and defence policy. It then examines the UK's role in launching ESDP in the late 1990s. The third section – and central focus of the chapter – analyses the UK's attitude and policy under Tony Blair toward three of the most significant elements of ESDP: institutions, capabilities and operations. The final section examines the UK's involvement in ESDP under Gordon Brown. The chapter concludes with a discussion of the implications of the changes under New Labour and argues that, given changing priorities and shrinking resources, this shift should be consolidated in the long term.

The chapter demonstrates that the UK has been an important player in shaping each of the three crucial areas of ESDP outlined above. This was a significant change from previous governments, which saw the UK shift from resisting any EU involvement in defence matters to leading, at least initially, the development of ESDP. By taking the lead, the UK has been better placed to try to align ESDP with its preferences. In order to accommodate the preferences of – and minimise competition from – its co-leader France, while also pursuing its key priority for a strong transatlantic security alliance, the UK ensured ambiguities were built into ESDP. This meant that the UK government could sell ESDP in different ways to different audiences: the EU, EU member states, the US, the UK Parliament and the British electorate. For example, by tackling the EU's collective capability gaps, the UK wanted to convince the US that the Europeans were serious about improving capabilities and that this would benefit NATO, while also trying to assure the other

EU states that they wanted the EU to be a global player in crisis management. This approach to ESDP suggests that, under Tony Blair, there was a clear change in strategy, but not a change in fundamental interests. Despite clinging to the 'special relationship' with the US as the principal British security and defence relationship, the shift towards the EU was both genuine and permanent.

Cold War Legacy and the 'Peace Dividend'

Europe and the Cold War

In both defence and European policy the UK has had different experiences to its continental neighbours, due to geography and history. As an island, the UK could base its defence and foreign policy, to a large extent, on a 'philosophy of choice', as opposed to its continental neighbours, which had to base it on a 'philosophy of necessity' (Wolfers, 1962, 244–5). In addition, the development of the British Empire meant that expeditionary forces were always a requirement. Distance, together with the difficulties of invading an island, meant that, aside from the two world wars, only a few of the UK's wars were about national survival. Most were elective wars, unlike those waged by other European states that are now in the EU (Chuter, 1997, 109).

While the UK has traditionally seen itself as different from its continental neighbours, Europe's importance was nevertheless evident in how the UK constantly strove to ensure a balance of power on the continent (Dorman, 2001). The UK's position was succinctly summarised in 1930 by Winston Churchill: 'We are with Europe, but not of it. We are linked but not compromised. We are interested and associated, but not absorbed' (Churchill cited in Urwin, 1991, 31). This attitude continued after 1945, with the UK's self-perception as a global player leading to a three way division of defence priorities. Europe continued to be the most important issue, but it had to compete with the UK's imperial role and its desire to ensure a 'special relationship' with the US. However, as the Cold War unfolded and British global defensive commitments declined, the primacy of Europe in UK defence policy became ever more apparent. The 1974–75 defence review elucidated the four 'pillars' upon which defence policy was founded, each with a European component: an independent element of strategic and theatre nuclear forces committed to the Alliance; the direct defence of the UK homeland; a major land and air contribution on the European mainland; and a major maritime effort in the Eastern Atlantic and Channel (Dockrill, 1988, 154). Another 'half pillar' was out-of-area action to protect dependent territories, as demonstrated in the Falklands Campaign of 1982. The four pillars demonstrated the extent to which Europe had become a dominant focus of UK defence policy in the second half of the Cold War. These pillars, reiterated in the 1981 Defence Review (Ministry of Defence, 1981), remained in place until 1992, guiding defence policy throughout the Thatcher years. However, despite the increased importance of Europe in the form of NATO, the UK continued to prioritise the 'special relationship' and remained, in Churchill's words, 'interested and associated, but not absorbed' by Europe, at this stage in the form of the European Community (EC).

Post-Cold War Europe: 'Peace Dividend' v. Crisis Management

At the end of the Cold War, the UK, along with the rest of Western Europe, rushed to realise the so-called 'peace dividend', despite uncertainty about the evolution of the new strategic environment. The perception of a reduced threat led to calls for cuts in defence spending and a shift towards a capability-based, rather than threat-based, policy (Croft, 2001, 21). The reassessments undertaken by the Conservative governments of Margaret Thatcher and John Major heeded the calls for cuts in the defence budget, largely through reductions in the size of the armed forces, but eschewed fundamental reform (King, 1990; Ministry of Defence, 1994). There was acknowledgement of a need to shift towards more expeditionary capabilities to 'contribute to promoting the UK's wider security interests through the maintenance of international peace and stability' (Sabin, 1993, 269), but tangible change was limited. The notion of a 'peace dividend' persevered, despite the outbreak of civil war in Yugoslavia, demonstrating all too clearly that peace had not come to all parts of Europe. The desire for this perceived 'peace dividend' was apparent in the 1994 'Frontline First' report, which reduced manpower across the support and logistical units at the very time the move to 'out of area' operations in the former Yugoslavia put greater emphasis on precisely these capabilities (Ministry of Defence, 1994; Croft, 2001, 22).

The increasing need for crisis management capabilities highlighted by the disintegration of Yugoslavia, together with broader changes in the strategic environment, was a catalyst for a greater European effort in coordinating security and defence arrangements. Already in 1991 the Conservative government acknowledged that a 'European security and defence identity was needed' but insisted it should be within NATO and/or the Western European Union (WEU), not the EU (Ministry of Defence, 1991). This was reiterated in 1995 with the government stating that 'Britain does not want the WEU to merge with the European Union … the WEU, not the European Union, should be the basis for cooperation in defence matters' (United Kingdom Government, 1995). This remained the government's position until the Conservatives left office in 1997, becoming an increasing source of tension between the UK and many of its European allies, which sought a greater role for the EU in security and defence policy. The UK, under the Conservatives, wanted to ensure a strong NATO and to preserve the 'special relationship' with the US and believed an explicit EU role in security and defence would jeopardise both of these objectives. However, UK–US relations were also under strain because of differences over the conflict in Yugoslavia. Hence, by the time of the 1997 General Election, the UK was caught between a peripheral role in the European institutional debate on defence and a weakening of the 'special relationship', as US priorities continued to shift ever further towards the Middle East and Asia-Pacific region

(Dorman, 2001). Tony Blair's accession to the office of Prime Minister in 1997 had a significant impact on this balancing act and fundamentally changed British defence policy in relation to the EU.

New Labour: The European Turn?

Assessing the Options: From Amsterdam to St Malo

Under Blair, British defence policy took a significant European turn, positioning the UK at the heart of the EU's security and defence ambitions. Blair was vital to the launching of ESDP and, while the UK lost some of its authority after his first term of office and then under Gordon Brown, it continues to influence the ESDP's evolution. Ironically, however, one of Blair's first major decisions on the issue was to veto the EU's incorporation of the majority of the WEU at the Amsterdam summit in July 1997, replicating the previous government's position. This rejection suggests that, while Blair had expressed his desire to be 'at the heart of Europe', it was not yet clear that defence would be the field which would take Britain there. Yet, the rejection probably owed more to the timing of negotiations than to any fundamental opposition to the idea. Having only been in office for a few weeks and done relatively little thinking on the issue, it was simpler for New Labour to continue the UK tradition of resisting a defence dimension for the EU.

The first signs of the growing importance of the EU for UK defence policy emerged in the 1998 SDR. The review stated that the UK was 'a major European state and a leading member of the European Union' (Ministry of Defence, 1998, 7). This suggested that New Labour wanted leadership in the EU, rather than the resistance and selective engagement seen under the Conservatives. The increased importance of the EU was implied in the SDR's claim that, on defence, 'the EU has a vital role ... through the common foreign and security policy' (Ministry of Defence, 1998, 10). While NATO remained the 'cornerstone' of UK defence policy and the 'special relationship' was still paramount, the SDR was an early indication of the greater 'Europeanisation' of UK defence policy.

These tentative shifts gained momentum through the summer and autumn of 1998. Driven, most importantly, by increasing concern over the EU's impotence in Kosovo, but also the desire for a more influential British role in the EU, the UK put forward a series of options on European defence. These ranged from strengthening NATO's European Security and Defence Identity (ESDI) to the creation of a new fourth pillar for the EU, alongside the traditional 'three pillars' of the EU (Whitman, 1999). By the time of the October informal EU summit in Portschach, an EU solution was gaining ascendency in the UK government's thinking about improving European military capabilities. At the same time, as the Kosovo crisis continued to escalate, the British and French were working well together on establishing the Kosovo Extraction Force to pull out observers from the Organisation for Security and Cooperation in Europe (OSCE) if required. This positive experience even led the MoD to be more enthusiastic about an EU defence project (Andreani, Bertram and Grant, 2001). It was clear by the end of 1998 that the UK government believed that the provisions for European defence under the Maastricht and Amsterdam Treaties were no longer sufficient (Whitman, 1999). This was confirmed at the December Franco-British Summit at St Malo.

St Malo the Defining Moment? Motivations and Implications

The declaration issued at the end of the St Malo summit was the springboard for ESDP. It is perhaps the defining moment in Blair's efforts to be at the 'heart of Europe' and demonstrated the profound change in UK government thinking on European security and defence issues. The Joint Declaration called for the EU to:

> have the capacity for autonomous action, backed up by credible military forces, the means to decide to use them, and readiness to do, in order to respond to international crises ... be given appropriate structures and a capacity for analysis of situations, sources of intelligence, and a capability for relevant strategic planning (Franco-British Summit, 1998).

The drivers behind this change were both internal and external. Internally, the change of leadership from a Conservative to a Labour government was vital. Labour's election manifesto spoke of the need to be at 'the heart' of Europe. At the Labour Party conference in 1997, Blair called for the UK to 'be a respected leading European nation' (Blair, 1997). Yet, bureaucratic politics also played a part. To find avenues for greater cooperation, initiative and leadership in Europe, Number 10 sent a memorandum to government departments asking for proposals (Dover, 2007, 29). Given the high reputation of the British armed forces – in 1996 President Chirac held them up as a model for the reform of the French armed forces – if the UK was to lead in any policy area then defence would be the most likely to be developed (Interview, 2008). Moreover, as Dover points out, defence was chosen because the MoD was the only department to respond to the memorandum (Dover, 2007, 29). There has been some debate about whether the UK took a lead on defence because it was staying out of the single currency, but this was probably only a peripheral factor, not a decisive one (Interviews, 2000 and 2008). More important was the role of Tony Blair in pushing for a stronger European lead and the part played by Richard Hatfield as the MoD's Policy Director in persuading then Defence Secretary George Robertson to pursue a European agenda (Interviews, 2000), overcoming the inertia usually found in large government departments. However, while bureaucratic politics and the desire for leadership within the EU were significant internal drivers, external factors were perhaps even more important in shaping UK policy towards ESDP.

The key external impetus for the UK's changing approach to an EU defence capability was the violent disintegration of Yugoslavia. This conflict – and the Europeans' inability to change the course of events – was such a strong catalyst that some officials labelled Slobodan Milosevic the 'father of ESDP' (Interview, 2008). As Yugoslavia imploded, the EC tried to take a lead in ending the violence, infamously declaring 'this is the hour of Europe' (Poos cited in Buchan, 1993, 67). Yet, despite negotiating numerous cease-fires, the EC/EU could not enforce the agreements because they lacked the political will, leadership and capabilities to back up their diplomacy. In particular, the lack of European military capabilities was decisive in convincing Blair of the need for ESDP. The conflict highlighted the continuing European reliance on US capabilities at the very time Europe was declining as a security priority for the US.

The break-up of Yugoslavia clearly illustrated the reduced importance of Europe in US security policy, as it became increasingly focused on the Middle East and Asia-Pacific region. The US had guaranteed Western Europe's security since 1945 and thereby facilitated the construction of a security community that now encompasses most of Europe. After the Cold War, as the likelihood of an existential state-based security threat diminished vastly and the EU developed its own security policies, the US shifted its security priorities elsewhere. Yet, the lack of EU capabilities to enforce its diplomatic efforts in Yugoslavia meant that the US was drawn reluctantly into the conflict in the mid-1990s. Although US capabilities were welcomed by the EU, its involvement created political divisions, particularly over the characterisation of the Serbs as the principal aggressors. This difference was exemplified by arguments over the US proposal for a policy of 'lift and strike', lifting the arms embargo on the Bosnian Muslims and striking the Bosnian Serbs. Regardless of the differences, it was apparent that the EU could not end the Bosnian war without American assistance. Only after US led NATO air-strikes against the Bosnian Serbs in September 1995 did the fighting end and negotiations begin, culminating in the Dayton Accords.

Just three years later, the need for US military capabilities was again apparent in the planning and implementation of Operation Allied Force (OAF) over Kosovo and Serbia. Once again, the NATO air campaign clearly demonstrated the chronic shortcomings in EU military capabilities. The opposition of the US to committing ground forces, coupled with the capability shortfalls of the Europeans, convinced Tony Blair that a European initiative to improve military capabilities was essential. By tackling their collective capability gaps so conspicuously exposed during the Yugoslav conflicts, the UK hoped to convince the US that the Europeans were serious about capabilities and burden-sharing, thereby also strengthening NATO and the 'special relationship'. Meanwhile, within the EU, Blair was trying to convince the UK's partners of his commitment to improving the crisis management capabilities available to the EU. This led many within the UK to argue that Blair was 'Europeanising' British defence policy.

The Europeanisation of British Defence?

This significant change represented a greater Europeanisation of British defence policy. Yet, by taking a leading role in ESDP, Blair ensured it was Europeanised largely in line with UK preferences. While the UK has had to make compromises at times, the need for unanimity in decision making and the importance of the UK in the defence field has limited its impact on key UK national interests. Indeed, on some issues, such as improving the capabilities of European states, they have been enhanced. Therefore, the increased Europeanisation of UK defence policy has been less about downloading preferences from the EU and more about the UK uploading a significant majority of its preferences to the EU. In three crucial areas – institutions, capabilities, and operations – the UK has been central to shaping the development of ESDP.

Institutions

Throughout its membership of the EU, the UK has been wary of the proliferation of EU institutions. However, Blair was supportive of establishing the institutions necessary to run ESDP effectively, as long as they were intergovernmental. As ESDP was embedded within the CFSP, itself largely intergovernmental, this was not too difficult to ensure and, importantly, it fitted with French preferences in this field. Therefore, the structures established in 2000 – the Political and Security Committee [COPS], EU Military Committee and EU Military Staff (EUMS) – were intergovernmental with decision-making based on unanimity.

However, arguments, compromise and ambiguity were evident in implementing these decision-making structures. The UK and France differed on committing to ambassadorial rank representation for COPS, with the UK preferring lower ranking representation and some form of dual-hatting with NATO representatives (Howorth, 2000; Duke, 2005). The compromise of 'senior/ambassadorial level' was ambiguous enough to allow France and the UK to appoint different levels of seniority (Duke, 2005). Similarly, for the post of High Representative (HR) for CFSP, the UK preferred a lower profile politician or civil servant, whereas the French wanted a high profile 'political heavyweight'. The UK concern was that high level political appointments would be seen by the US as real autonomy for the EU and a challenge to NATO's pre-eminence. The agreement on Javier Solana as the first HR for CFSP was acceptable to the UK because, despite being a high profile personality, he had been NATO Secretary-General. He was, therefore, seen by the UK as an 'Atlanticist' and a pragmatist who had contributed to holding the Alliance together through OAF.

Despite appointing Solana, leadership of ESDP has remained largely in the hands of key member states, notably the UK and France, but also Germany and, occasionally, Italy (Interview, 2008). Other states do provide leadership on specific initiatives, but the UK and France are the lynchpin states for ESDP. The influence of the UK on ESDP's institutions can also be seen in the development of the European Defence Agency (EDA). Despite initial reservations, the UK was, alongside France, 'instrumental' in its establishment (House of Lords, 2005). Despite divisions over Iraq, at the Le Touquet summit in February 2003 Tony Blair and Jacques Chirac proposed the creation of an EU defence agency with the aim of promoting 'a comprehensive approach to capability development across all EU nations' (Declaration on Strengthening European Cooperation in Security and Defence, 2003) The agency would not only focus on armaments procurement, but would also seek to harmonise military requirements and coordinate research and development. Through these roles, the EDA would 'help to direct and assess member-states' progress towards meeting their capability commitments' (Keohane, 2004). These capability based objectives meshed neatly with the UK's preferences. With this focus the EDA, in the UK's eyes, would 'coordinate mutually convenient and advantageous projects as they occurred', whereas the French wanted a more prescriptive approach to common procurement that would also promote the European defence industrial base (Keohane, 2004). The compromise was that the EDA was endowed with the power to request and fund new projects, but its budget was decided on by unanimity (Dover, 2007, 124). The UK's preferences were also evident in the composition of EDA's steering board, ensuring it is made up of national defence Ministers. Finally, the UK successfully promoted Nick Witney, a British official, as the EDA's first Chief Executive, a key post for shaping the institution's design (Dover, 2007, 121). However, by 2007, the compromises were under strain as differences over the focus and direction of the EDA re-emerged, with the UK only approving a one year budget, blocking a three-year proposal because, as one British official put it, it did not want to 'back a budget without seeing what we are paying for' (Goldirova, 2007).

EU–NATO Relations

The biggest institutional concern for the UK with regard to ESDP has been the potential impact on NATO and the 'special relationship' with the US. In particular, the UK was keen to ensure that ESDP did not risk undermining or competing with NATO, something the US wholly opposed. This concern was already evident in the St Malo Declaration, which stated that 'acting in conformity with our respective obligations in NATO, we are contributing to the vitality of a modernised Atlantic Alliance, which is the foundation of the collective defence of its members', and insisting the EU would only act 'where the Alliance as a whole is not engaged' (Franco-British Summit, 1998). However, this did not reassure senior members of the Clinton administration or US Congress who were unhappy with the UK's apparent *volte-face* on European defence (Interviews, 2002). They supported improved European military capabilities, but were angered by the notion of an 'autonomous' capability. Four days after St Malo, at the North Atlantic Council, Madeline Albright, then US Secretary of State, made it clear that the US 'welcomes a more capable European partner', but warned that ESDP must avoid 'delinking ESDI from NATO, avoid duplicating existing efforts, and avoid discriminating against non-EU members' (Albright, 1998). The 'three Ds', as they became known, shaped US policy towards ESDP under Clinton and George W Bush. As Stanley Sloan put it, this was a 'yes, but …' response; yes to capabilities, but no to genuine leadership or autonomy (Sloan, 2000).

At the Cologne European Council in 1999, in an attempt to reassure the US, the EU made it clear that this initiative was being developed 'without prejudice to actions by NATO' (European Council, 1999a). This was strengthened at Helsinki later that year when the EU reiterated the St Malo pledge that ESDP operations would only take place 'where NATO as whole is not engaged'. Blair latched on to this, suggesting to a North American audience that NATO had a 'right of first refusal', as the 'initiative on European defense … applies only where NATO has chosen not to act collectively' (Blair, 2001). However, this was rather disingenuous as, while in practise it was highly likely that NATO would be consulted before the EU acted, the EU was not obliged to do so. Nevertheless, the UK worked hard to improve increasingly strained political relations between the EU and NATO. A central problem has been the continuing impasse in Greek-Turkish relations. The UK was central to negotiating the 2002 agreement between the Turks and Greeks that allowed the EU assured access to NATO capabilities, thereby facilitating the launch of the EU's first military operation in the Former Yugoslav Republic of Macedonia (FYROM) in 2003.

Despite partially resolving one impasse in EU–NATO relations in 2002–03, the build up to and launch of the US led war in Iraq severely derailed any rapprochement. Blair's unwavering support for George W Bush's decision to invade Iraq put him in direct opposition to President Chirac of France, the other key state leading ESDP, and Chancellor Schroeder of Germany. These divisions were a major set back for EU–NATO and EU–US relations and for UK leadership on ESDP. Disappointed by the perceived lack of autonomy for ESDP, the slow development of further defence integration and by the way the US and its partners decided ultimately to act without an explicit UN mandate, the French turned to their long-term EU partners, the Germans, to move the European defence project forward. This led to the mini-summit of April 2003, dubbed the 'chocolate summit' by critics, where France, Germany, Belgium and Luxembourg made a number of proposals for a European Security and Defence Union, including an operational headquarters (OHQ) and a mutual defence pact. The desire for greater autonomy from NATO, through the development of an OHQ, and the possibility of a defence union seemed to challenge NATO's primacy in the European security architecture. The UK strongly opposed an OHQ, believing it unnecessary because the EU has assured access to the Supreme Headquarters Allied Powers Europe (SHAPE). In the second half of 2003, despite the fallout from Iraq, the UK eventually negotiated a compromise. This agreement established an EU Cell within SHAPE and a NATO Permanent Liaison Team within the EUMS. While the compromise demonstrated the continuing influence of the UK it did not resolve the underlying differences and demonstrated that several key EU states were willing to challenge the UK's leadership and vision for ESDP. This episode badly damaged Anglo-French relations and further soured EU–NATO relations. The EU–NATO relationship has also been affected by the differences within NATO over the 'national caveats' being attached to the troop deployments of many NATO members in Afghanistan. This has raised questions about burden-sharing and risk-sharing and seems to have exacerbated the Atlanticist–Europeanist divide in transatlantic relations. In particular, a sense of mistrust and competition between higher-ranking officials in NATO HQ and the Council of the EU has been damaging. On operations such as in the Balkans, however, the two organisations have continued to work reasonably well together (Interviews, 2008).

This cooperation on the ground helps the UK government to continue to argue that the EU and NATO are complementary and that ESDP does not undermine or duplicate what NATO is doing. This line of argument has continued even after the signing of the Lisbon Treaty in 2007. Des Browne, then Secretary of State for Defence, said in January 2008 that 'we are conscious that those capabilities if they are generated by members of both organisations will be available to NATO, but there is no duplication' (House of Commons, 2008b). Even with the inclusion of the mutual assistance clause in the Lisbon Treaty, the UK government continues to stress the primacy of NATO within the European security architecture, with Des Browne (2008) declaring:

> I am in no doubt that NATO will remain the cornerstone of the United Kingdom security policy and the only organisation for collective defence in Europe. The Reform Treaty does not change that. The Reform Treaty text makes clear that NATO is the foundation for collective defence of its members.

However, the Conservative Party has a very different view. Specifically, they argue that ESDP is focused on institution building and undermines NATO. Their argument is highlighted in their opposition to the Lisbon Treaty and its reform of ESDP (House of Commons, 2008a). Liam Fox, Shadow Defence Secretary, argued that 'This treaty proposes giving the EU a defence capability that will duplicate many of the functions of NATO. Worse, it will potentially compete with, rather than complement, NATO' (Fox cited House of Commons, 2008a). In the same debate, William Hague, Shadow Foreign Secretary, argued that the Labour government had continually conceded ground on EDSP during the Lisbon Treaty negotiations and had understated the implications of such changes for the UK (House of Commons, 2008a). Yet, in his speech on the future of British foreign policy in 2009, Hague barely mentions the EU. When he does so he merely reiterates his claim that 'EU defence arrangements ... too often involve the "rehatting" or duplication of NATO structures' (Hague, 2009). Finally, despite the concerns over ESDP expressed by Fox and Hague, David Cameron's promise to negotiate 'three specific guarantees' (Cameron, 2009) to claw back powers from the EU did not include foreign, security or defence policy. Regardless of whether the Conservatives succeed in getting their guarantees on the Social Chapter, the Charter of Fundamental Freedoms and Criminal Justice, a Conservative government is unlikely to be able to reverse what has been achieved thus far. As one official stressed, 'ten years have passed since

St Malo and ESDP is not reversible' (Interview, 2008). The Conservatives would, however, slow the development of ESDP, possibly moving the UK back to the sidelines on an issue where its leadership credentials are strong.

The long term problem for Labour or the Conservatives is that the continual desire to keep the US onside through this institutional balancing act is unsustainable. In terms of capabilities, financial resources and global priorities, the UK can no longer keep pace with US defence policy. Despite this, the UK has tried a similar balancing with crisis management capabilities, pursuing greater cooperation with EU partners while selling it to the US as improving NATO.

Capabilities

For the UK, capabilities, particularly for expeditionary crisis management operations, have been the main motivation for its support of ESDP. European military shortcomings exposed during the Yugoslav wars were glaring. However, since ESDP was launched, the lessons learnt through its operations have led to civilian capabilities and especially a civil-military focus becoming increasingly important to the UK's vision of ESDP.

Military Headline Goals   Improving European military capabilities was a central driver behind the UK's launch of ESDP. Yet, the UK's objective was not just about improvements for the EU. Improvements to European capabilities would also mean an improvement for NATO, which would reassure the US. Within the UK, the EU capability has always been provided 'to complement NATO, rather than compete with it' (Ministry of Defence, 2003, 6). Blair and the MoD believed that the Europeans would do more about capabilities if the issue was raised and developed within the EU, rather than in NATO, where it would be seen as a US project (Ministry of Defence, 2003, 6). The best way forward was seen as setting targets (similar to the methodology used for Economic and Monetary Union (EMU)) to which states had to aspire.

The UK was central in setting these targets through the establishment of 'headline goals'. In 1998–99, it was two British officials, Emyr Jones-Parry and Richard Hatfield, along with their French counterparts, including Gerard Errera, who put forward the proposals that became the Helsinki Headline Goal (HHG) (Interview, 2008). Unsurprisingly, they drew heavily on NATO's operations in the Balkans, setting a target of 50–60,000 troops which would be deployable in 60 days and sustainable for at least a year. The UK was also crucial in establishing the associated requirement and force catalogues for EU military capabilities (Interview, 2008). In July 1999, the Anglo-Italian summit put forward a 'joint proposal to set criteria' for 'European wide goals for enhanced military capabilities to undertake crisis management, including peacekeeping' (Joint Declaration Launching European Defence Capabilities Initiative, 1999). This would include 'national capability objectives' and 'peer review'. For the UK, the capabilities issue was not simply a quantitative, but also a qualitative one, with the focus on interoperability, sustainability and deployability, developing smaller but more capable expeditionary forces (Interview, 2008). The objective was to give the EU the potential to act autonomously when necessary, thereby closing the capabilities-expectations gap (see Hill, 1993) and allowing it to become a regional, and possibly even global, security actor, while also improving burden-sharing within NATO.

As part of its push for improved military capabilities, the UK was at the forefront of the commitments to the HHG at the first Capability Commitment Conference in 2000. The UK was the second largest contributor, behind Germany, committing 12,500 troops plus 72 aircraft and 18 naval vessels (Salmon and Shepherd, 2003, 75). Despite the agreed commitments exceeding the HHG, it was clear that a significant number of capability shortfalls remained and the qualitative elements showed little improvement. While the HHG was not abandoned, the UK was instrumental in planning for a 'future headline goal' (Ministry of Defence, 2003). The announcement in 2004 of Headline Goal 2010 and the associated Battlegroup concept reemphasised UK capability priorities: actual rather than rhetorical commitments of a meaningful size, available quickly and for a sustained period (Whitman, 2006). The 1500 strong Battlegroups, to be deployable in 15 days, were both more realistic and more practical for EU member states. In hindsight, some UK officials believed the HHG of 60,000 troops had become a millstone for ESDP, especially as an operation of that scale was (and still is) not yet realistic for the EU (Interview, 2008). While the HHG remains as an overarching framework, Headline Goal 2010 focuses on more qualitative improvements to deployability, sustainability and interoperability (Interview, 2008). The Battlegroup concept was a better vehicle for getting these improvements, setting very specific criteria and expectations, especially with regard to deployability, while what the HHG meant in practise was always rather ambiguous.

The UK's Spearhead Battalion was the model for these Battlegroups. When presented to the EU, the concept vividly illustrated what was expected in terms of deployability and sustainability (Interview, 2008). Subsequently, the Battlegroup concept has been decisive in driving defence reform in several European states, including Sweden, which subsequently refocused its defence structures, capabilities and spending (Interview, 2008). As with the HHG, the UK supported its initiative with significant commitments, putting forward a national Battlegroup for six months in 2005, 2008 and 2013, and a UK–Dutch Battlegroup in 2010. The UK has also used the concept to support pooling and/or specialising of military capabilities by other EU states. However, the UK, seeing itself as a large independent power with global interests, is not willing to consider this option (Interview, 2008). This may have to change. As political and economic conditions continue to constrain defence spending further integration with other European military forces, including the possibility of pooling, will need to be seriously considered by the UK in the longer term.

The UK's ability to shape ESDP can also been seen in the development of structured cooperation, which emerged during the European Convention. The UK was concerned that a smaller group of 'self-selected states could short-circuit decision-making "at 25" and that the initiative was really an alternative to NATO' (Howorth, 2004, 488). The UK, along with a number of other states, having failed to block structured cooperation, managed to ensure it became a capability focused exercise. Specifically, the criteria for membership were based on the ability to provide a national Battlegroup or a component of a multinational Battlegroup by 2010 (Biscop, 2008).

Civilian Headline Goals   The civilian side of ESDP was initially pushed very strongly by the Swedes and Finns. In 1999, the Finnish Presidency ensured that the military HHG was complemented by a less specific and lower profile statement on 'non-military crisis management of the European Union' (European Council, 1999b). In 2000, the Feira European Council outlined the four priority areas for civilian capabilities: police, rule of law, civilian administration and civilian protection. The summit set a target of 5,000 police officers by 2003 for conflict prevention and crisis management operations, 1,000 of which should be deployable in 30 days (European Council, 2000). The June 2004 European Council published a draft action plan, which outlined the need for a civilian headline goal, a capability commitment conference and a broadening of the expertise available to include human rights, political affairs, security sector reform, mediation, border control, disarmament, demobilisation and reintegration and media policy (European Council, 2004a). The quantitative side of the civilian equation was met at the November 2004 commitment conference with 5,761 police, 631 rule of law experts, 562 administration experts and 4,988 civil protection personnel pledged (European Council, 2004a).

Since the launch of ESDP, these civilian capabilities have become increasingly important. Military capability improvements across Europe are still essential, but the civilian side has become increasingly important as the UK pushes for a civil-military ESDP. During the UK Presidency of the EU in 2005 the civil-military aspect of ESDP was the 'top priority' (Interview, 2008). The 'comprehensive' approach of ESDP and the EU more broadly has become more important than purely military capabilities. A civil-military ESDP gives the EU a capability that few other organisations have, thus demonstrating the 'added value' of an EU security policy (Interviews, 2008). The EU is seen as having the potential to be a 'comprehensive' security actor with the 'full tool-kit' for stabilisation and nation-building (Interview, 2008). Conveniently for the UK, this positioning of ESDP also helps sell the policy domestically and to the US in that a less military dominated ESDP is seen as less of a direct threat to NATO's role. ESDP has also been constructed by the UK to reduce the perceived threat to NATO through the types of operations it is mandated to undertake.

ESDP Missions and Operations

The UK supports the framework within which ESDP operates, namely the Petersberg Tasks and the 2003 European Security Strategy (ESS) (Treaty of Amsterdam, 1999;

European Council, 2003). As the Petersberg Tasks originated within the WEU, the UK had few problems with the EU incorporating them into the Amsterdam Treaty and was happy for them to be expanded in 2003 to include: 'joint disarmament operations', 'military advice and assistance tasks', 'post-conflict stabilisation' and 'supporting third countries in combating terrorism' (Treaty of Lisbon, 2007). However, the upper end of the tasks, 'combat forces in crisis management, including peace-making', did raise questions of overlap with NATO and whether this was overly ambitious for many EU states. The problem is not only capabilities but also the lack of political will to put troops in harm's way (Interviews 2008). The UK would like to see more troop contributions in less benign and limited roles and it has challenged several states to do more of the 'harder' operations such as in Afghanistan, a challenge the French have taken up under President Sarkozy (Interview 2008). Yet, the domestic circumstances of some states, especially Germany, make it very difficult to change their approach to the use of the armed forces. However, change is slowly occurring and, significantly, there is an increasing confidence within parts of the UK government that the EU can effectively undertake tougher operations, such as in Bosnia and Kosovo (Interview, 2008).

The second framework for ESDP missions is the ESS. Largely drafted by Javier Solana's Chief of Staff, Robert Cooper, a former UK diplomat, it fitted well with the UK's view of the challenges and threats facing Europe and the means to address them. One official believed that the ESS was a 'visionary' document, providing a long-term overview for European security, although others have been less complimentary (Interview, 2008). Improved capabilities and the importance of NATO were both stressed and the language was ambiguous enough to satisfy most states and audiences. The revision of the ESS in 2008 was supported by the UK, which thought it sensible to review the implementation of the strategy and reassess the threats (Interview, 2008). The result was an updated set of challenges and threats to include energy security, climate change and cyber security, as well as more specific issues of piracy and small arms proliferation (European Council, 2008b). Geographically, the UK believes the main focus for EU operations should be the so-called 'arc of crisis' in the EU's neighbourhood, encompassing primarily Africa and the Balkans (Interviews, 2008). However, as with CFSP, the operation in Aceh, Indonesia, demonstrated that there is no geographical limit to ESDP's remit.

Despite being one of the most militarily capable EU states, the UK has been criticised in some quarters for not contributing enough personnel or capabilities to EU operations. However, officials argue that this is due less to a lack of political will on the part of the UK government and more to a lack of resources (Interview, 2008). In 2006, the percentage of UK troops deployed through ESDP or NATO stood at 19 per cent, while, in France, it was just 5 per cent (Interview, 2008). With the UK military severely overstretched by commitments in Afghanistan and elsewhere, more personnel are already on deployment more frequently than they should be. Nevertheless, the UK continues to contribute when it can, such as in 2003, providing engineers for the EU's first autonomous military mission, Operation Artemis, in the Democratic Republic of Congo (DRC). Officials also make it apparent that the key to the UK contributing is having a clear and achievable security objective, rather than merely making a political statement (Interview, 2007). For example, the UK refused to contribute to EUFOR Tchad in 2008 as it saw the operation as more of a political statement than an operation with clearly defined objectives that would make a significant difference (Interview, 2007; Interview, 2008).

Under the Lisbon Treaty the role of the EU in defence and security was broadened and deepened through the inclusion of the Solidarity Clause and the Assistance Clause. The Solidarity Clause commits the EU to 'mobilise all the instruments at its disposal, including the military resources made available by the member states' if a member state suffers a terrorist attack or natural or man made disaster. The Assistance Clause states that 'if a member state is the victim of armed aggression on its territory, the other member states shall have toward it an obligation of aid and assistance by all means in their power', although it notes, significantly, that 'commitments and cooperation in this area shall be consistent with commitments under the North Atlantic Treaty Organisation, which, for those states who are members of it, remains the foundation for their collective defence and the forum for its implementation' (European Council, 2008). Even with these caveats, the Assistance Clause in particular suggests the EU may encroach on NATO's core collective defence role, potentially questioning the primacy of NATO. The Conservative Party see these developments as confirmation of their fears that ESDP is undermining NATO (House of Commons, 2008a). However, UK officials have stressed that the Lisbon Treaty 'does not duplicate NATO's function as a mutual defence pact' and may be 'to the potential benefit of the UK' (House of Commons, 2008a). Former Labour Defence Secretary Des Browne reiterated this by claiming that 'NATO will remain ... the only organisation for collective defence in Europe' (House of Commons, 2008a).

The UK and ESDP Post-Blair

The transition from Tony Blair to Gordon Brown as Prime Minister in 2007 signalled changes in priorities and preferences domestically and internationally. While the UK and France managed to re-establish some semblance of a working relationship after the deep rifts created by the 2003 Iraq War, matters were only effectively resolved after a change of leadership in both countries in May and June 2007. Ironically, it was the election of Nicolas Sarkozy as President of France rather than Gordon Brown replacing Tony Blair that was more perhaps more significant for the UK's role in ESDP.

British Defence Policy and ESDP under Gordon Brown

In contrast to Tony Blair, Gordon Brown's international profile was relatively low. To the extent he was engaged in international affairs, it was economic issues (as demonstrated during the economic and financial crisis of 2007–09), African and humanitarian issues and global poverty that were his primary focus. In the security field he was seen to be more of a natural Atlanticist than Europeanist, with little apparent interest in defence or Europe (Interview, 2008; Interview, 2009). Through the second half of 2007, the MoD seemed to be invisible to Brown, especially the department dealing with international organisations (Interview, 2008). ESDP appeared to register barely any interest. However, things began to change in January and February 2008, as more requests for information began to filter through from the PM and Cabinet Office. The focus for Brown, and the Cabinet Office's key initiative, was making a reality of the ESS's notion of 'effective multilateralism', by putting forward proposals to improve coordination between international organisations in response to crises (Interview, 2008). This was evident in the 2008 UK National Security Strategy, which highlights collective action through the UN, EU and NATO as the most effective way of managing the threats faced by the UK (Cabinet Office, 2008, 7–8). This document also acknowledged the vital role of the EU in securing a safer world within and beyond the borders of Europe (Cabinet Office, 2008, 8).

On ESDP more specifically, Brown seemed to step back from the leading role played by the UK under Blair. In November 2007, Brown 'humiliated' Foreign Secretary David Miliband by forcing him to change a speech he was due to give in Bruges calling for the EU not to reject the use of hard power and to establish a 'military capabilities charter' (Coates, 2007; Wintour, 2007). Brown seemed to have a much more cautious attitude towards the EU and a more sceptical view of ESDP's potential. Despite this, in 2008, responding to the lead taken by an increasingly proactive Sarkozy, there were signs of a slightly more positive attitude, with both the Foreign and Defence secretaries supporting French proposals for a strengthened ESDP. In July, Miliband stressed that 'the countries of Europe need to be better at using their hard power' adding that he supported Sarkozy's call for the 'EU to play a greater role in crisis management' (Miliband, 2008b). In October, then Defence Secretary, John Hutton labelled those who dismissed ESDP as 'pathetic', adding that working with the EU on military missions was 'perfectly sensible' (Oakeshott, 2008). Then, in October 2009, Miliband made the most robustly pro European speech of Brown's time in office. He argued 'that is it very strongly in the British national interest for the EU to develop a strong foreign policy' and that 'Britain should embrace it, shape it and lead it' (Miliband, 2009). His key point was that the UK is no longer able to be a global power in its own right and it had to 'lead a strong European foreign policy or – lost in hubris, nostalgia and xenophobia – watch our influence in the world wane' (Miliband, 2009). However, this forceful speech was overtaken by internal Labour politicking over the posts of President of the European Council and EU 'Foreign Minister', which Blair and Miliband were both associated with for some time. However, neither Miliband's speech nor the eventual appointment of a British woman, Baroness Ashton, to the role of EU 'Foreign Minister' seemed to change Brown's position of generally supporting ESDP, but failing to provide the strong leadership seen in Blair's first term. Instead, France increasingly took the lead on ESDP.

The UK, Sarkozy and ESDP

Nicolas Sarkozy's Presidency had a significant impact on ESDP for the UK, with the French administration moving closer to the UK on European security issues. The 2008 French Defence White Paper outlined reform of defence policy and the armed forces similar to that in the UK's SDR. On ESDP the French have focused more on deliverables rather than high level rhetoric, being less wedded to 'autonomy' meaning separation from NATO (Presidence de la Republique, 2008). This more pragmatic approach to ESDP is much closer to the UK's position when ESDP was launched. The French have also mirrored Blair's early approach to ESDP with a more centralised style, as the Élysée, rather than the Quai d'Orsay, became the principal point of contact for those in UK government working on ESDP (Interview, 2008). In contrast, under Gordon Brown, key government departments (Cabinet Office, FCO and MoD) are assuming the main responsibility for ESDP in the UK. This suggests an increased importance for ESDP in France and declining importance in the UK. The significance of ESDP for France can also be seen in its move to fully rejoin the NATO command structure in April 2009 after its withdrawal in 1966. Whereas Chirac seemed to be using ESDP to move away from NATO, Sarkozy has used ESDP as a way of moving closer to NATO. There are still concerns about American dominance of NATO yet this change is, for the UK, a significantly better attitude (Interview, 2008).

Conclusion: A European Turn but Not a U-Turn

Driven primarily by the desire for improved European military capabilities, UK defence policy has clearly taken an EU turn. While this has involved some 'Europeanization' of defence policy, it has been relatively limited. By assuming joint leadership of ESDP, the UK has significantly shaped its development to better suit British objectives. The majority of the important ESDP proposals have been drafted or shaped by UK policy makers. Even where the UK has not instigated or led, where it has had to react to other states initiatives, such as the proposed OHQ in 2003, it has managed to ensure compromises that were compatible with its interests. That the UK managed to broker a compromise, however ambiguous, is evidence of its importance to ESDP. On the other hand, the fact that four states threatened to push ahead with an OHQ suggested that UK leadership was being tested.

The UK's objective for ESDP has been relatively consistent throughout New Labour's time in office, despite the upheavals of 11 September, the war in Iraq, divisions within Europe over NATO's operation in Afghanistan and a change of Prime Minister. The UK engaged with the EU in order to enhance European crisis management capabilities, initially solely military and then civil-military instruments. This has consistently been promoted as also strengthening NATO. The focus has been on pragmatic capability improvements, although, in hindsight, the HHG 2003 was perhaps a little ambitious. While not opposing other states' desires to develop more 'high-end' capabilities, such as space-based assets, the UK has tried to ensure the focus remains on the key issues of deployability, interoperability and sustainability as the most cost-effective way of improving European capacity (Interview, 2000).

Despite the move towards the EU, NATO remains the UK's, and probably most of Europe's, preferred institution for collective defence. Nonetheless, the EU now appears regularly in UK defence policy documents. This more overtly European dimension to UK defence policy is a significant shift. This change is partly due to the transformed strategic and budgetary environment, but the role of key individuals is also an important factor. The change in leadership when New Labour took office in 1997 was crucial, especially as Tony Blair took a personal interest in the development of ESDP. Within the MoD the role of Richard Hatfield can also be highlighted as an important factor in the European turn in UK defence policy. The degree of change can be seen in parts of the MoD, if not in the armed forces, which seem to be more comfortable with the EU (Interviews, 2000; Interviews, 2008).

This may suggest a gradual acceptance within UK government that in foreign and defence policy the UK can rarely act alone. Gordon Brown's push for 'effective multilateralism' is consolidating a trend that has been developing intermittently since the end of World War II and the importance of multilateralism will grow as political and economic constraints on British defence policy tighten. As the US further develops its capabilities, ESDP should become an ever more significant forum for this multilateralism and for UK defence policy. The importance of ESDP is that, combined with other EU instruments, the organisation has the potential to become a 'holistic' and 'comprehensive' security actor.

It is clear that the US–UK 'special relationship' and NATO are still the principal security relationships for the British government. Nevertheless, ESDP is becoming an increasingly important element of defence policy, especially as the UK sees EU capabilities as strengthening NATO, thereby assisting the US. This complementary relationship between the EU and NATO that the UK seeks is central to its European turn. The key method for achieving this objective has been ambiguity. With consensus decision-making, the agreements on ESDP are, naturally, compromises. This often means there is a great deal of ambiguity in key words and phrases, such as 'autonomy'. This ambiguity allows the UK to tell slightly different stories to different audiences. The enduring question is: how long can these balancing acts last? Tony Blair saw the UK as the 'bridge' between Europe and the US (Blair, 2003). However, several commentators, such as William Wallace, believe the bridge has already collapsed (Wallace, 2005). Miliband elevated further the UK's self-perception when he talked about 'Britain as a global hub' (Miliband, 2008a). These kinds of comments suggest that the UK has not really recognised its diminishing importance in international affairs in general and to the US more specifically. The UK needs to build into its defence policy the fact that it is no longer a global power and that the 'special relationship' with the US is a little more one-sided than currently acknowledged. Hence, politicians, policy-makers and commentators should be more pragmatic about the need for greater cooperation and even integration in defence policy at the European level. This would be easier to acknowledge if it were realised that the 'Europeanization' of British defence policy has been rather limited and that British preferences have actually significantly shaped EU defence policy. The EU should, in the long term, become the key partnership for British defence policy. While, ideologically, this will be opposed by many, pragmatically it is the logical long term solution to declining defence resources and to an America that is widening the military gap across the Atlantic.

Regardless of questions about the UK's continuing ability to balance the US and EU one thing is clear – 'ESDP is not reversible' (Interview, 2008). The policy shift under Blair is a genuine and permanent change in UK defence policy. The significance of the shift is that, after years of resisting an EU defence role, the UK has been central to 'letting the genie out of the bottle' (Interview, 2008). It does not spell the end of UK attachment to NATO or the 'special relationship'; these remain, for the foreseeable future, the 'cornerstones' of UK defence policy. Yet, the European turn in UK defence policy is indisputable.

For the time being, it is less a fundamental transformation of the UK's core interests than a shift in the way the UK ensures and promotes its interests. The European turn in UK defence policy changes national instruments not (at least not yet) national interests. It is, rather, a change in the way the interests are pursued. What is clear is that the UK has been central in banishing the taboo of an EU defence policy and, in doing so, has raised the longer term prospect that the UK will not just be 'with Europe', but 'of' Europe.

Bibliography

Albright, M (1998), *Statement by the US Secretary of State to the North Atlantic Council* (Brussels: NATO)

Andreani, G, Bertram, C and Grant, C (2001), *Europe's Military Revolution* (London: Centre for European Reform)

Baylis, J (ed.) (1977), *British Defence Policy in a Changing World* (London: Croom Helm)

Baylis, J (1989), *British Defence Policy: Striking the Right Balance* (London: Macmillan Press)

Biscop, S (2008), 'Permanent Structured Cooperation and the Future of ESDP', *Egmont Paper* 20

Blair, T (1997), *Speech by the Prime Minister to the Labour Party Conference on 30 September* (London: Labour Party)

Blair, T (2001), *Speech by the Prime Minister to the Canadian Parliament on 23 February* (London: HMSO)

Blair, T (2003), *Speech by the Prime Minister to the Foreign Office Conference on 7 January* (London: HMSO)

Bolton, D (1991), 'Defence in Transition: Options for Change', *RUSI Journal*, 136/3, 1–3

Buchan, D (1993), *Europe: The Strange Superpower* (Aldershot: Dartmouth)

Cabinet Office (2008), *The National Security Strategy of the United Kingdom: Security in an Interdependent World* (London: HMSO)

Cameron, D (2009), *A Europe Policy that People can Believe in – Speech by the Leader of the Opposition on 4 November* (London: Conservative Party)

Chuter, D (1997), 'The United Kingdom', in Howorth, J and Menon, A (eds), *The European Union and National Defence Policy* (London: Routledge)

Coates, S (2007), 'Another Bruges Speech Stirs up Controversy as Brown Weighs In', *The Times* 16 November

Croft, S (ed.) (1991), *British Security Policy: The Thatcher Years and the End of the Cold War* (London: HarperCollins Academic)

Croft, S, Dorman, A, Rees, W and Uttley, M (2001), *Britain and Defence 1945–2000: A Policy Re-evaluation* (Harlow: Pearson Education)

Declaration on Strengthening European Cooperation in Security and Defence (2003), Franco-British Summit, Le Touquet

Dockrill, M (1988), *British Defence since 1945* (Oxford: Basil Blackwell)

Dorman, A (2001), 'Reconciling Britain to Europe in the Next Millennium: The Evolution of British Defence Policy in the Post-Cold War Era', *Defense Analysis*, 17/2, 187–202

Dover, R (2007), *The Europeanization of British Defence Policy* (Aldershot: Ashgate)

Duke, S (2005), *The Linchpin COPS: Assessing the Workings and Institutional Relations of the Political and Security Committee – Working Paper 2005/W/05* (Maastricht: European Institute of Public Administration)

European Council (1999a), *Declaration of the European Council on Strengthening the Common European Policy on Security and Defence in Cologne on 3–4 June 1999* (Brussels: European Council)

European Council (1999b), *Presidency report on Non-Military Crisis Management of the European Union in Helsinki on 10–11 December* (Brussels: European Council)

European Council (2000), *Presidency Report on Strengthening the Common European Policy on Security and Defence at Feira on 19–20 June* (Brussels: European Council)

European Council (2003), *A Secure Europe in a Better World – The European Security Strategy on 12 December* (Brussels: European Council)

European Council (2004a), *Civilian Capabilities Commitment Conference – Ministerial Declaration on 22 November* (Brussels: European Council)

European Council (2004b), *Annex III – The Way Ahead for Civilian Crisis Management – Action Plan in Presidency Report on ESDP on 18 June* (Brussels: European Council)

European Council (2008a), *Consolidated Versions of the Treaty on European Union and The Treaty on the Functioning of the European Union on 9 May* (Brussels: European Council)

European Council (2008b), *Report on the Implementation of the European Security Strategy – Providing Security in a Changing World on 11 December* (Brussels: European Council)

Featherstone, K and Radaelli, C (eds) (2003), *The Politics of Europeanisation* (Oxford: Oxford University Press)

Franco-British Summit (1998), *Joint Declaration on European Defence on 3–4 December 1998* (London: HMSO)

Freedman, L (1999), *The Politics of British Defence, 1979–98* (London: St Martin's Press)

Goldirova, R (2007), 'EU defence ministers give boost to military spending', *EUOberserver.com* 20 November

Hague, W (2009), *The Future of British Foreign Policy with a Conservative Government – speech by the Shadow Foreign Secretary to the International Institute for Strategic Studies on 21 July* (London: International Institute for Strategic Studies)

Heisbourg, F (2008), 'Knowledge Holds Key to French Defence', *Financial Times* 18 June

Hill, C (1993), 'The Capabilities-Expectations Gap, or Conceptualising Europe's International Role', *Journal of Common Market Studies*, 31/3, 305–28

House of Commons (2008a), *House of Commons Debate on the Lisbon Treaty, Hansard on 20 February 2008* (London: Hansard)

House of Commons (2008b), *The Future of NATO and European Defence – The Ninth Report of the Defence Select Committee on 20 March 2008* (London: HMSO)

House of Lords (2005), *European Defence Agency: The Ninth Report of the European Union Committee on 16 March 2005* (London: HMSO)

Howorth, J (2000a), 'Britain, France and the European Defence Initiative', *Survival*, 42/2, 33–55

Howorth, J (2000b), 'Britain, NATO and CESDP: Fixed Strategy, Changing Tactics', *European Foreign Affairs Review*, 5/3, 1–20

Howorth, J (2004), 'The European Draft Constitutional Treaty and the Future of the European Defence Initiative: A Question of Flexibility', *European Foreign Affairs Review*, 9, 483–508

Howorth, J and Menon, A. (1997), *The European Union and National Defence Policy* (London: Routledge)

Joint Declaration Launching European Defence Capabilities Initiative (1999), British-Italian Summit (London)

Keohane, D (2004), *Europe's New Defence Agency* (London: CER)

King, T (1990), *Options for Change – Statement by the Secretary of State for Defence to the House of Commons on 25 July* (London: Hansard)

Miliband, D (2008a), *Key Note Speech at Fabian Society Conference 'Change the World' by the Foreign Secretary on 19 January* (London: HMSO)

Miliband, D (2008b), *Europe – Speech by the Foreign Secretary to the Progress Magazine series on 2 July* (London: HMSO)

Miliband, D (2009), *Strong Britain in a Strong Europe – Speech by the Foreign Secretary to the International Institute for Strategic Studies on 26 October* (London: HMSO)

Ministry of Defence (1981), *The United Kingdom Defence Programme: The Way Forward* (London: HMSO)

Ministry of Defence (1991), *Statement on the Defence Estimates, Britain's Defence for the 90s* (London, HMSO)

Ministry of Defence (1994), *Front Line First: The Defence Costs Study* (London: HMSO)

Ministry of Defence (1998), *The Strategic Defence Review: Modern Forces for a Modern World* (London: HMSO)

Ministry of Defence (2003), *Delivering Security in a Changing World – Defence White Paper* (London: HMSO)

Oakeshott, I (2008), 'John Hutton Backs European Army', *The Sunday Times* 26 October

Ovendale, R (1994), *British Defence Policy since 1945* (Manchester: Manchester University Press)

Presidence de la Republique (2008), *The French White Paper on Defence and National Security* (Paris: Presidence de la Republique)

RUSI (1994), 'The Defence Costs Study: Undermining the Front-Line?', *RUSI Newsbrief*, 14/7

Sabin, PA (1993), 'British Defence Choices Beyond Options for Change', *International Affairs*, 69/2, 267–88

Salmon, TC and Shepherd, A (2003), *Toward a European Army: A Military Power in the Making?* (Boulder: Lynne Rienner)

Sloan, S (2000), 'The United States and European Defence', *Chaillot Papers* 39

The Economist (2008), 'Let's Get Real' 19 June

The European Convention (2005), *Final Report of Working Group VIII Defence on 16 December 2002* – http://european-convention.eu.int/docs/wd8/5914.pdf

The Independent (2008), 'The Big Question: What is the New French Defence Strategy, and Should we Follow Suit?' 18 June

The Treaty of Amsterdam Amending the Treaty on European Union, the Treaties Establishing the European Communities and Certain Related Acts (Brussels: European Council, 1997) – http://www.europarl.europa.eu/topics/treaty/pdf/amst-en.pdf

The Treaty of Lisbon amending the Treaty on European Union and the Treaty Establishing the European Communities (Brussels: European Council, 2007) – http://eur-lex.europa.eu/JOHtml.do?uri=OJ:C:2007:306:SOM:EN:HTML

The United Kingdom Government's Memorandum of 2 March 1995 on the Treatment of Defence Issues at the 1996 Intergovernmental Conference – www.europarl.europa.eu/igc1996/pos-en_en.htm

Urwin, D (1991), *The Community of Europe: A History of European Integration Since 1945* (London: Longman)

Wallace, W (2005), 'The Collapse of British Foreign Policy', *International Affairs*, 81/1, 53–68

Whitman, R (1999), 'Amsterdam's Unfinished Business? The Blair Government's initiative and the future of the Western European Union', *Institute for Security Studies Occasional Papers*, 7

Whitman, R (2006), 'United Kingdom and ESDP', in Brummer, K (ed.), *The Big 3 and ESDP: France, Germany and the United Kingdom* (Gutersloh: Bertelsmann Stiftung)

Wintour, P (2007), 'Miliband: EU Must be Prepared to Use Military Power', *The Guardian* 15 November

Wolfers, A (1962), *Discord and Collaboration: Essays on International Politics* (London: The Johns Hopkins University Press)

Chapter 4

'A World Full of Terror to the British Mind': The Blair Doctrine and British Defence Policy

Steven Haines

When Tony Blair rose to speak to the Economic Club in Chicago on 22 April 1999, it was not generally expected that he would use the opportunity to launch a strategic policy doctrine. However, that is precisely what he did. His speech was immediately seen as a significant statement, framing what rapidly came to be referred to as the 'Blair Doctrine'. He did not use that label himself, it must be said, but he certainly referred to an emerging 'doctrine of the international community', which was translated by commentators into the shorthand 'Blair Doctrine' as the speech was being delivered.

The articulation of a doctrine in this way came as a surprise. British leaders are not noted for such things. Indeed, one might even argue that the British are emotionally disinclined to be 'doctrinaire'. As Oscar Wilde once observed, it is a 'word full of terror to the British mind' (Holland, 1993, 178). 'Doctrine' is often erroneously assumed to be synonymous with 'dogma' – and that suggests inflexibility and an absence of pragmatism. The pragmatism of Lord Palmerston, who famously stated that it was simply his duty at all times to pursue British interests, whatever they might be (Woodward, 1962, 225), is regarded as more typically British. The articulation of a strategic policy doctrine could impose unhelpful constraints on action, thus endangering the more flexible pursuit of British interests. The aim must surely be to keep one's policy options as open as possible.

This general approach is confirmed by reference to the recent history of British external policy. Where are the Attlee, Churchill, Eden, Macmillan, Home, Wilson, Heath, Callaghan, Thatcher and Major doctrines? Nothing of the sort is ever referred to in accounts of British foreign policy. While it might have been possible to convert the themes from Macmillan's 'Winds of Change' speech into something approaching a strategic policy doctrine for decolonisation, it was never articulated in that way. Anthony Eden had previously developed the 'three unities' in foreign policy. Frequently described as the 'three circles' and often ascribed to Churchill, they were the Commonwealth and Empire, Western Europe and the US, three unities that Eden stressed were 'not disparate, not incompatible, but complementary' (Eden cited in Rhodes James, 1986, 330). However, even if one considers his musings as tantamount to the articulation of a doctrine, the result was more an exception that proved the rule, rather than significant evidence of a doctrinal tendency in the framing of British external policy.

Of course, Blair's audience that day in Chicago may well have been somewhat less surprised and more open to such a suggested doctrine than a similar audience gathered in London might have been. Students of US foreign policy are familiar with the range of strategic doctrines promulgated by successive presidents since Harry Truman and his closest advisers came up with the Truman Doctrine (notwithstanding the early nineteenth century Monroe Doctrine, the grand-daddy of them all). The strategy of Containment, the Eisenhower Doctrine, the Johnson Doctrine, the Nixon Doctrine, the Ford Doctrine, the Carter Doctrine, the Clinton Doctrine and the most recent – and controversial – offering, the Bush Doctrine, are milestones along the road of understanding America's general strategic posture. We await the 'Obama Doctrine' with interest. Nor is it only US presidents who feel inclined to articulate what they or others choose to label as 'doctrine'. During the Reagan-Bush era, both Defense Secretary Caspar Weinberger and Chairman of the Joint Chiefs, Colin Powell articulated sets of criteria to be met in deciding to intervene abroad with military force. The Weinberger and Powell doctrines chime well with the most memorable aspect of Blair's speech, outlining similar decision-making criteria. However, in the British context, Blair's reference to doctrine was exceptional. Over a decade later, with his premiership well behind us, it is perhaps time to consider the impact of his message then and since. What exactly was the Blair Doctrine? Did it define British strategy during the years that followed? Does it retain any relevance today and, if so, will its legacy endure?

The Doctrine of International Community

The day in Chicago when Mr Blair introduced the world to his thinking about the international community and its responsibilities was also the 29th day of NATO's air campaign against Serbia over Kosovo, a campaign destined to last a further 50 days. John Kampfner tells us that the appointment in the Economic Club was a long-standing commitment for Blair. Planned before NATO's Operation Allied Force (OAF) commenced, Blair was nevertheless keen to go ahead with his visit to Chicago, seeing it as an opportunity to articulate some of his broader foreign policy goals (Kampfner, 2003, 50). Yet, since NATO was fighting its first war, taking a lot longer over it than it should have done and, with no UN authorisation, doing so in legally contentious circumstances, it would have been surprising indeed if the speech had not contained some justification of the air campaign then in train. It did, and what it is best remembered for is Blair's list of five essential criteria for intervention, all of which he naturally considered to be met in the case of the air campaign then underway.

Blair's Five Criteria for Military Intervention

As already noted, the most widely quoted aspect of the so-called 'Blair Doctrine' is the extract of the Chicago speech in which he articulated his criteria for military intervention, offering an answer to the questions of when should one intervene and how might one decide that the time was right to do so. To quote Blair himself:

I think we need to bear in mind five major considerations:

- First, are we sure of our case? War is an imperfect instrument for righting humanitarian distress; but armed force is sometimes the only means of dealing with dictators.
- Second, have we exhausted all diplomatic options? We should always give peace every chance, as we have in the case of Kosovo.
- Third, on the basis of a practical assessment of the situation, are there military operations we can sensibly and prudently undertake?
- Fourth, are we prepared for the long term? In the past we talked too much of exit strategies. But having made a commitment we cannot simply walk away once the fight is over; better to stay with moderate numbers of troops than return for repeat performances with large numbers.
- And finally, do we have national interests involved? The mass expulsion of ethnic Albanians from Kosovo demanded the notice of the rest of the world. But it does make a difference that this is taking place in such a combustible part of Europe. (Blair, 1999)

It is worth considering the origins and antecedents of this proposal. It was Professor Sir Lawrence Freedman of King's College, London, who came up with the five criteria, having been asked to contribute to the speech by Jonathan Powell, Blair's Downing Street Chief of Staff. Ideas associated with the notion of humanitarian intervention formed the backdrop to this request. According to Kampfner, some of these ideas were resulting from the work 'being done by a group called the International Commission on Intervention and State Sovereignty (ICISS)' (Kampfner, 2003, 51). This is incorrect, as the ICISS was only convened to look into the issue of humanitarian intervention some months after NATO's legally ambiguous intervention in Kosovo. Kosovo and the Chicago speech preceded the ICISS's work by almost two years. As also noted, the Blair criteria were very similar in concept to the so-called Weinberger Doctrine that Ronald Reagan's Secretary of Defense had produced some years earlier.

The Weinberger Doctrine was made public in 1984, as a response to the US military's unfortunate experience in Lebanon the year before. It insisted that US forces should only be committed as a last resort measure and only then if it was in the national interest. The objectives of military intervention must be both defined and achievable, the action must have public support and the forces intervening must be of sufficient capability to ensure success (Weinberger, 1984). The doctrine was highly controversial at the time and was opposed by then Secretary of State George Schultz, who regarded it as a rather negative product of the Vietnam Syndrome, namely a marked reluctance to deploy US forces as an effective instrument of US power (Herring, 2008, 875). Colin Powell had been one of the authors of the Weinberger doctrine, in his then capacity as military adviser to the Secretary of Defense, and he deployed very similar thinking as Chairman of the Joint Chiefs following the Iraqi invasion of Kuwait in 1990. Powell's updated version of the doctrine stressed the need for the US to deploy disproportionate or overwhelming force and added a requirement for an exit strategy. He opposed US intervention in the Gulf, arguing that such involvement was not fundamental to US interests (Herring, 2008, 909).

These three groups of criteria (Weinberger, Powell and Blair) are essentially guides or frameworks for political decision-making in relation to military intervention. They point to when intervention will be considered appropriate and when it will not. Although all three groups differ in precise content, they are also very similar. Arguably they represent statements of the obvious or simply common sense. Indeed, they are all merely frameworks for applying pragmatism to particular sets of circumstances. Nevertheless, the actual policy results of their application may well be controversial, in that one person's answers to any or all of the implied questions posed by all three groups of criteria may not be another's. There is also one very significant difference between the Weinberger and Powell doctrines on the one hand and the Blair Doctrine on the other. Whereas the first two were crafted as an intentional attempt to restrict the use of force by the US, when Blair articulated his version in Chicago his intention was quite the opposite. He was seeking a justification for Britain to use force and not a reason for not doing so. In that sense, both Weinberger and Powell were motivated by pessimism whereas Blair was optimistic about the utility of force. While Blair's five criteria largely chimed with both Weinberger and Powell, he took issue with Powell's approach in important respects. Powell was concerned with defining objectives, particularly in relation to an exit strategy. Blair was quite openly critical of this, suggesting that talk of exit strategies undermined long term goals. Indeed, his comment that it would be better to stay with moderate numbers than to return in larger numbers at a later date seemed to contradict Powell's preference for overwhelming force at the outset. He seemed relaxed about long term commitment, quite a different approach from that of Powell.

One can, of course, expend too much energy deconstructing the various criteria. Ultimately, all three groups, if applied to the same set of circumstances, could conceivably return the same result. Alternatively, the application of just one group to one set of circumstances by different decision makers could also produce different answers to the same set of questions. Blair's final criterion, for example, which refers to national interest, notoriously rests in the eyes of the beholder and is impossible to pin down definitively – a matter of opinion, not a matter of fact (except, of course in extremis). Engagement in the Balkans was in Britain's national interest as viewed by Blair. There were opponents in Britain who viewed the national interest quite differently. As for the issue of last resort and exhaustion of diplomatic options: were they really exhausted in relation to Kosovo by the Rambouillet talks? Some thought not. Four years later, in relation to Iraq, were other means effectively exhausted by the passing of UN Security Council Resolution 1441? Blair clearly thought so. Neither President Chirac nor Chancellor Schroeder agreed; nor, for that matter, did his former Foreign Secretary, Robin Cook.

Blair's Strategic Vision – or World View

Blair's five criteria are in general assumed to be the crux of the Blair Doctrine. However, it is possible to view it existing on two levels. Clearly it is strategic, but there have traditionally been two levels within strategy: the grand strategic and the military strategic. The former, and higher, of these is emphatically located within the political realm, while the latter is the level at which political and military decision-makers tend to interact. While the grand strategic is largely about policy, the military strategic combines both policy and military doctrine, the former being ultimately the responsibility of the political leadership of the state while the latter is ultimately the responsibility of the most senior military commanders. A simple distinction between 'policy' and 'doctrine' is that, while policy will determine what the military will do, doctrine determines how the armed forces will go about doing it. There is, of course, a fundamental relationship between policy and doctrine at the military strategic level. Quite obviously, the armed forces can only do what their overall capability (including their doctrine) will allow them to do, something acknowledged within the Weinberger, Powell and Blair criteria. Policy is constrained by military capability, such that political decision makers should never charge the armed forces with doing something beyond their ability to deliver. The essential interaction between political decision making and military decision making for the use of force represents the fundamental relationship between political and military that defines the military strategic level.

One needs to regard the Blair criteria as sitting on the policy side of that relationship. They are emphatically not, for example, to be confused with military strategic level military doctrine. When this author set about writing the UK's military strategic level doctrine for the Armed Forces in early 2000, he never seriously considered incorporating the Blair criteria in the draft, nor did they get inserted by others as that draft went on to achieve endorsement by the Chiefs of Staff and final signature by the Chief of Defence Staff (CDS). As a statement of an approach to policy making, the Blair criteria are perhaps best regarded as one means of operationalising a particular way of looking at the world. Blair undoubtedly had a 'world view' that served as a backdrop to the emergence of those criteria. Although that 'world view' did not constitute a grand strategy in and of itself, it served as the essential intellectual underpinning to inform both the development of grand strategy and an approach to dealing with issues of importance in an international system understood from that perspective.

Blair's world view has emerged over time and is not, it must be said, revealed in its entirety in the Chicago speech, although that was an important starting point. As has been noted already in this volume, Blair had demonstrated an almost total lack of interest in foreign affairs or defence prior to reaching Downing Street and was on a steep learning curve in his first months in office (Kampfner, 2003, 9–17). Yet, subsequently, there were pertinent pronouncements right up to the year of his resignation as Prime Minister. The Chicago speech in 1999 was followed by a significant speech to the 2001 Labour Party Conference, in the immediate aftermath of the events of 11 September (Blair, 2001; Kampfner, 2003, 123). In the summer of 2003, following the invasion of Iraq, a Downing Street document was circulated among foreign leaders who were visiting London for a summit of 'progressive' governments (McSmith and Dillon, 2003). Until then, each of his major pronouncements had coincided with a significant deployment of military force; subsequently, of course, all had Iraq as a backdrop. In March 2004, he delivered a speech to his Sedgefield constituents about his approach to combating global terrorism (Blair, 2004). A series of three further connected speeches, in the spring of 2006 (Blair, 2006a–c), was followed by another major foreign policy statement in Los Angeles to the World Affairs Council in August of that year (Blair, 2006d). Also in 2006, he published a lengthy pamphlet through the Foreign Policy Centre, in which he further outlined his vision and approach to foreign affairs (Blair, 2006e). Finally, in January 2007, as he was becoming increasingly conscious that his time in Downing Street was drawing to a close, he spoke onboard the Royal Navy's new amphibious warship HMS Albion, to initiate what he hoped would be a vigorous debate about Britain's role within the international system (Blair, 2007).

In Chicago, with Kosovo very much in mind, he made severely critical reference to Bismark's famous remark that the Balkans were not worth the bones of a single Pomeranian grenadier and went on to state emphatically that NATO's action against Serbia over Kosovo was 'a just war, based not on any territorial ambition but on values'. Going on to speak of global interdependence and globalisation, he insisted that 'we are all internationalists now', declaring that 'we are witnessing the beginnings of a new doctrine of the international community' (Blair, 1999). He privileged global security over national security, insisted that most Western states were not under existential threat and suggested their actions should be 'guided by a more subtle blend of mutual self interest and moral purpose in defending the values we cherish'. As such, he was picking up ideas that had already been expressed in the 1998 SDR process. Arguing that 'the spread of values makes us safer', he advocated a process where we should 'spread the values of liberty, the rule of law, human rights and an open society' – all of which would be in the national interests of liberal democratic states. Adding a note of caution, he said that the principle of non-intervention should not be jettisoned too readily but, at the same time, insisted it was no longer acceptable to assume the internal affairs of states were necessarily the business of themselves alone (Blair, 1999). In his view, minority rule equalled illegitimacy

– and illegitimacy breeds conditions that justify intervention. In July 2003, in the initial aftermath of the Iraq invasion, he insisted that:

> Where a population is suffering serious harm, as a result of internal war, insurgency, repression or state failure, and the state in question is unwilling or unable to halt or avert it, the principle of non-intervention yields to the international responsibility to protect. (Blair cited McSmith and Dillon, 2003)

This, of course, reflected the conclusions of the post-Kosovo report of the Canadian initiated ICISS, presented to UN Secretary General Kofi Annan in December 2001 (ICISS, 2001). The report went on to become a source document for the Secretary-General's High Level Panel and was influential in the report that Annan presented to world leaders at the 2005 World Summit. Annan's UN reform agenda chimed well with Blair's desire to see a general reform of international institutions. In 2003, that agenda was very much alive and there was much hope that the ambitions of the reformists would eventually prevail.

In his Sedgefield speech, Blair asserted that his own thinking had begun to evolve sometime before his Chicago speech. He noted that, even before Kosovo and certainly before the terrorist attacks on the World Trade Center and the Pentagon on 11 September 2001, 'the world's view of the justification of military action had been changing'. Prior to 2001 he 'was already reaching for a different philosophy in international relations from a traditional one that (had) held sway since the treaty (sic) of Westphalia in 1648'. However, 11 September had been a revelation for him: 'What had seemed inchoate came together'. Importantly, he then remarked that:

> It may well be that under international law as presently constituted, a regime can systematically brutalise and oppress its people and there is nothing anyone can do, when dialogue, diplomacy and even sanctions fail, unless it comes within the definition of a human catastrophe ... This may be the law, but should it be? (Blair, 2004)

On the subject of the threat from terrorism and Weapons of Mass Destruction (WMD), echoing the pre-emptive message in the US National Security Strategy of 2002, he went on to assert that:

> we have a duty and a right to prevent the threat materialising; and we surely have a responsibility to act when a nation's people are subjected to a regime such as Saddam's ... It means getting the UN to understand that faced with the threats we have, we should do all we can to spread the values of freedom, democracy, the rule of law, religious tolerance and justice for the oppressed, however painful for some nations that may be: but that at the same time, we wage war relentlessly on those who would exploit racial and religious division to bring catastrophe to the world. (Blair, 2004)

In his 2006 speeches, Blair railed against the mainstream world view, which he characterised as a doctrine of 'benign inactivity' (Blair, 2006b). In contrast to this he called for 'a policy of engagement not isolation; and one that is active and not reactive'. He portrayed progressive views – associated with the neo-conservatism of the right – as stronger and more effective at dealing with the world's new problems than mainstream conservatism, which viewed interventionism as 'dangerous and deluded' and believed that 'provided dictators don't threaten our citizens directly, what they do with their own, is up to them'. Not only that, but, looking wider than the military sphere, 'progressives are stronger on the challenges of poverty, climate change and trade policies' (Blair, 2006b).

As a final thought, before he gave up office in 2007, in his speech onboard HMS Albion (a significant platform for the launching of expeditionary warfare) he called for a debate about Britain's future world role. He pleaded for a military posture geared to war fighting rather than merely peacekeeping. He talked of the new security context in which 'our armed forced will be deployed in the lands of other nations far from home', combating global threats that can only be countered with a strong combination of hard and soft power (Blair, 2007). The debate he called for was about how Britain should respond to these threats and contribute to their defeat. Would it be 'benign inactivity', as he had previously called it, or would it be a strong and influential combination of effective hard and soft power, incorporating what he had called 'progressive pre-emption' in his Foreign Policy Centre pamphlet? (Blair, 2006e, 9) In other words, should Britain continue to be an influential great power, with all that implied, and an activist one at that, leading from the front and influencing the development of the international system for the benefit of all or should it retreat from that status and merely follow? He may have been calling for a debate, but he was very clear on which side he placed himself – progressive not benign.

In summary, Blair's world view is liberal and interventionist. Ideologically committed to the liberal approach to international affairs, his pronouncements while Prime Minister pointed to a firm belief in the responsibility of liberal democratic states to accept the burden of advancing that cause – and to be activists in its pursuit. A noticeable strand of idealism permeates through all these pronouncements. Blair is undoubtedly an optimist, who believes in the possibility of progress towards a better world, and an activist who believes that all right thinking liberals should take positive action to achieve such change.

It is, of course, entirely possible to be an optimistic idealist while remaining passive. Indeed, there is a strong element of liberal philosophy that suggests that the condition within states is rightly the preserve of those inhabiting them. One can either see intervention as depriving citizens of the right to determine their own future without interference or as forcible change imposed by external agents providing a recipe for failure – if a people are not themselves ready or able to effect change, it is most unlikely they will be able to sustain it without supportive force once it is imposed (for a wider discussion of such views, see Vincent, 1974). An alternative world view is based on a pessimistic attitude to progress. The world is the way it is because human nature makes it that way – while change is inevitable, positive change in a particular direction should not be anticipated or predicted. Pessimism certainly breeds realism and the naturally realist are emphatically pragmatic. Even if personally committed to liberal democratic ideals, the pragmatist would not regard it as by any means essential actively to impose those ideals on others. Indeed, he would regard it as essential not to intervene for reasons of order. In managing the international system, the pessimistic and pragmatic realist seeks order before justice, because order can be imposed while justice can only emerge in an ordered world. The optimistic idealist, in contrast, pursues order through justice. One of the great dilemmas of international politics is the search for both order and justice. A combination of the two would be wonderful, but there is a question mark over whether such a combination is possible, given that, while order is a matter of fact, justice will invariably be a matter of opinion. In essence, one can be objective about order but only subjective about what is just. British policy has traditionally sought order before justice, despite a commitment to the idea of liberal democratic progress, which helps explain the enduring influence of Palmerston. In contrast, Blair would place Palmerston firmly in the Westphalian past.

The Blair Doctrine and British Defence Policy

While Blair's world view and his determination that liberal interventionism should be the guiding basis for British military activism became very clear as his premiership progressed, they were not reflected in anything tangible or explicit in terms of overarching strategy. What were explicit were the five Chicago criteria, constituting what can be described as a military strategic level means of operationalising that world view. Indeed, if they are taken in isolation from that world view, they are arguably relatively meaningless – just five questions that might produce widely differing answers depending on the identity and instincts of those providing them. It was Blair's greater vision – optimistic, activist and committed to achieving a better world – which rendered his five criteria distinct from the similar criteria articulated by Weinberger and Powell. His optimism prompted a desire to utilise force, just as their pessimism caused them to advocate reining in interventionist tendencies elsewhere in the US administrations in which they served. As a result, the totality of the 'Blair Doctrine' is best seen as the five criteria for intervention set against the world view, with the latter shaping the likely answers to the questions those criteria served to posit. However, the question remains as to what extent the 'Blair Doctrine' actually influenced the formulation and direction of policy.

In 1997, two years before Kosovo and the Chicago speech, the New Labour government had ordered a full review of defence policy. The subsequent SDR has gained a reputation for having been one of the most thorough in memory, for being one of the most open, with much opinion being sought from outside government, for being foreign policy led and based on a clear assessment of the international security environment, rather than merely being driven by budgetary considerations. It also marked a significant shift towards genuinely joint approaches to operations. The author believes there to be substantial flaws in most of these claims, although this is not the place to expand on them. Suffice it to say that the SDR process was well managed and its public projection benefited from sound presentation, with a noticeable and commendable attempt to ensure that what was decided for defence would chime with the government's approach to foreign policy. The latter had been articulated immediately after the election, by Foreign Secretary Robin Cook in his FCO Mission Statement. In the brief speech he used to launch this, Cook remarked that in this 'age of internationalism' one of the goals of Labour's foreign policy would be:

> to secure the respect of other nations for Britain's contribution to keeping the peace of the world and promoting democracy around the world ... Our foreign policy must have an ethical dimension and must support the demands of other people for the democratic rights on which we insist for ourselves. The Labour government will put human rights at the heart of our foreign policy ... (Cook, 1997)

George Robertson, Labour's first Secretary of State for Defence, in his introduction to the SDR, echoed these ideas, stating that:

> The British are by instinct an internationalist people. We believe that as well as defending our rights we should discharge our responsibilities in the world. We do not want to stand idly by and watch humanitarian disasters as the aggression of dictators goes unchecked. We want to give a lead. We want to be a force for good. (Ministry of Defence, 1998, 4)

The SDR itself went on to reiterate this theme in its text, mentioning the need for Britain to be a 'force for good' and stressing the 'immense importance' attached to the 'international community as a whole, working together through the many international organisations, above all the United Nations' with one of the eight defined missions of the Armed Forces being 'Peace Support and Humanitarian Operations' (Ministry of Defence, 1998, 7). In the 1999 Defence White Paper there was a further reference to Britain having 'a responsibility to act as a force for good in the world' and the Armed Forces' very existence was stated as being 'to make the world a safer, better place'. The text went on to state that:

> as a Permanent Member of the UN Security Council and a country both willing and able to play a leading role internationally, we have an important wider interest in supporting international order and in promoting freedom, democracy and prosperity. (Ministry of Defence, 1999, 6)

Despite this document being drafted in the months following Kosovo and the Chicago speech, there was no real hint of the Blair Doctrine in its text. This is especially notable. The first occasion on which a major defence policy statement was published following the Chicago speech would have been perhaps the most obvious point at which to endorse what the Prime Minister had said. One would have thought that, from a presentational point of view, the five criteria would have been a most apposite insert to the White Paper.

A further publication, in February 2001, outlined what the MoD considered to be the 'future strategic context'. This also contained nothing especially significant that could be construed as reflective of the 'Blair Doctrine', which, by then, had been a subject for public discussion for almost two years. While it is important to stress that these post-SDR publications were not reflecting major reviews of defence, but were merely periodic restatements of the existing policy promulgated in SDR or statements supportive of it, it might nevertheless strike one as odd that they were devoid of any reference to the 'Blair Doctrine', in particular to the five criteria.

Following the 11 September 2001 attacks on New York and Washington, the MoD set about the production of what it called a 'New Chapter' of the SDR. The implication here was that, while the assumptions underpinning the SDR still stood, an additional chapter reflecting some consideration of international terrorism would be appropriate. In fact, the New Chapter work certainly had the feel of a mini-defence review for those of us who were serving on the Central Staff at the time. The results of this mini-review were published in July of 2002; once again, the New Chapter contained no material making any direct reference to the Blair Doctrine or, indeed, anything that could be construed as reflecting its distinctive features (Ministry of Defence, 2002). Following the invasion of Iraq, the government published a further White Paper in December 2003, which repeated the existing pattern, making no specific mention of or reference to the 'Blair Doctrine' (Ministry of Defence, 2003). One must of course admit that the 2003 White Paper, in envisaging an overall military capability to mount short-term high and low intensity operations up to divisional level was, in its substance, not inconsistent with the ambitions encapsulated within the 'Blair Doctrine', which makes its absence all the more significant (Cornish and Dorman, 2009).

Since 2003, the government has effectively abandoned the past practice of regular (usually annual) White Papers on defence and has instead opted to produce periodic policy papers on issues of significance (those on the Defence Industrial Strategy (Ministry of Defence, 2005) and on the future of Trident (Ministry of Defence, 2006) being examples). In addition, the conduct of the operations in both Afghanistan and Iraq has been a major pre-occupation. So too has been a decision to produce a National Security Strategy (NSS), from which one might expect a restatement of defence policy to flow. In fact, the NSS, when it was published in 2008, was revealed as very little more than an extremely wide threat assessment, with nothing remotely approaching a coherent 'strategy' for dealing with the threats described therein (Cabinet Office, 2008). Indeed, it is difficult to see how anyone could possibly arrive at a single strategy for dealing with such a broad range of threats. This document was the first that post-dated the Blair premiership. Arguably, if Blair's world view had had any impact of an enduring nature at all, it might have been expected that the very first NSS document produced in Whitehall would have made mention of it, yet once again they are notable by their absence. While the five criteria sat most appropriately at the level of defence policy, the broader world view would have sat very comfortably in an overarching NSS document.

The Influence of the 'Blair Doctrine'

The most remarkable feature of the collection of policy statements since 1997, and up to date, is that none of them reflect the apparently passionate intensity of Blair's formulation of his grand strategic world view. Nowhere is there any mention of the five criteria for military intervention articulated in Chicago in 1999. There is scant read across from the Prime Minister's speeches into defence policy statements. For the 'Blair Doctrine' not to get any mention in periodic defence policy statements seems stark evidence of its lack of influence. Significant mention of 'internationalism' and Britain and its armed forces acting as a positive 'force for good' were contained in the earliest documents examined and there is arguably more evidence to support the influence in those of Robin Cook's ideas than those of Tony Blair. Indeed, they are, on reflection, signposts pointing in the direction in which Tony Blair went, as he became increasingly involved with the international dimension of his job and came to his own understanding of the nature of the international system. This suggests that Blair, almost entirely new to foreign affairs in 1997, was initially influenced by the internationalism displayed by his then Foreign Secretary, Robin Cook. Kosovo was a turning point, however. From that point on, Blair assumed the leading role, with Cook losing influence. As Oliver Daddow has observed, after Kosovo, Blair was 'a more confident, proactive leader genuinely committed to grounding British foreign policy in the theory of liberal interventionism' (Daddow, 2009, 548)

Blair was a Prime Minister securely in office for ten years, a winner of three general elections and the most successful Labour leader ever, a major international figure and a statesman of significance. There is some justification, therefore, in asking ourselves what led to his pronouncements on international affairs and the utility of military force in pursuit of an activist interventionist agenda being apparently ignored in formally promulgated policy documents. By way of contrast, if the US President were to make a similar series of speeches to those referred to above, they would more than likely have a notable influence on the national security strategy emanating from the White House and the single service strategies emanating from the Pentagon. It is verging on inconceivable that a presidential world view and articulation of principles for military intervention would have been effectively ignored by branches of the US government in the way that the 'Blair Doctrine' seems to have been in Whitehall. This is despite the fact that US presidents frequently find themselves checked in their power and influence by powerful forces within Congress – which, unlike a British Prime Minister in relation to Parliament, they emphatically do not dominate through the mechanisms of tight party discipline.

The British Prime Minister is powerful and influential in relation to Parliament, but noticeably weaker in relation to his own colleagues. His Cabinet is not a collection of appointees entirely dependent on him for their positions. Whereas a US cabinet member (the Secretary of Defense, for example) will be a presidential appointee and placeman, there to serve the President, a British Cabinet Minister is usually a figure of political substance – possibly even a rival – whose direction of his or her department may well be a means of exercising significant influence. There is a limit to the extent to which Prime Ministers can simply direct Cabinet members to do their bidding. Constitutionally, the Prime Minister is a primus inter pares within the Cabinet. A US President is constitutionally in a much more revered and powerful position relative to Cabinet colleagues. A presidential command or directive carries constitutionally significantly greater weight than a prime ministerial decision or expressed preference about policy. This has effect at lower levels. Whereas the Pentagon would feel obliged to reflect the substance of presidential speeches in strategic policy papers, the MoD in London is not so tied.

Another factor to be taken into account is that, while the top end officialdom within US departments are largely political appointees, holding their positions because they have been so appointed by or on behalf of the President, the top officials in Whitehall are almost all career civil servants who may well have held the same position under the previous government. Permanent officials are responsible for the drafting of major policy documents; they are less inclined than would be political appointees to fill them with text reflective of a party leader's prejudices. The staffing processes by which key policy documents (such as Defence White Papers) achieve departmental endorsement are almost entirely driven by officials, with Ministers having little opportunity to shape the end product. It is not too strong a claim to make that the totality of officialdom in the MoD tends towards pragmatism rather more so than idealism. The collective product of their labour tends, not surprisingly, to reflect that.

It is important to make these points because one detects a tendency among pundits and political 'scientists' to overstress the extent to which government has become more 'presidential' in recent years, highlighting that political appointees within the ranks of officialdom in government departments have greatly increased in number and influence and that even Cabinet Ministers no longer wield the same power and influence that once they might. These shifts may well have occurred and may even seem seismic to those closest in time and space to them. However, when processes in Britain are contrasted with processes in Washington, for example, the distinct British political realities are seen in different light. Very obviously, the style of government does change from administration to administration, but there are some enduring verities. The Prime Minister is emphatically not the US President and experiences both the advantages and disadvantages of that truth. One Prime Minister may be more a chair of equals in Cabinet while another may lord it over colleagues. Yet another – and this is reputedly the case with Mr Blair

– may well exclude Cabinet colleagues by forming small cabals of favoured Ministers and Downing Street advisers or may engage in surprisingly informal forms of decision making on his office sofa. Nevertheless, the reality remains that no Prime Minister can assume that his or her philosophical musings will filter inexorably down into major, formally endorsed and published policy statements. For this to happen requires a conviction on the part of Cabinet colleagues and their determination, in turn, to insist on this within their departments. There is no reference in any of the sources consulted of any measure of Cabinet discussion of the 'Blair Doctrine'. This may, paradoxically, be one of the reasons why it had legs for some observers of the political scene but failed to gain traction in the deeper recesses of government.

Finally, one needs to appreciate precisely what periodic defence white papers and other related documents are actually for. They are partly an element of the government's approach to public relations, partly an intra-departmentally negotiated set of literary hooks for the services' desired equipment programmes, and only partly about national strategy. Over the last 30 or 40 years, the content and substance of white papers has been progressively reduced to the point where they are now relatively thin and 'glossy' documents consisting largely of a series of brief paragraphs and bullet points – with at times the right looking set of bullets having the appearance of being produced before the policy has been fleshed out around them. They are invariably not substantial statements of strategic intent. Surprisingly, despite Blair's five criteria for military intervention representing what might have been regarded as a useful set of bullets, they still found no way into a major policy document.

The conclusion one is inexorably drawn to is that the Blair Doctrine obtained no recognisable form of endorsement in the formal policy process within government. Some have argued that the Blair Doctrine was a 'fully fledged doctrine'; others believe it 'hardly qualifies as a fully worked out doctrine' (Daddow, 2009, 548–9). Clearly this author is more inclined to the latter assessment than he is to the former. Nevertheless, this does not necessarily mean that it had absolutely no impact at all. While it did not influence the writing of formal policy documents, it would be most surprising if a world view as strongly articulated as Blair's had had no discernible influence on the decisions he made.

Conclusions

There is no doubt whatsoever that the Blair government was one of the most militarily interventionist of post-Second World War British administrations. Military actions against Iraq, against Serbia, in Sierra Leone and in Afghanistan have been the subject of much analysis, debate and both domestic and international controversy. The key question is not, therefore, about the extent to which Blair was generally prepared to deploy the military instrument but rather about the extent to which such interventions that did take place were consistent with the principles underpinning his doctrine. It is perfectly possible to posit an argument that all 'Blair's wars' were consistent with his articulated doctrine. One could run through the main features of his world view and tick off the elements of it that were reflected in his decisions to deploy military force, and the five criteria can also be interpreted in ways that would confirm this. Notwithstanding this, it cannot be denied that some British military interventions were undoubtedly more consistent than others with the idealism and humanitarianism that were such important themes in the Chicago speech and the other principal sources quoted above.

Both Kosovo and Sierra Leone seem strongly to fit the bill – Kosovo as the backdrop when Blair originally enunciated his ideas, and Sierra Leone, which seemed to confirm his thinking by its immediate military success. Both served to persuade many that there was something of substance in his approach. Both were strongly altruistically humanitarian in motive, rather than governed purely by British self interest. However, in the aftermath of 11 September, there was a noticeable shift in emphasis away from the idea of doing good towards taking action in expressed defence of the national interest. This is not to imply criticism necessarily; it is merely an observation. Indeed, many in Britain and abroad (including this author) were strongly in favour of the decision to join the US in the intervention against the Taliban and Al Qaeda in Afghanistan. The real schism in opinion emerged with the decision to join the US in the invasion of Iraq.

That invasion was a real test for the 'Blair Doctrine', a test which arguably it not only failed but which also effectively destroyed it. Iraq was not an intervention for humanitarian purpose. As for general internationalist motives, the distortion of international law by the British government in the process of justifying its involvement put paid to any claims by Blair that he was supportive of the UN (although, to be fair, he had challenged the value of the law as it stood and had also been critical of an unreformed UN). In the context of the 'Blair Doctrine' – including the wider vision that underpinned it – the real impact of Iraq was not these concerns, however, but its opportunity cost. If Britain's armed forces had not been so consumed with the effort in Iraq, it would have been possible to maintain a much higher commitment in Afghanistan. Even more dramatically in tune with the idealistic rhetoric behind the 'Blair Doctrine', it may alternatively also have been possible for Britain to deploy serious military capability elsewhere, including into Darfur – even if a Chinese veto in the Security Council would have meant intervention without a Security Council mandate, resulting in a very similar 'illegal but legitimate' justification to that argued in the case of Kosovo (Haines, 2009).

It is ironic that a doctrine born out of humanitarian motive, against a backdrop of an illegal but arguably legitimate intervention in Kosovo, should be sacrificed in an illegal and illegitimate invasion of Iraq, almost at the same time that a genuine and massive humanitarian catastrophe was unfolding in Sudan. The experience of Iraq may also have had the longer term effect of reducing public support for the very sort of progressive pre-emption that Blair was advocating in his various articulations of his world view. One may, of course, be wrong about this; the British people as a whole are not generally inclined to oppose the use of the military instrument or regret too much the loss of British military lives in genuinely heroic endeavour. However, it is certainly worth asking the question: following the war in Iraq, would an intervention in Sudan today, without UN Security Council mandate, obtain the majority support of the Cabinet, of Parliament or of the voting public in general? One hopes that it might but fears it would not. The tragedy for Blair is that the world view he so passionately advocated was ultimately undermined by the war he so passionately pursued. On the evidence to date, it seems that the Westphalian world has survived for now – and for Britain it is Palmerston's, rather than Blair's, instinct that prevails.

References

Blair, T (1999), *Doctrine of the International Community – Speech by the Prime Minister to the Economic Club of Chicago on 24 April* (London: HMSO)

Blair, T (2001), *Speech by the Prime Minister to the Labour Party conference on 2 October* (London: Labour Party)

Blair, T (2004), *Iraq and the Threat of International Terrorism – Speech by the Prime Minister to his Sedgefield constituents on 5 March* (London: HMSO)

Blair, T (2006a), *Clash about Civilisations – Speech by the Prime Minister to the Foreign Policy Centre on 21 March* (London: HMSO)

Blair, T (2006b), *Global Alliance for Global Values – Speech by the Prime Minister to the Australian Parliament in Canberra on 27 March* (London: HMSO)

Blair, T (2006c), *We Must Modernise Institutions to Meet Challenges – Speech by the Prime Minister at Georgetown University, Washington on 26 May* (London: HMSO)

Blair, T (2006d), *Complete Renaissance – Speech by the Prime Minister to the Los Angeles World Affairs Council on 1 August* (London: HMSO)

Blair, T (2006e), *A Global Alliance for Global Values* (London: Foreign Policy Centre)

Blair, T (2007), *Our Nation's Future: Defence – Speech by the Prime Minister onboard HMS Albion at Devonport Dockyard on 12 January* (London: HMSO)

Cabinet Office (2008), *The National Security Strategy of the United Kingdom: Security in an Interdependent World* (London: HMSO)

Cook, R (1997), *Speech by the Foreign Secretary regarding the government's commitment to an ethical dimension to foreign policy on 12 May 1997* (London: HMSO)

Cornish, P and Dorman, A (2009), 'Blair's Wars and Brown's Budgets: From Strategic Defence Review to Strategic Decay in Less than a Decade', *International Affairs*, 85/2, 247–61

Daddow, O (2009), 'Tony's war? Blair, Kosovo and the Interventionist Impulse in British Foreign Policy', *International Affairs*, 85/3, 547–60

Haines, S (2009), 'The Influence of Operation Allied Force on the Development of the Jus ad Bellum', *International Affairs*, 85/3, 477–90

Herring, G (2008), *From Colony to Superpower: US Foreign Relations Since 1776* (Oxford: Oxford University Press)

Holland, M (1993), *Oscar Wilde: Stories* (London: Folio Society)

International Commission on Intervention and State Sovereignty (2001), *The Responsibility to Protect* (Ottawa: International Development Research Centre)

Joint Doctrine and Concept Centre (2001), *British Defence Doctrine Second Edition: Joint Warfare Publication 0-01* (Shrivenham: Joint Doctrine and Concepts Centre)

Kampfner, J (2003), *Blair's Wars* (London: Free Press)

McSmith, A and Dillon, J (2003), 'Blair Seeks New Powers to Attack Rogue States', *The Independent*, 13 July

Ministry of Defence (1998), *The Strategic Defence Review: Modern Forces for the Modern World* (London: HMSO)

Ministry of Defence (1999), *Defence White Paper* (London: HMSO)

Ministry of Defence (2001), *The Future Strategic Context for Defence* (London: HMSO)

Ministry of Defence (2002), *The Strategic Defence Review: A New Chapter* (London: HMSO)

Ministry of Defence (2003), *Delivering Security in a Changing World: Defence White Paper* (London: HMSO)

Ministry of Defence (2004), *Future Capabilities: Defence White Paper* (London: HMSO)

Ministry of Defence (2005), *Defence Industrial Strategy: Defence White Paper* (London: HMSO)

Ministry of Defence (2006), *The Future of the United Kingdom's Nuclear Deterrent: Defence White Paper* (London: HMSO)

Naval Staff (1999), *British Maritime Doctrine: Second Edition* (London: Directorate Naval Staff)

Rhodes James, R (1986), *Anthony Eden* (London: Weidenfeld and Nicolson)

Vincent, J (1974), *Non-intervention and International Order* (Princeton: Princeton University Press)

Weinberger, C (1984), *Speech by the US Secretary of Defense to the National Press Club in Washington on 28 November* (Washington: Department of Defense)

Woodward, L (1962), *The Age of Reform 1815–1870* (Oxford: Oxford University Press)

Chapter 5

Britain and the Politics of Counter-Terrorism: The 2002 New Chapter and Beyond

David Brown[1]

Introduction

In July 2002, the MoD produced its policy framework to combat the more prominent threat of international terrorism, the New Chapter to the 1998 SDR process. This document outlined the effects based structure that was to guide a military contribution to the government's overall efforts to combat international terrorism in the wake of the horrific events of 11 September 2001. It was stressed at the outset that this was not a new review, coming less than four years after the conclusion of the initial SDR process, but was merely an update on the pre-existing SDR assumptions to take into account the greater threat posed by Al Qaeda, its associated groups and wider network (although Steven Haines, who was heavily involved in the production of the New Chapter has noted, elsewhere in this volume, that it felt like a 'mini-review' for those that were engaged in the process at the time).

Interestingly, the New Chapter, despite being the foundation document for the controversial use of armed force as a primary mechanism for combating terrorism, has not received the academic analysis that it deserves. For example, in their otherwise welcome tour d'horizon of developments in British Defence Policy during the New Labour era, Cornish and Dorman skim over the content and consequences of the New Chapter relatively quickly (Cornish and Dorman, 2009). This despite the fact that the underlying assumptions and arrangements contained within this document provide part of the justification for the deployment of troops to both Afghanistan and Iraq, as part of the wider 'war on terror', with all the wider consequences for the reputation of the UK, the management of the Armed Forces more generally – particularly the British Army, which will be the primary focus of this chapter – and the wider physical security of the UK. Combating terrorism has become one of the central concerns of contemporary governance, both within the UK and wider, with a range of international organisations, from NATO (D Brown, 2005) to the EU (D Brown, 2010) to the UN, seeking to help justify their 'security credentials' with reference to the contribution they can make to combating terrorism.

---

1   The views contained within this chapter reflect solely those of the author, and are not representative of the views of the Royal Military Academy Sandhurst, the British Army, the Ministry of Defence or the British government more widely.

This can be seen in even the briefest survey of relevant statistics. In budgetary terms, overall spending on security is expected to rise from £2.5bn in 2007 to £3.5bn by 2011, with the Security Services doubling in size since the initial attacks in the US in 2001 and the number of police personnel dedicated to counter-terrorism increasing by over 70 per cent since 2006 (G Brown, 2007; Home Office, 2009, 12, 62). The Joint Terrorism Analysis Centre (JTAC), established in 2003 as part of a wider co-ordinated approach for the assessment and dissemination of intelligence on international terrorism, has also seen its staffing rise by 60 per cent during its relatively brief lifetime (Home Office, 2009, 62). In addition, within the military sphere specifically, terrorism is a central feature of defence activity, as noted by the 2003 Defence Aim – 'to deliver security for the people of the United Kingdom and the Overseas Territories by defending them, including against terrorism; and to act as a force for good by strengthening international peace and stability' (Ministry of Defence, 2003, 4). Given its continued importance to the development of both British Defence Policy and its wider security policy more generally, the New Chapter needs to be taken more seriously. This chapter hopes to rectify this imbalance, by placing the underlying assumptions of the New Chapter under the microscope.

This will be done in a number of ways. Firstly, the chapter will briefly look at the underlying motivations for organising a New Chapter in the first place, considering what the requirement to 'update' underlying assumptions within four years of a process that was initially supposed to provide a much wider and longer term strategic overview says about the nature of policy-making more generally. This is particularly important given that all three main political parties have committed themselves to a further Strategic Defence Review following the 2010 General Election. Having placed the New Chapter within a wider policy-making context, and explained the central objectives and arrangements contained within, the chapter will then critically examine two key assumptions underpinning the New Chapter. Firstly, it will explore the nature of the threat posed by international terrorism, particularly as encapsulated by the Blair administration. It will ask whether the Blair conception of international terrorism – which culminated in the controversial labelling of such matters as a 'clash about civilisation' (Blair, 2006, 2007a) – is accurate and trace to what extent the Blair approach to the nature of the problem has survived his departure from the British political scene, in relation to both his successor, Gordon Brown, and also the views of the Conservative Party on this issue. Secondly, the role of the state as the central focus of such an interventionist approach will be considered in some depth, particularly in relation to the prominence given to the contribution of state sponsors, of both an active and passive variety, within the New Chapter as a whole, possibly at the expense of other potential targets, notably the ever more prominent category of fragile, failing or even failed states. In doing so, the chapter aims to assess where UK Armed Forces can make a contribution to the wider aim of combating international terrorism.

Two brief caveats need to be highlighted before commencing the more in-depth analysis. Firstly, the primary focus, understandably, given the length of his tenure in Downing Street and his central role in forming both the initial response and the wider intellectual and political justifications for such interventions, will be on the Blair administration. Where appropriate, comparisons will be drawn with his successor and the position of David Cameron's Conservative Party. Secondly, the focus will be primarily on external power projection, rather than the role of the UK Armed Forces within homeland defence. This has been done for a number of reasons. Firstly, it fits within the wider ethos of the New Chapter and the government's stated approach to projecting military force, as seen in the fundamental, but ultimately flawed, objective to 'deal with the threat at source, rather than waiting for the threat to arrive in the UK' (Hoon cited House of Commons, 2003, 42). The approach of 'going to the crisis rather than have the crisis come to you' exemplifies much of the initial approach, and is still inherent in the defence of a continued – and expanded – UK military presence in Afghanistan. Secondly, notably the Army's involvement in homeland defence has been both more limited and yet, as exemplified by certain key instances, such as the decision to place a more visible military presence at Heathrow Airport in February 2003, controversial (Blunkett, 2006, 447). Its more limited involvement can be seen, for example, in the fact that the Army is not named as a 'first responder' in the 2004 Civil Contingencies Act. In fact, in the 2007 review of the UK military's role in wider counter-terrorism, commissioned by Gordon Brown on arrival at Number 10 Downing Street and executed by former Armed Forces Minister, Adam Ingram MP, the scope of the initial review had to be widened to even formally take into account specific aspects of the homeland dimension, notably the issue of resilience to terrorist attacks (Interview, 2009). In addition, the Civil Contingencies Reaction Force (CCRF) – initiated in the New Chapter as part of a wider Reservist role in homeland security and standing at 13 units as of mid-2009 – was considered by CGS, General Sir David Richards, to be 'perhaps the one measure falling out of the SDR New Chapter that has not been exploited', because the situation has not arisen to warrant its involvement, assisting civilian agencies during an emergency (House of Commons, 2009). Finally, in terms of the structure of this volume, much of the relevant discussion with regard to the military's role within homeland defence against potential terrorist threats relates more specifically to Northern Ireland, which is handled in Trevor C Salmon's chapter.

A Necessary Chapter: The SDR and the Politics of Prediction

While this is not the place to go into the SDR process and its outcomes in any depth (for details, see McInnes, 1998), a brief comparison between some of the SDR's central conclusions and the amendments made within a couple of years will give some food for thought as to the appropriate process and outlook to adopt for the future. Certainly, the commitment by all parties to hold a more regular review of the underlying assumptions and projections that are likely to appear from the 2010 process, however it is undertaken, is to be welcomed. While it was claimed that this is what the government has effectively done on a less formal basis during its time in office – 'one way you keep vigilance is to keep coming back and restudying problems' (Simon Webb cited House of Commons, 2003) – giving it a more formal structure to review and reappraise assumptions against reality is surely a sensible precaution, particularly given the range of challenges posed in the intervening period between the SDR and the New Chapter.

While there are clear elements of continuity and consistency between the two documents, such as the continued emphasis on jointery, defence diplomacy and wider power projection, some key SDR assumptions did not survive unscathed, highlighting once again the difficulties that the wider defence community, both practitioner and academic, has when it attempts to predict the developing nature of the international system. Firstly, the New Chapter is arguably even more internationalist in its outlook than its founding document, with Hoon noting that the events of 11 September have 'demonstrated that we cannot dictate the geographic areas where our interests may be engaged' (Hoon, 2001). While the SDR had a clear and explicit internationalist core, there was always an underlying assumption that certain parts of the world posed no immediate interest for the UK, such as South-East Asia and Latin America. In fact, the SDR highlighted that the key areas for future defence operations were likely to be Europe, the wider Mediterranean and the Gulf region. Such limitations were effectively withdrawn in the New Chapter, where it was asserted – as part of the underlying maxim of 'going to the crisis rather than having the crisis come to you' – that 'we will have to be prepared to become diplomatically or militarily involved more often than before in parts of the world where, perhaps, we have not played an active role in the more recent past' (Hoon, 2002). Afghanistan was a specific case in point, with Hoon admitting that, in 1998, it was not seen as a likely focus for future military operations, although he defended this position by noting that 'we were not alone in making that assumption' (Hoon cited House of Commons, 2003).

A potential consequence of such a widening of the UK's overall horizons relates to the declared 'scale of tasks' – or harmony guidelines – which were the stated limitations on deployment contained within the SDR. In 1998, it was declared that, in addition to the continuing commitment to a military presence in Northern Ireland, the UK could successfully undertake one large scale operation (similar in scale and duration to the UK commitment in the 1991 Gulf War) or two simultaneous medium scale engagements, 'a more extended overseas deployment', on the scale of the commitment to Bosnia, as well as retaining the 'ability to mount a second substantial deployment – which might involve a combat brigade and appropriate naval and air forces' (Ministry of Defence, 1998). Time limits were placed on the level of involvement, with the medium scale commitment officially limited to a six month period, with no expectation of war fighting. Once again, the realities of the post-11 September world – a more prominent international terrorist threat, a more active and aggressive stance adopted in the White House, combining with the underlying internationalist and interventionist instincts of Blair himself – meant that there needed to be a change of focus, both rhetorically and then more formally in the 2003 White Paper process. Geoff Hoon, the then

Defence Secretary, accepted that 'we need to examine the number, size and nature of operations we may be called on to undertake, perhaps simultaneously or in quick succession' (Hoon, 2002). In 2003, as part of a further ad hoc amendment process to the underlying SDR assumptions, the White Paper formally amended pre-existing guidelines, committing the UK instead to a greater combination of small and medium scale operations, arguing that the UK should be able to operate on three simultaneous and enduring small to medium level commitments (Ministry of Defence, 2003). Given the manner in which the initially stated limitations on both the scope and duration of military activity were overcome by events, it does potentially call into question the effectiveness of such an approach in the future. While supporters will argue that they were never meant to be taken as hard and fast limits – 'the assumptions are not intended to constrain or precisely describe the actual pattern of operational commitment at any point in time' (Hutton, 2009) – the fact that they have been surpassed in each of the last seven years – with all of the ensuing implications for managing existing commitments and preparing for future operations – hardly inspires confidence if such a process is repeated in the future.

One of the most significant statements made in the SDR concerned the government's assessment that, for the duration of the SDR process, it did not foresee the possibility of an attack on either the UK or the surrounding region – 'there is today no direct military threat to the United Kingdom or Western Europe' (Ministry of Defence, 1998). As NATO effectively recognised the events of 11 September as a threat to its members, invoking Article Five for the first time in its history, this prediction seems more difficult to sustain. While it could be argued that – given the overt and lingering state focus of defence policy even within a post-Cold War 'strategic review' – the SDR was referring specifically to conventional warfare, that position seems difficult to sustain in light of subsequent evidence. In 'Defence Policy 2001', for example, no distinction is made when asserting, as part of its brief overview of the state of defence policy, that 'we assess that, for the foreseeable future, it is unlikely that *a direct threat* to the UK could re-emerge' (emphasis added) (Ministry of Defence, 2001). Also, Hoon effectively admitted that the initial prognosis had been a little optimistic, noting that 'one assumption that was clearly challenged by the events of 9/11 was that there was no longer a direct threat to the UK. Quite clearly there is' (Hoon, 2002).

There also seems to be some confusion over the level of importance placed on assessing terrorism in the SDR, with government spokesmen effectively trying to ride two horses going in different directions at once. On the one hand, there is a need to determine the nature of the terrorist threat as quantifiably different, if for no other reason than to justify a New Chapter in the first place. Yet, somewhat defensively, there is also an underlying need to defend against claims that, in its initial strategic review, it underestimated the threat posed by international terrorism. In effect, it led to some rather confusing arguments, on one occasion within the same speech. For example, when Hoon launched the New Chapter at the Royal United Services Institute (RUSI) in 2002, he pointed out first that, with regard to the SDR, 'the events of the last few years have largely vindicated its assumptions', before adding that the impact of 11 September 'altered' the nature of terrorism 'in many ways which, despite our best planning, we could never have anticipated' (Hoon, 2002).

It does pose the question – should a self-ordained 'strategic review' have given greater prominence to considering the implications of international terrorism, both for the UK's wider security policy and the military more specifically? In the SDR, it is listed as a potential risk, with the review highlighting the possibility of 'new and horrifying forms of terrorism, which can cause dangerous instabilities' (Ministry of Defence, 1998). The inclusion of the word 'new' is of particular interest here, and is worth a more detailed assessment. What aspects of the 11 September attacks were, in effect, new – save the obvious that, on this occasion, the Islamist terrorists involved had successfully completed their objective? This was not the first attempted attack on the World Trade Center, as Ramsi Yousef had attempted unsuccessfully to bring down the Towers in 1993 with a truck bombing. Nor was it the first Al Qaeda attack on either US citizens or property – the timeline leading up to the events of 11 September includes the 2000 attack on the USS Cole as well as the 1998 Embassy bombings in Tanzania and Kenya (National Commission, 2004; Wright, 2006). In fact, it was not even the first time that a terrorist group had attempted the tactic of using hijacked planes to crash into notable landmarks, as the Algerian terrorist group, Groupe Armee Islamique (GIA) planned to crash a hijacked Air France plane into the Eiffel Tower in December 1994. Rohan Gunaratna, one of the world's leading experts on suicide terrorism and the development of Al Qaeda, has estimated that there had been over 240 land and maritime suicide attacks prior to the events of 11 September (between 1968 and 2001) (Gunaratna, 2001). In effect, Osama Bin Laden did not emerge from the ether in 2001; perhaps, given the implications of holding a more 'strategic' review, with a wider frame of reference and a greater baseline of analysis (having widened the levels of participation beyond the traditional limits of Whitehall to incorporate the voices of a greater number of practitioners from the worlds of academia, industry and the media), expectations were a little higher.

Yet, in fairness, this assessment is done with the much advantageous benefit of hindsight, where a more coherent narrative can be placed on far more disparate events and developments. In addition, a debate has raged in the US as to whether the Clinton administration could have done more to prevent the threat developing to the level it did or whether – in the early days of the Bush administration – that administration took its eye off the ball in the first nine months in office (Clarke, 2004; Feith, 2009). Leaving aside much of the partisan analysis that has discoloured the debate, the National Commission established to examine the events leading up to 11 September tried to avoid naming and shaming any one group in particular, preferring instead to criticise both administrations for 'a lack of imagination' with regard to this developing threat (National Commission, 2004, 339). Given that the US were effectively caught unprepared by the tragic events of 11 September, it may be unfair to criticise the UK for failing to place more emphasis on such threats.

The New Chapter – Objectives and Roles

Before considering in more depth the three underlying assumptions of the 2002 New Chapter, it is necessary to explain in a little more detail what precisely the document had to say, both about the nature and objectives to be achieved and the main mechanisms for managing a military contribution to countering primarily international Islamist terrorism (the technological aspect of the New Chapter, particularly its focus on network-centric capabilities, is covered in a later chapter by Michael Codner). The central goal, as stated in the New Chapter, is 'to eliminate terrorism as a force for change in international affairs' (Ministry of Defence, 2002a). In placing the emphasis on the impact and effectiveness of terrorism within the wider international arena, not only was the Blair administration giving yet another indication of its greater internationalist perspective – a theme that had coloured its approach to foreign policy generally, not just the response to international terrorism – but had also subtly differed from the initial position taken by the Bush administration, which initially advocated the aim of eliminating terrorism per se – 'the only way to defeat terrorism as a threat to our way of life is to stop it, eliminate and destroy it where it grows' (Bush, 2001). In fact, this chimes with Sperling's assessment earlier in this volume; although much of the debate within the UK is affected by developments in the US, there are still differences between the two, qualifying the claim that they effectively share a 'security culture'. While they may arrive at the same end point, for example the controversial decision to target Iraq in 2003, they may not approach it from quite the same direction. For example, the US debate at the time focused on the need for 'regime change' – believed by some, notably Vice President Cheney, as the only means to secure an end to the 'cheat and retreat' approach of the Hussein regime to the question of WMD development – and the perceived, if heavily disputed, links between Saddam Hussein's Iraq and Al Qaeda. In contrast, the UK – although concerned about the development of WMD – placed more emphasis on the humanitarian aspect of the intervention (Blair, 2003) and made no attempt of note to specifically link Iraq and the events of 11 September.

This has led some, notably Malcolm Chalmers, to claim that 'the UK did not see Afghanistan and Iraq as part of a counter-terrorist strategy; it saw it as part of an Alliance commitment' (Chalmers cited House of Commons, 2009). This seems a little simplistic, not least because there is rarely a monocausal explanation for such decisions, particularly decisions as complex and controversial as the application of force without a specific UN mandate and in the teeth of considerable opposition within the wider international community. The UK government, in both its New Labour guises, has never hidden the fact that part of the rationale for its involvement was to 'stand shoulder to shoulder' with the US, to provide advice and seek, potentially, to curb the more unilateralist tendencies within the Bush administration that had caused so much disquiet within sections of the international community – 'There is fear of US unilateralism ... the way to deal with it is not rivalry, but partnership' (Blair, 2003). In addition, to elevate the relationship with the US – which presumably is Chalmers' focus rather than a wider Alliance structure, given NATO's non-involvement in either the initial stages of the Afghan intervention or in Iraq per se – is potentially to fall into the trap of seeing Blair as effectively a 'poodle' of the Bush administration, led reluctantly to war by its larger partner, which does not necessarily accord neatly with the facts (D Brown, 2008). Not only that, but it is a little misleading, not least because it seeks to conflate the two operations, assuming they have the same single underlying motivation. At its most basic, there would be no International Security Assistance Force (ISAF), nor would there be up to 10,000 UK troops in Afghanistan if it was not for the terrorist attacks of 11 September, and the belief – firmly held, if not always supported by the evidence, which has subsequently pointed more directly at Pakistan than Afghanistan (as pointed out by the departing government Minister Lord Malloch-Brown (Malloch-Brown, 2009) – that the UK's continued efforts to stabilise and provide support to the fledgling Afghan National Army (ANA) was preventing future terrorist attacks in the UK – 'Our aim in 2009 is the same as it was in 2001. We are in Afghanistan as a result of a hard-headed assessment of the terrorist threat facing Britain' (G Brown, 2009a). While the situation with Iraq is less straightforward, it should also be remembered that Iraq had been declared a state sponsor of terrorism for three consecutive Presidencies, from 1990 until the overthrow of the Hussein regime. Given the importance placed – rightly or wrongly – on state sponsors within the contours of the Bush-Blair led 'war on terror' (a matter that will be discussed in greater depth later in the chapter), while the decision to invade Iraq had disastrous consequences, both in diplomatic and security terms, both for the region itself and, arguably, for the UK, it was not as bizarre a decision as Clarke colourfully claimed, in arguing that it was the equivalent of 'invading Mexico after the Japanese attacked us at Pearl Harbor' (Clarke, 2004, 31). In some senses, it may come down to a difference between *a* 'war on terror' – which would not necessarily be specifically targeted solely at the perpetrators of the 11 September attacks – and *the* 'war on terror', which arguably would have a more narrow focus.

There is a related question, particularly important given that the UK – and indeed the EU more generally – is threatened to different extents by a range of terrorist groups, emanating from all shades of the ideological spectrum. Was the 'war on terror', of which the New Chapter was part, concerned with all terrorism or just a specific variant? In the US, the debate seemed to be initially very confused, with the President suggesting an Al Qaeda first approach, as part of a wider campaign to tackle terrorism more widely, and the Vice President – bizarrely – providing an initially very minimalist approach, focusing not on the wider Islamist network or even Al Qaeda as a specific variant, but on the person of Osama Bin Laden specifically – 'If Osama Bin Laden is in a cave and we get a hit, people won't care what's going on elsewhere' (Cheney cited in Woodward, 2001 218). Eventually, in the US, alongside the continued focus on states who 'harbor or sponsor', the occasionally fractious Bush administration resolved on the phrase 'terrorism with a global reach', a wider concept than international terrorism per se, with an understandable focus on terrorism that was of direct threat to the US. In the UK – as Salmon explains in more depth in a later chapter – there remains an additional and long-standing concern with the different variants of terrorist activity in Northern Ireland. While such activity declined steadily during the Blair-led peace process, the situation requires careful monitoring, as developments in the latter half of 2009 demonstrated, with M15 more than doubling its presence to counter-act a rise in Republican dissident activity (O'Neill and Sharrock, 2009).

However, having established that the central aim of the UK was to 'eliminate terrorism as a force for change', the focus of such efforts, militarily or otherwise, was going to be based on 'those groups whose aims are to establish strict Islamic regimes and expel Western influences from their regions (Ministry of Defence, 2002). Interestingly, in the Anti-Terrorism, Crime and Security Act (ATCSA) – published in the same year as the New Chapter – the Provisional Irish Republican Army (PIRA) was even excluded from the definition of 'international terrorists' used in the legislation. International terrorists have traditionally been defined as a group that targets action against foreign citizens or property within the terrorist's country of origin, has taken action in a third country or attempted to influence the policies of a foreign government or has received support from international sources. While there was substantive evidence of PIRA's wider international linkages – in terms of allegations regarding its relations with the Basque separatist group Euskadi Ta Askatasuna (ETA), its controversial involvement in Columbia and its well documented support from Libya and sources of financing within the US (Moloney, 2003), the UK government excluded 'terrorism … concerned with the affairs of part of the United Kingdom' from the definition of international terrorism (ATCSA, 2002). Rightly or wrongly, New Labour's involvement in the 'war on terror' was focused outside the UK.

Having assessed the initially stated objectives, it is now worth outlining how the New Chapter fitted in to a much wider government effort. The document outlines a range of potential roles for the military, embracing both the preventative side of military intervention (such as post-conflict reconstruction and wider defence diplomacy and training teams) and a more aggressive posture, detecting terrorist activity within states, obstructing such activity and, if necessary, ultimately destroying the terrorists ability to act and the states ability to assist them. The New Chapter has, at its core, five principal activities that make up the spectrum of counter-terrorism – to prevent, deter, coerce, disrupt and destroy – applied 'both against the international terrorists directly and, where necessary, against state regimes that support or sponsor them' (Ministry of Defence, 2002a, 9). Containment, at that time a dirty word within the US debate particularly, was not considered as a potential military effect worthy of inclusion, although it later makes an appearance as part of the wider development of potential effects, as part of the 2003 White Paper (only to be dropped from consideration once again by then Defence Secretary John Hutton in February 2009). The conceptual framework is explained in depth in Chapter Six of the supporting information and what is immediately striking is the level of involvement of state sponsors throughout, even featuring as a potential indicator under the heading of 'prevention', although the specific roles outlined in detail focus on 'defence diplomacy', particularly 'working with new partners' to combat terrorism, capacity building and the prevention of 'security vacuums' which terrorists could seek to exploit. It is also a central theme of the more aggressive end of the spectrum, in terms of coercion – using the threat of military force either to dissuade from current activity or from future involvement – disruption, notably of terrorist training camps, and destruction, using 'military action to destroy terrorist cells, entire terrorist networks and … state sponsored facilities and infrastructure' (Ministry of Defence, 2002b, 14–16). The role of the state, both as sponsor and secure location, will be returned to later in the chapter. Before that, however, the first of the two highlighted assumptions will be considered – the scale and nature of the terrorist threat more generally.

The Scale of the Terrorist Threat – Then and Now

Although not explained in any depth, neither in the main document nor in the supporting material, it is clear that the New Chapter is predicated on a particular view of the nature of the terrorist threat that confronted the international community more plainly after 11 September 2001. In asserting that the nature of the threat was so significant that it warranted the potential use of military force (as part of a much wider governmental effort to combat the threat), the New Chapter fits within the wider view of the Blair government. The central elements were thus: the threat posed was significant, unique in its scale and scope – to the point of eventually warranting the label a 'clash about civilisation' (Blair, 2006) – global in nature and unrelenting in its determination to expose and exploit the potential vulnerabilities of the modern globalised international community, with a particular emphasis on the Western world. As the underlying motivation for such an assault was portrayed as being the underlying values and beliefs of a modern society, such as the UK or US, with its emphasis on fairness, equality in all its forms, freedom and capitalism, there was little chance of finding any common ground by which to find even some element of accommodation, as had been the case with the much more limited PIRA. In fact, one of the central contributions that Blair has made to the development of the 'war on terror' is to attempt – not always successfully – to reconceptualise the campaign as a 'battle for global values', isolating the terrorists as a dangerous minority, out of step with the wider process of modernity that was shared across the international system as a whole (Blair, 2006). In essence, by placing identity – as expressed through shared values and belief systems, which need to be both preached and practiced as consistently as possible – at the centre of international efforts to combat the terrorist threat, Blair sought to adopt the scale, severity and underlying rationale of Samuel P Huntington's 'clash of civilisations' model, but not the wider division into a series of 'large scale cultural entities' (Huntington, 1998).

Such a characterisation remained a central theme of the Blair approach throughout, from his initial response to the Labour Party Conference in October 2001 – 'there is no compromise possible with such people, no meeting of minds, no point of understanding with such terror. Just a choice – defeat it or be defeated by it. And defeat it we must' (Blair, 2001) – to his final parting words in *The Economist*, when he returned to much the same theme – 'There is no alternative to fighting this menace wherever it rears its head. There are no demands that are remotely negotiable. It has to be beaten – period' (Blair, 2007, 30). Before considering the accuracy of such an approach, within the limited space available, it is interesting to note how such an overarching theme has remained as part of the wider political discourse even after Blair has departed the main stage. As one of the wider themes of this volume is to consider the impact not only of 11 September – self-evident in this case, as there would arguably not have been a New Chapter without it – but also of Blair himself, it is significant that some of the central themes of his initial characterisation were carried over by his successor and are likely to remain should the Conservatives enter office in 2010. For example, Gordon Brown seemed equally comfortable utilising the almost Manichean language and imagery that had characterised the speeches of both his predecessor and President Bush, even as he sought – for obvious tactical political reasons – to place some greater distance between himself and the unpopular Bush administration. In a series of speeches prior to becoming Prime Minister, Brown outlined his own view of the threat that was facing the UK and the wider international community, and emphasised much the same points as Blair, including the global nature of the struggle – 'there should be no safe havens anywhere in the world for terrorism' (G Brown, 2006a) and the obdurate nature of the opposition, who were motivated by 'a hatred of our very existence' (G Brown, 2006b). As with Blair, Brown posed the choice in terms of values – 'between justice and evil, humanity and barbarism, no-one should be impartial, neutral or disengaged' (G Brown, 2006b).

Interestingly, while Brown expressed an early desire, on taking office, that the controversial term 'war on terror' – with all it implied in terms of the priority given to a military response – no longer be used for official purposes, this must be placed within the context of the continuity of conceptual approach and the continued, and indeed, increased military commitment to Afghanistan (even as the UK was steadily – and then finally in April 2009 – withdrawn from Iraq). Given the controversy that was engendered by such a labelling, few eyebrows were raised by the newly inaugurated President Obama's similarly tough language on terrorists, if not their state sponsors – 'We will not apologise for our way of life, nor will we waver in its defence and to those who seek to advance their aims by inducing terror ... we will defeat you' (Obama, 2009a). While some may dismiss this as simply rhetoric, it should also be noted that, in the first nine months of his administration, President Obama authorised as many Predator air strikes in Pakistan as were initiated in the final three years of the Bush administration (and would arguably have been even greater, had Vice President Biden got his way in the three month discussion over the nature of Afghan strategy that gripped the

Obama administration during the latter part of 2009 (Mayer, 2009)). The position adopted by New Labour has also effectively been adopted by the Conservative Party – even as they seek to establish a belief in liberal conservatism, with its greater scepticism over the ability of the military to deliver specific effects, such as the consolidation of democracy within a society, they are drawn to much the same diagnosis of the problem – 'these extremists hate us for who we are – our values, our way of life' (Fox, 2008).

Where there may be a greater distancing by the Opposition is in relation to the wider geographical scope of the terrorist threat, although there has been little public follow-up on Cameron's initial scepticism – 'the danger is by positing a single source of terrorism – a global jihad – and opposing it with a single response – American backed force – we will simply fulfil our own prophecy' (Cameron, 2006). Leaving aside the somewhat generalised stereotyping of the nature of the response thus far, it may be beneficial in the longer term to scale back the rhetoric surrounding the 'global' nature of the threat, looking instead to deconstruct, to explore the individual motivations of specific terrorist groups, to 'think local' – and, as a corollary, 'act local'; in effect, to consider what Justine Rosenthal has called 'jigsaw jihadism' (Rosenthal, 2007). In doing, so, not only do you present a less frightening conception of the threat, but arguably a more accurate one as well. This author has conducted a substantive quantitative analysis of the geographical spread of terrorist incidence within the EU, as a subset of the wider international system, and has argued that, rather than even view the threat as a 'common concern' of all 27 states, a more accurate description would be that of 'cluster terrorism', focused on a much smaller group, including the UK (D Brown, 2010). The most recently available complete statistics – for 2008 – seem to verify this trend, indicating that, of 515 terrorist attacks carried out – registered in only seven states – only one had a specifically Islamist motivation (Europol, 2009, 12). This was a 24 per cent reduction on the previous year, and chimes with the formal assessment within the UK that, contrary to the more alarming rhetoric of the Blair era, there is potentially a decline – or possibly a lull – in terrorist activity. The 2009 CONTEST assessment, while advocating continued vigilance, predicted that the wider Al Qaeda movement was 'likely to fragment and may not survive in its current form', diversifying towards smaller, more independent self-starter groups, the likes of which were to blame for the events of 7 July 2005 (Home Office, 2009, 10). As this was a more positive assessment than in the original CONTEST document – which judged the threat to be 'potentially still increasing' and 'not likely to diminish significantly for some years' (Home Office, 2006, 1) – it emphasises once again both the difficulties of prediction and the need to maintain regular and accessible assessment.

The number of incidents – in quantitative and geographical terms – is only one potential indicator of the nature of the threat. One of the wider issues regarding the politics of counter-terrorism that the international community, not simply the UK, continues to wrestle with, is what are the most effective metrics by which to calculate not only the nature and scale of the threat, but also the level of progress being made in countering it. A quantitative analysis will, by definition, only take you so far, whether it be the number of incidents, the geographical concentration or the number of fatalities accrued (Al Qaeda arguably having turned Brian Jenkins' dictum regarding terrorism – that they wanted a lot of people watching rather than a lot of people dead – on its head, by accepting that the latter will effectively generate the former anyway on an ever grander scale). The Europol analysis also considers the number of arrests – for an array of terrorist related offences – and convictions, as a means of demonstration, while there is also the issue of foiled plots to consider. For example, in the most recent iteration of CONTEST, it was claimed that the UK security and policing services had disrupted 12 potential terrorist plots since 11 September, with over 200 individuals convicted of terrorist related offences between 2002 and 2008, with a further 40 awaiting charge at the time the report was published (Home Office, 2009, 9, 28). This has helped justify the continued threat level assessment of 'severe', indicating an attack is 'highly likely', from 2006 on – with only two exceptions, in August 2006 and July 2007, when it was raised to critical (Home Office, 2009, 37). There is also the wider issue of radicalisation to consider. Donald Rumsfeld, former US Secretary of Defense, famously placed the equation in these terms – 'are we capturing, killing, deterring and dissuading more terrorists every day than the madrassas and the radical clerics are recruiting, training and deploying against us? (*USA Today*, 2003). Yet, there are, by his own terms, too many 'known unknowns' in this scenario – how many killed or captured were actually or potentially terrorists, or part of a wider terrorist logistical support network (particularly given the difficulties caused by the use of Guantanamo Bay as an indefinite detention centre (Wittes, 2008, 66–84)? What is the scale of radicalisation, defined as increased scepticism of the government's actions, passive opposition, support or radical action?

No-one is suggesting that a tangible threat to certain key states in the international system does not exist. To move too far down the road to a reductionist position, particularly one based on eye-catching but ultimately misleading statistical comparisons (such as Mueller's statistical analysis of comparable fatalities in the US, which, while initially intriguing, fails to take into account the wider concepts of fear creation, political and economic impact and the intent to kill that are part and parcel of a terrorist incident (Mueller, 2006, 2–13)), would be to deny the evidence from across the world that is placed before us with an all too worrying regularity. Accusations that certain states, particularly the US and UK during the Bush-Blair eras most notably, are constantly 'crying wolf' need to be taken in context. It should always be remembered that the moral of the story was that there was a wolf waiting at the end and people no longer believed the warnings they were being given. However, there were dangers inherent in the Bush-Blair approach as well; by trying to avoid complacency on the part of wider society, they may have ended up creating the very atmosphere of fear that was part of the terrorist agenda in the first place. There is a need to balance the avoidance of complacency with the maintenance of accuracy when portraying the nature of the wider threat, and there has been a move away from some of the more alarmist rhetoric prevalent in Blair's speeches. The publication of both regular National Security Strategies – even if they have tended to list all potential grievances in an all inclusive, but not always analytically supportive, manner – and the CONTEST documents (described by the then Home Secretary Jacqui Smith as 'one of the most comprehensive and wide-ranging approaches to tackling terrorism anywhere in the world' (Home Office, 2009, 5) are a welcome addition, as will be the more regular Strategic Defence reviews promised by all parties. Keeping a regular and publicly accessible assessment of the nature of the threat can only be of benefit. Given that one of the foundation steps in any counter-terrorist strategy is to 'understand and make collective policy responses to the terrorist threat' (European Council, 2005), it is even more important not to get carried away by exaggerated rhetoric, nor to simply accept at face value the assumption of a global, or indeed – considering the statistics on offer – regional threat. Not only that, but, with their credibility already damaged by the fall-out from the 2003 invasion of Iraq, with its discredited claims of actual WMD, rather than plans, programmes or potential intent, wider society may be less receptive to such siren calls in the future. Tim Hames has lamented that the worst consequence from the 2003 intervention in Iraq is that it may never be able to be undertaken again (Hames, 2006), although, as will be demonstrated in a later section of this chapter, the lack of credible or politically acceptable state targets in any wider 'war on terror' should close off this avenue anyway and lead to a potential reprioritisation of military effect in the longer term.

Coerce and Destroy – The Focus on State Sponsors of Terrorism

This leads us to our second assumption underpinning the New Chapter, that it is too traditional in its explanation of security, with too overt a focus on states, particularly state sponsors of terrorism, at the expense of the wider threat from international terrorism. From the outset, in the Bush and Blair approach to countering terrorism, terrorist groups and the states that sponsor or harbour them shared equal billing (as was noted earlier, the concept of state sponsorship appears in four of the five roles outlined for the military within the New Chapter). In part, this is understandable. Politically, states are somehow easier to deal with, with traditional instruments of statehood structured around inter-state relations, and are more visible when it comes to determining the nature of the enemy and the level of progress made (particularly in comparison to a more amorphous, shifting terrorist threat, based around a shared ideological belief, although without necessarily having specific linkages between the various localised groups or individuals).

Yet, as Daniel Byman has argued in relation to the Bush approach to countering terrorism – which essentially is part of the linked approach adopted in the UK by Blair in the New Chapter – it 'rests on a flawed understanding of the problem' (Byman, 2008), namely that state sponsorship has been – and remains – a central element of the 'war on terror'. Given the linkages between the two states – discussed in wider terms by James Sperling earlier in this volume – the best guide to use in determining the actual nature of the problem is the annual appraisal of global terrorist trends produced by the US State Department, which contains a specific section on declared 'state sponsors'. In 2002, in its first full reaction to the events of 11 September, it denoted seven states as sponsors – Cuba, Iran, Iraq, Libya, North Korea, Sudan and Syria. Of these, three have been subsequently removed, with North Korea – which the 2001 report accepted had not sponsored any terrorism since 1987 (State Department, 2002) – being withdrawn as part of the Bush administration's wider negotiations over its nuclear programme. Iraq – for obvious reasons – and Libya, as part of the wider process of renovating relations with the Gadaffi regime (it last appeared as a designated state sponsor in the 2006 report), were also withdrawn from the list. While there is not sufficient space to consider each declared candidate, it is worth looking at a number of the remaining examples in a little more detail.

At one end of the scale, there is Cuba, designated a state sponsor in 1982, and therefore the longest serving member of a dwindling group. It seems to be an egregious case of inclusion on the grounds of US foreign policy more generally, rather than any specific linkage to the wider terrorist problem. Although making reference to permitting up to twenty ETA members to live in Havana as 'guests', as well as wider support to the Revolutionary Armed Forces of Columbia (FARC) and National Liberation Army (ELN) groups, it is difficult to sustain this as a basis for inclusion. Leave aside the fact that both the US and UK were primarily focused on international Islamist terrorism, rather than the shifting threat posed by ETA and contained bilaterally by France and Spain, there is little evidence offered to suggest that these supporters of Basque independence were in any way actively involved in the violent separatist campaign that has veered between activity and ceasefire over the past few years. Additionally, the following year, the report admitted that Columbia had actually 'acquiesced' in the arrangements and was content with Cuba's assistance, particularly in terms of the mediation it was undertaking with the ELN (State Department, 2003). This does call into question why there was a need to mention it in the first place, as it was not perceived as a hostile act even by the Columbian government. More bizarrely, the report chose to highlight the fact that 'Cuba did not protest the use of Guantanamo Bay base to house enemy combatants' as part of its case, suggesting that failure to criticise US foreign policy served as part of their overall case (State Department, 2002). In its most recent report, while still continuing to include it on the list, the report noted that 'Cuba no longer actively supports armed struggle in Latin America', and that some of the ETA and FARC representatives that had featured in previous reports had arrived 'in connection with peace negotiations with the governments of Spain and Columbia' (State Department, 2009).

At the other end of the scale are Iran and Syria, with the former consistently branded 'the most active state sponsor of terrorism', via its links to Hezbollah, Hamas and other Palestinian groups. In the most recent report – only emphasising the previous paucity of information about some of the other candidates – it notes specifically that, in 2008, Iran had provided more than $200m to Lebanese Hezbollah and had assisted in the training of over 3,000 Hezbollah fighters in

camps within Iran (State Department, 2009). Similar general accusations are
levelled at Syria, with a section of the report detailing Syria's continued links with
Iran – as if guilty by association – but there is notably less specific detail than is
the case for Iran. Yet, the changing political atmosphere, notably under the Obama
administration – from which many other states, including the UK, will take its lead
– needs to be factored in here.

Recent developments suggest that they are not politically or militarily
acceptable targets for pursuing a military contribution to countering terrorism. Just
as politics explains the continued inclusion of Cuba on the list, so politics and the
Obama preference for 'softer' options, including potentially direct negotiations,
changes the calculus here as well, regardless of the wider evidence contained
within the reports. As was noted earlier, while Obama continued to strike a
more robust stance with regard to the terrorist groups that threaten US security
and interests, he was notably more conciliatory when it came to the other side
of the counter-terrorist coin, namely the 'state sponsors' of terrorism. Such an
approach was effectively confirmed by a senior UK political figure, who had been
heavily involved previously in counter-terrorist policy, noting that 'any thinking
Western nation has to have a different approach', one based around negotiation
and encouragement (Interview, 2009). There is insufficient space here to address
in any depth the nature of the US-Iranian relationship (see, for example, Murray,
2009). However, building on a much quoted passage in his inauguration speech
to 'extend a hand if you unclench your fist' (Obama, 2009a), there has been a
noted change of tone, if not concrete achievements as yet. Whether it be his direct
message to the Iranian people in March 2009 – with its call for 'engagement that is
honest and grounded in mutual respect' (Obama, 2009b) – or greater consideration
of direct negotiations with the Iranian regime, depending on the outcome of the
wider international efforts to curtail Iran's suspected nuclear ambitions – there are
concerted attempts to move on to a new phase in addressing the problems of states
and terrorism. In addition, with a specific UK angle, the UK Foreign Secretary,
David Miliband was engaged in talks with Syria in November 2008, part of the
purpose of which was 'to bring Syria in from the cold' (Harris, 2008).

It is worth considering in a little more depth the specific phrasing of the
stated New Chapter objective, as there is a wider element to the New Chapter's
coverage. In declaring that it is 'our intention to hold to account regimes which
directly support or condone international terrorist groups *or allow their presence
within their borders*' (emphasis added) (Ministry of Defence, 2002) it widens the
potential coverage to embrace what Byman has called 'passive sponsors', those
states that either turn a blind eye to developing terrorist activity – an issue of
intent – or lack the governing structures and capabilities to respond effectively
(Byman, 2005). In effect, the New Chapter – potentially because of the lack of
formal targets, as discussed above and confirmed in its Annex, which concluded
in 2002 that 'state sponsored terrorism' was 'in decline' (Ministry of Defence,
2002) – endorses a potentially far wider ranging group of candidates. For example,
in the US in the mid-1990s, both Greece and Pakistan – which will be discussed

at the end of this chapter – were considered by the National Commission for Terrorism to be examples of states that were not fully co-operating with wider international counter-terrorist efforts. Within Europe, there was a long held belief that the phenomenon of right-wing terrorism – in abeyance at present but of greater significance during the 1990s, when it was particularly prominent in Germany, Sweden and Italy – has been linked, in some cases, to the belief that the state authorities were not doing enough to tackle either the problems of immigration or deal effectively with the rival threat of left-wing terror. In addition, in the case of Italy, a strong case was made that it had been 'blind in the right eye', suggesting that certain elements of the Italian security apparatus had condoned such activity, particularly in comparison to the manner in which they responded to left wing activity (Sheehan, 1981).

When asked about the inclusion of this phrase within the New Chapter, one key figure who had been involved in discussions at the time seemed to struggle with the concept, eventually returning to the more traditional concepts of state sponsorship discussed earlier, highlighting North Korea, Iran and Libya as the best examples (Interview, 2009). Yet, the manner in which the definition is worded suggests that permitting terrorist activity on your territory is an additional category or even alternative to traditional methods. That said, even with this definitional confusion remaining, there is even less chance of the UK 'holding to account' such regimes – potentially by military means, given the nature of the document it was located in – if it is not prepared to do so for more active sponsors, such as Iran.

Prevention is Better than Cure?

Interestingly, the definition used above blurs the categories between states that are willingly assisting and those that simply lack the capabilities to counter a potential growing threat within their borders. It is the latter group, considered as part of the New Chapter's Prevent category, that may turn out in the longer term to be a more productive area than the more aggressive posturing associated with the latter end of the New Chapter's scale of military involvement. There are effectively three options here: Defence Diplomacy and wider military training, which was promoted to a specific mission of defence policy as part of the SDR, the possibility of increasing humanitarian intervention, as part of an overall policy of tackling the problems of failed or failing states or the controversial process of democratisation advanced by the Bush administration, which some claim to be a means by which international terrorism can be tackled at its roots (Windsor, 2003; Gregory Gause, 2005) but which has subsequently fallen out of favour, an ideological casualty of the 2003 Iraq invasion. In the aftermath of 11 September, partially fuelled by the prominence given to Afghanistan, a far greater emphasis has been placed on failed and failing states, the so-called 'rotten boroughs' of international politics, where the state is ultimately 'unable' to prevent terrorism from flourishing. As Jack Straw, former Foreign Secretary, has noted, 'turning a blind eye to the breakdown of order in any part of the world, however distant, invites direct threats to our national security and well-being' (Straw, 2002).

While this may be a more productive line of inquiry in the longer term – particularly at the lower end of the military spectrum, in terms of providing training teams, military assistance and defence diplomacy support – there are a number of concerns that remain to be fully resolved. Firstly, and perhaps more importantly in this case, there remains a problem of definition. Although the literature, both primary and secondary, has developed apace, particularly in the post-11 September world, a consensus has not really developed regarding the key criteria for specifying what should alert the international community to a potential state failure. The literature is awash with laundry lists of criteria across the spectrum – from economic to political to issues regarding law and order, the monopoly over the use of force within their given territory, the safety of borders and citizens within them, human rights, migration, the delivery of public goods and services, the nature of the body politic and levels of corruption (a particular concern in post intervention Afghanistan), ethnic or other social cleavages – without indicating how such criteria should be monitored, prioritised and operationalised in terms of providing a future guide to military intervention in whatever form.

The Institute for Public Policy Research (IPPR), in its widely publicised report into global security, produced a matrix of 14 different criteria, including 'evidence of a youth bulge', levels of human development, vulnerability to climate change and the 'potential for terrorist attacks'. It then argued that if a state was demonstrating eight of the 14 then it should be classified by the international community as a failing state, with all the potentially negative – in terms of status – and positive – in terms of offers of wider assistance – consequences that would entail (IPPR, 2008, 56). However, does it matter which of the eight criteria? Are some more important than others, both for the likely development and trajectory of failure and for the security of the wider international community? What happens if the international community cannot agree, either on the underlying priorities or the evidence being examined? The aim, according to Straw, was to 'bring our influence to bear at the point when a state begins to display the symptoms of failure, rather than when it is a lost cause' or certainly when its lax security arrangements impinge directly on the security of the UK (Straw, 2002). Yet, seeking an early assessment may be even more difficult, in terms of assessing a combination of criteria. As a consequence, even with the greater research and modelling that has gone into this subject in recent years, Straw remained pessimistic – 'I doubt it will ever be possible to develop the tools to pinpoint precisely the next Afghanistan' (Straw, 2002).

The emphasis on Afghanistan is an interesting one, and highlights the second concern, namely an assumed link between failing or failed states and terrorist activity. At first glance, this seems straightforward – the laxity with which law and order tasks are being undertaken creates areas where government control has effectively disappeared, allowing a whole range of non-state actors, including terrorists, to literally set up camp, protected by the legal shell of sovereignty (from outside intervention in most cases) and the failure to exercise practical sovereignty inside. The greater focus once again placed on both Somalia and Yemen in the early part of 2010 seems to only further emphasise such linkages. Yet, as Patrick has argued, the possible lack of oversight has to be weighed against the potential lack of essential infrastructure, the economic, technological, transportation and communication links that international terrorists require to execute their campaigns (Patrick, 2006, 35–6). In 2009, in a trenchant editorial, *The Economist* argued that the international community had become 'too obsessed' with the linkage between the two concepts, emphasising – as the geographical range and diversity of terrorist targets has shown – that 'functioning states do not necessarily equal a nation inhospitable to terrorism' (*The Economist*, 2009). Much of the underlying assumption is predicated primarily on the linkage between the Taliban regime in Afghanistan and Al Qaeda, as noted by Straw, with the assumption that – as the Taliban were failing across a range of indices – this status had allowed terrorist training camps to flourish. Yet, this fails to understand the true nature of the relationship between the two groups – while it may very well be the case that Afghanistan under the Taliban were failing across a range of indicators, including human rights standards, Al Qaeda were not exploiting the laxity of Taliban law and order, but the protection of Mullah Omar's sense of hospitality. In effect, Afghanistan – at that time – more accurately fulfils the traditional definition of a state sponsor, as is suggested by the ultimatum delivered by President Bush to the Taliban at the outset of the 'war on terror':

> The United States makes the following demands on the Taliban – Deliver to the United States authorities all the leaders of Al Qaeda who hide in your land … Close immediately and permanently every terrorist training camp in Afghanistan and hand over every terrorist and every person in their support structure to appropriate authorities … They will hand over the terrorists or they will share in their fate. (Bush, 2001)

While there may be a productive role to play, in terms of assisting states that require – and request – assistance, as has been the case in Pakistan, for example, this is a further step back from assuming that, even if we could firstly accurately define a 'failing' state and then muster the combined political will to respond effectively, it would be the ultimate solution to our problems.

Conclusion

A greater exploration of the 2002 New Chapter than has been carried out thus far highlights a number of issues regarding not only the manner in which international terrorism should be countered, but also wider concerns of defence policy more generally. Firstly, it places into context the very nature of a strategic review, demonstrating its limits as well as its virtues. While it makes sense – as much as is practicable to do – to seek as long a time-frame as possible, not least because of time-lags in the procurement process, the shifts in emphasis between the 1998 SDR and the 2002 New Chapter indicate all too clearly the potential drawbacks of such an approach, in terms of the practicality of prediction. Secondly, there are significant questions still to be answered in terms of both the portrayal of the nature and scale of the terrorist threat confronting the UK and the wider efficacy of a policy of military intervention as a means to counter it at distance. Part of the problem here is one of the underlying credibility of the messenger, as well as the nature of the message, a position that even Blair ruefully accepted, having told Sir John Stephens, then Metropolitan Police Commissioner in February 2003 that 'they'll believe what you say, but not what I say' (cited Seldon, Snowdon and Collings, 2005, 367). As this came before the full fall-out from the conduct of the Iraq war – the subject of a third independent inquiry, chaired by Sir John Chilcot, which commenced at the time of writing this volume – and the wider cynicism about politicians more generally, inspired by the 'annus horribilis' of widespread expenses scandals in 2009, the precious commodity of credibility seems to be in ever shorter supply. Yet, the political class – whoever is ultimately in power – must rise to the challenge posed by the likes of Paul Robinson, who calls into question the veracity of the assumptions underpinning contemporary British defence policy, if they wish to maintain public support for an interventionist policy aimed at protecting the UK's shores. Given the polling evidence emerging in 2009 regarding continued and growing scepticism over the asserted linkages between the military campaign in Afghanistan and the wider protection of the UK from terrorist activity – as well as the somewhat mixed signals sent by the Brown government as it committed a further 500 troops to that conflict in December 2009 – this will be an uphill task.

What is needed, therefore, as part of the proposed SDR process, is a rigorous re-examination of the underlying rationales for the New Chapter, as the framework document for a military contribution to counter terrorism. It may lead, as has been suggested here, towards a reworking and reprioritisation of military activity, away from the aggressive end of the spectrum towards a more limited, but potentially more effective contribution, in terms of assisting with the training and preparation of other states, to effectively allow them to tackle potential problems on their own in the longer term – 'the best course of action in our own defence will often be to help others to help themselves' (IPPR, 2008, 104). A combination of changing political circumstances and security realities may help to bring that about. In the case of the latter, a combination of a lack of suitable or politically acceptable targets in the longer term – particularly with the changed emphasis in the US on the role of the state within a wider counter-terrorist campaign – effectively closes off some of the main routes explored in the New Chapter. In addition, both Gordon Brown – witness the drawdown in Iraq, as well as the caveated commitment to additional troops in Afghanistan – and the Conservative Party are less committed to the use of military intervention than the Blair administration was. In the case of the latter, Dame Pauline Neville-Jones, the Shadow Security Minister, would like to see a far greater emphasis on other instruments within the national security apparatus, particularly softer instruments of diplomacy and aid, believing they are likely to be significantly less expensive and potentially more effective in the long run – 'for a fraction of the £1.2bn that the UK spent on military operations … we could have a lot of soft power' (Conservative Party, 2006, 8). She is likely to play a central role in UK national security policy more widely, if the Conservative Party are returned to government in 2010, and has suggested that an overt military role should almost be considered a sign of failure, effectively confirming that 'we have lost ground if we have to intervene militarily' (Neville-Jones, 2008). Interestingly, as a point of comparison, Geoff Hoon, when considering what would constitute a 'failure' with regard to the military's role in countering terrorism in 2002, took a different line – 'we must prevent our enemies from tying up our forces in defence of the home base – otherwise they have won' (Hoon, 2002).

Of the five principal roles outlined in the New Chapter, the most likely and most promising development in the longer term seems to be in the area of Prevention, even with the potential difficulties in both defining and determining the role of failing states, particularly within the development of the wider international terrorist threat. Given the limited scope – in both actual and political terms – for further prioritisation of the more aggressive end of the spectrum outlined in the New Chapter, and the wider considerations in terms of both manpower and budgetary constraints, a scaling back, in terms of both rhetoric and reality, may be called for. While it would be a step too far to adopt the exceptionally narrow limitations of the Robinson approach to defence policy – as can be seen in the initially hostile reaction to the suggestion by former Minister Kim Howells that the UK withdraw its troops from Afghanistan and reorient Britain's defence posture more towards traditional territorial defence (Howells, 2009) – a greater focus on where the military can genuinely add value, in reconstructing a state's defences and assisting it in ultimately defending itself, through greater use of defence diplomacy and military training teams, would seem to be in order – 'terrorism which threatens the UK … will continue to depend less on state sponsorship and more on state failure' (Home Office, 2009, 48).

A case in point is Pakistan. Bridging the divide between sponsor of terrorist activity – if not actively by central government then by agencies within the state, notably the Pakistani intelligence agency, the Inter Services Intelligence (ISI) (Rachid, 2009) – and failing state, it has proved far too sensitive to consider for the sort of military intervention utilised in Afghanistan and Iraq. This has long been the case – in 1996, the Clinton administration refused to even accept the National Commission on Terrorism's assertion that Pakistan be declared, not a 'state sponsor', but as a state that was 'not co-operating' with wider counter-terrorist efforts (Rediff, 1996). The Bush administration, allegedly, were slightly blunter, with then Deputy Secretary of State Richard Armitage allegedly threatening to 'bomb Pakistan back to the stone age' if it did not contribute effectively to the immediate stages of the 'war on terror' (Musharref, 2006; Reid, 2006). Yet, it did not lead to significant military intervention in Pakistan. Under the Obama administration, the level of sensitivity regarding even political intervention in Pakistani affairs was seen in the reaction to a decision to increase the level of aid Pakistan was to receive from the US to $1.5bn annually, as part of the 2009 Enhanced Partnership with Pakistan Act. The Act has engendered a certain amount of hostility, in part because it contains specific riders seeking to ensure civilian and democratic control over Pakistan's military. Interestingly, there is a far greater number of conditions that seek to encourage Pakistan to demonstrate more actively that it is countering terrorism, including dismantling terrorist camps, as well as the assertion that Pakistan's military is not 'materially or substantively' seeking to subvert political or judicial processes. This chimes with analysis within the UK, which has increasingly accepted that Pakistan, whether actively or passively, is part of the problem. For example, it is estimated that three quarters of the most serious plots discovered within the UK have Pakistani links (Cabinet Office, 2009 5). Even as Gordon Brown sought to justify an increased military commitment to Afghanistan, he admitted that 'for the past eight years, Al Qaeda has been able to send instructions from Pakistan to the rest of the world and organise from Pakistan terrorist attacks that have affected every continent' (G Brown, 2009b).

Yet, partly as a result of the level of Pakistani co-operation that was to follow in the wake of such demands – culminating eventually in the long awaited Pakistani military campaigns into Waziristan – partly for political reasons, there is no question of Pakistan being targeted in the same way as Afghanistan and Iraq. While a consensus develops that the stability of Pakistan is central to the longer term security of the international system, in terms of countering terrorism as well as wider regional and nuclear stability, the considered response of the UK particularly is to focus on assisting the Pakistani government, encouraging it in its efforts and making it the recipient of the 'largest bilateral programme of counter-terrorist support and capacity building' (Cabinet Office, 2009, 24). This, coupled with ever greater emphasis on an 'Afghanisation' strategy of speeding up the training and preparation of the Afghan Army and police forces, suggests the longer term future for the military contribution to counter-terrorism.

Bibliography

Anti Terrorism, Crime and Security Act (2002) (London: HMSO)

Blair, T (2001), *Speech to the Labour Party Conference on 4 October 2001* (London: Labour Party)

Blair, T (2003), *Speech by the Prime Minister Opening the Debate Authorising the Use of Military Force in Iraq on 18 March 2003* (London: HMSO)

Blair, T (2006), *Speech by the Prime Minister to the Foreign Policy Centre on 21 March 2006* (London: HMSO)

Blair, T (2007a), 'A battle for global values', *Foreign Affairs*, January–February, 79–90

Blair, T (2007b), 'What I've learned', *The Economist* 2 June

Blunkett, D (2006), *The Blunkett Tapes: Life in the Bear Pit* (London: Bloomsbury Press)

Brown, D (2005), 'The War on Terrorism would not be possible without NATO: A critique', *Contemporary Security Policy*, 25/3, 409–29

Brown, D (2008), 'Britain: Cheerleader for the US in the "War on Terror"?', in Eder, F and Senn, M (eds) *Europe and Transatlantic Terrorism: Assessing Threats and Counter-Measures* (Berlin: Nomos)

Brown, D (2010), *Unsteady Foundations: The European Union's Counter-Terrorist Framework 1993–2007* (Manchester: Manchester University Press)

Brown, G (2006a), *Meeting the Terrorist Challenge – Speech by the Chancellor of the Exchequer to Chatham House on 10 October 2006* (London: HMSO)

Brown, G (2006b), *Speech by the Chancellor of the Exchequer to the Royal United Services Institute on 13 February 2006* (London: HMSO)

Brown, G (2007), *Statement by the Prime Minister on National Security on 14 November 2007* (London: HMSO)

Brown, G (2009a), *Speech by the Prime Minister on Afghanistan on 4 September 2009* (London: HMSO)

Brown, G (2009b), *Statement by the Prime Minister to the House of Commons on Afghanistan and Pakistan on 30 November 2009* (London: HMSO)

Bush, GW (2001), *Address by the President of the United States to a Joint Session of Congress following the 11 September attacks on 20 September 2001* (Washington, DC: Office of the White House)

Byman, D (2005), 'Passive sponsors of terrorism', *Survival* 47/4, 117–43

Byman, D (2008), *The Changing Nature of State Sponsorship of Terrorism* (Washington, DC: Brookings Institute)

Cabinet Office (2009), *UK Policy in Afghanistan and Pakistan: The Way Forward* (London: HMSO)

Cameron, D (2006), *Speech by the Leader of the Opposition to the British American Project on 11 September 2006* (London: Conservative Party)

Clarke, R (2004), *Against All Enemies: Inside America's War on Terror* (London: Free Press)

Conservative Party (2006), *Security Issues: Interim Policy Position Paper – Report by the National and International Security Policy Group* (London: Conservative Party

Cornish, P and Dorman, A (2009a), 'Blair's wars and Brown's budgets: From Strategic Defence Review to strategic decay in less than a decade', *International Affairs*, 85/2, 247–61

The Economist (2009), 'Why focus on failed states?', *The Economist* 16 September

European Council (2005), *The European Union Counter-Terrorism Strategy* (Brussels: European Council)

Europol (2009), *TE-SAT 2009 – EU Terrorism Situation and Trend Report* (The Hague: Europol)

Fox, L (2008), *Honouring our Armed Forces – speech by the Shadow Defence Secretary on 28 September 2008* (London: Conservative Party)

Gregory Gause III, F (2005), 'Can democracy stop terrorism?', *Foreign Affairs* September–October, 62–76

Gunaratna, R (2001), 'Terror in the skies', *Jane's Intelligence Review 2001* – http://www.janes.com/security/international_security/news/jir/jir010924_1_n.shtml

Feith, D (2009), *War and Decision: Inside the Pentagon at the Dawn of the War on Terror* (London: Harper Paperbacks)

Hames, T (2006), 'Three years on: The tragedy of the Iraq war is that there won't be another one', *The Times* 20 March

Harris, E (2008), 'Miliband mission to bring Syria out of diplomatic cold', *Evening Standard* 18 November

Home Office (2006), *The United Kingdom's Strategy for Countering International Terrorism* (London: HMSO)

Home Office (2009), *The United Kingdom's Strategy for Countering International Terrorism* (London: HMSO)

Hoon, G (2001), *11 September – A New Chapter for the Strategic Defence Review – Speech by the Defence Secretary on 5 December 2001* (London: MoD)

Hoon, G (2002), *The New Chapter: A Blueprint for Reform – Speech by the Defence Secretary to the Royal United Services Institute on 30 July 2002* (London: MoD)

House of Commons (2003), *A New Chapter to the Strategic Defence Review: Sixth Report of the Defence Select Committee on 7May 2003* (London: HMSO)

House of Commons (2008), *Joint Session of the Defence and Foreign Affairs Select Committees on Iraq and Afghanistan – Testimony of Foreign Secretary David Miliband and Defence Secretary John Hutton on 28 October 2008* (London: HMSO)

House of Commons (2009), *The Defence Contribution to UK National Security and Resilience: Testimony of Chief of the General Staff General Sir David Richards to the Defence Select Committee on 27 January 2009* (London: HMSO)

Howells, K (2009), 'It's time to pull out of Afghanistan and take the fight to Bin Laden in Britain', *The Guardian* 3 November

Huntington, S (1998), *The Clash of Civilisations and the Remaking of World Order* (London: Simon and Schuster)

Hutton, J (2009), *Ministerial Statement by the Defence Secretary to the House of Commons on 11 February 2009* (London: HMSO)

Institute for Public Policy Research (2008), *Shared Destinies: Security in a Global World. Interim report from the Commission on National Security in the Twenty-First Century on 27 November 2008* (London: IPPR)

Kampfner, J (2004), *Blair's Wars* (London: Free Press)

Makarenko, T (2007), 'International Terrorism and the UK: Assessing the Threat', in Wilkinson P and Gregory, F (eds), *Homeland Security in the UK: Future Preparedness for Terrorist Attacks since 9/11* (London: Routledge)

Mayer, J (2009), 'The predator war: What are the risks of the CIA's covert drone program?', *The New Yorker* 26 October

Ministry of Defence (1998), *The Strategic Defence Review: Modern Forces for the Modern World* (London: HMSO)

Ministry of Defence (2001), *Defence Policy 2001* (London: HMSO)

Ministry of Defence (2002a), *The Strategic Defence Review: A New Chapter* (London: HMSO)

Ministry of Defence (2002b), *The Strategic Defence Review: A New Chapter – Supporting Information and Analysis* (London: HMSO)

Ministry of Defence (2003), *Delivering Security in a changing world: Defence White Paper* (London: HMSO)

Moloney, E (2003), *A Secret History of the IRA* (London: Penguin)

Mueller, J (2006), *Overblown: How Politicians and the Terrorism Industry Inflate National Security Threats and Why We Believe Them* (New York: Free Press)

Murray, D (2009), *US Foreign Policy and Iran: American-Iranian Relations Since the Islamic Revolution* (London: Routledge)

Musharref, P (2006), *In the Line of Fire: A Memoir* (London: Free Press)

National Commission on Terrorist Attacks on the United States (2004) – http://www.9-11commission.gov/

Neville-Jones, P (2008), *Speech to the Plenary Session of the International Institute for Counter-Terrorism on 9 September 2008* (London: Conservative Party)

Obama, B (2009a), *Inaugural Speech by the President of the United States on 20 January 2009* (Washington, DC: Office of the White House)

Obama, B (2009b), *Message by the President of the United States to the Iranian people on 21 March 2009* (Washington, DC: Office of the White House)

O'Neill, S and Sharrock, D (2009), 'MI5 doubles Ulster presence as elite forces foil murder attempt', *The Times* 24 November

Patrick, S (2006), 'Weak states and global threats – Fact or fiction?', *The Washington Quarterly*, Spring

Rachid, A (2009), *Descent into Chaos: The US and the Disaster in Pakistan, Afghanistan and Central Asia* (London: Penguin)

Rediff (1996), 'US administration differs with terrorism commission on Pakistan', 16 June – http://www.rediff.com/news/2000/jun/16us.htm

Reid, T (2006), 'We'll bomb you back to Stone Age, US told Pakistan', *The Times* 22 September

Robinson, P (2005a), 'Are we wasting money on defence?', *The Spectator* 9 July

Robinson, P (2005b), *Doing Less with Less: Making Britain More Secure* (London: Imprint Academic)

Rosenthal, J (2007), 'Jigsaw Jihadism', *The National Interest* 1 March

Sageman, M (2004), *Understanding Terror Networks* (Pennsylvania: University of Pennsylvania Press)

Sageman, M (2008), *Leaderless Jihad: Terror Networks in the Twenty-First Century* (Pennsylvania: University of Pennsylvania Press)

Seldon, A, Snowdon, P and Collings, D (2007), *Blair Unbound* (London: Simon and Schuster)

Sheehan, T (1981), 'Italy: Terror on the right', *The New York Review of Books*, 27/21–22

State Department (2003), *Patterns of Global Terrorism 2002* (Washington, DC: State Department)

State Department (2009), *Country Reports on Terrorism 2008* (Washington, DC: State Department)

Straw, J (2002), *Failed and Failing States – Speech by the Foreign Secretary to the European Research Institute, Birmingham on 6 September 2002* (London: HMSO)

USA Today (2005), 'The Rumsfeld memo', *USA Today* 20 May

Windsor, JL (2003), 'Promoting democratisation can combat terrorism', *The Washington Quarterly*, 26/3, 43–58

Wright, L (2006), *The Looming Tower: Al Qaeda and the Road to 9/11* (London: Knopf)

Chapter 6

Securing Stability, Ensuring Change:
British Defence Policy in Northern Ireland

Trevor C Salmon

Introduction

Northern Ireland deserves consideration in this volume for a number of reasons. Firstly, the development and maintenance of the 'Good Friday' peace process was a central feature of the Blair government and arguably one of his main achievements in office. To not consider it would unbalance the overall assessment. Secondly, as will be demonstrated, both from an examination of Northern Ireland's wider history and the specific New Labour period, there are a number of lessons – both military and political – that can at least be identified, if not formally and exhaustively learned, from the experiences gained in the Province, that may have resonance for the wider handling of New Labour's foreign and defence policy. Thirdly, it is arguably the drawdown in military involvement in Northern Ireland, as a direct consequence of the enduring peace process, which has helped provide the foundation for the wider interventionist defence policy so associated with the Blair government. Finally, as events in 2009 showed all too clearly, it would be foolish and perhaps a little complacent to assume that, even with a power sharing agreement between the Democratic Unionist Party (DUP) and Sinn Féin still in place, the ultimate aim of 'normalising' the situation in Northern Ireland once and for all has been achieved. This chapter will aim to consider these issues, beginning with the wider lessons identified, before going on to explore the crucial issue of what constitutes a 'normalisation' of violence and the military's role within it, a useful consideration that can be applied more widely than just in Northern Ireland.

Before beginning that process in more depth, it is worth briefly explaining some of the wider context, particularly within the Labour Party prior to Blair's accession to party leadership and eventually premiership (particularly given that one of the main themes of this volume is the impact that Blair has had on wider defence policy developments). Some key events in the peace process happened before Tony Blair entered Number 10 Downing Street in 1997. The first was the replacement of the perceived 'green' Shadow Secretary of Northern Ireland, Kevin McNamara, with Mo Mowlam. Although she had been a junior spokesperson on Northern Ireland, Mowlam was not initially identified with either side in the dispute, whereas McNamara had believed that Britain should act as persuader for Irish unity, trying to impose or enforce a united Ireland. As

Shadow Spokesman he worked to secure Irish unity by consent – which had been Labour Party policy of the time. Tony Blair, with a Protestant grandmother from Donegal, an Orangeman grandfather, a boyhood visitor to Northern Ireland and a Roman Catholic wife, had given thought to the problems of Northern Ireland and acted upon them on becoming leader of the Labour Party in July 1994. Blair believed absolutely in the principle of consent – a central element of the UK's approach to the peace process more generally – by which he meant the consent of the majority in Northern Ireland. As such, Britain could facilitate negotiations and hopefully agreement, but should not be a persuader in the cause of Irish unity. As Leader of the Opposition, one of Blair's most significant acts was to drop Labour's support for a united Ireland, bringing it more in line with traditional UK views on the Northern Ireland peace process. In fact, Powell records Tony Blair as saying in 1994 that he believed 'the most sensible role for us is to be facilitators, not persuaders in this, not trying to pressure or push people towards a particular objective' (Powell, 2008, 312).

There was also a wider context than internal Labour Party politics, relating to the peace process itself; in effect, the inheritance of the Blair administration. It is worth considering briefly the main efforts to bring peace to the Province between 1968 and 1997. Even though none would ultimately prove to be as successful as the 1998 Belfast Agreement (colloquially known as the 'Good Friday Agreement' – GFA), they would provide the foundations on which New Labour would have to build, either by learning from the errors of others, or from the flexibility of negotiating approaches or adopting those aspects that were significant in bringing a cohesive and lasting cross-community agreement (it should be recalled that Seamus Mallon, Northern Ireland's first Deputy First Minister of the post-GFA era caustically referred to the hard-negotiated agreement as 'Sunningdale for slow learners', making reference to the underlying similarities between the eventual agreement and its 1973 Sunningdale predecessor (Mallon cited Maginnis, 2004). It is worth highlighting both the errors made – and hopefully learned from – as well as the underlying structures that would help shape the Blair approach to Northern Ireland.

It seems clear with hindsight that, in the initial years of 'The Troubles', in 1968–1969, the UK government did not understand Northern Ireland, particularly that there was no homogeneous support for the forces of law and order. At best, there were two communities who gave their allegiance to different states, different norms and different cultures and creeds. The state structure in Northern Ireland was divided on political, religious, national and cultural/linguistic lines, including the use of symbols such as flags and different versions of football, both Gaelic and Association. Such a failure to appreciate the wider environment, both political and cultural, that the UK was about to intervene in – even within its own territory – should, in some senses, place in context what would subsequently develop almost 25 years later, in the UK's controversial interventions in both Iraq and Afghanistan. Equally, it suggests that lessons were not being learned, even as elements within the UK political and military community suggested that their experiences in Northern Ireland made them better prepared and more adaptable to the post-11 September conflict environments that they found themselves committed to (Aylwin-Foster, 2006). Yet, by 1997, experience had clearly been built up within Northern Ireland, at times learning the hard way. These lessons had been learnt – or at least identified, to use the formal phrasing – by the British Army as an institution, as well as the other elements of law and order within the Province, most notably the Royal Ulster Constabulary (RUC) and the intelligence services. Additionally, there was a new generation of political leaders in the UK, in Northern Ireland and in the Republic.

However, this did not happen all at once. Unfortunately, it took a while for the British to understand that there was a link between the use of military power and the political tasks of restoring order, and that 'their own occasionally hostile interface with the communities ... and the tactics that they sometimes employed became a problematic of the conflict itself' (Fitzduff, 2002, 79). As former Chief of the General Staff (CGS) General Sir Mike Jackson has admitted 'it is no less important to learn from mistakes, where they were made, and to ensure they are not repeated' (Ministry of Defence, 2006). Some of the mistakes were:

> the heavy-handed colonial approach of the 1970s that utilised ... hard interrogation, curfews and area searches was massively counter-productive and generated deep sympathy for the IRA ... One of the greatest achievements of the armed forces was the ability to evolve and fall more closely into step with political progress, becoming a vital, but always subordinate part of the overall campaign. (Sneddon, 2007 3)

Another mistake was the introduction of internment in 1971. Although internment had been tried before – interestingly both North and South of the border between 1957 and 1962 – the introduction of internment on the 9 August 1971 was to prove to be a disaster, particularly in terms of trying to win over the 'hearts and minds' of the wider community in which the Army operated. Although it was recognised at the time as a political risk, with the military significantly advising against it, a political decision was taken. However, the scheme was badly conceived, poorly prepared, based on old or faulty intelligence – which also has contemporary resonance – and the detention facilities were disgusting.

A third mistake was the lack of coordination between the military, police and intelligence community (a forerunner of some of the problems that Gordon will be discussing in terms of the wider in vogue phrase of the 'comprehensive approach'). Even after the imposition of direct rule in 1972, the formal relationship between the Army and the RUC was not well defined, nor indeed was the relationship between Secretary of State and the General Officer Commanding (GOC). This is epitomised by an interview with the then GOC, Major General Sir Frank King, regarding the army's role in not ending the Ulster Worker's Strike in 1974:

> we never had any aggro at all with the strikers. They never stopped an army vehicle – as far as we were concerned it was almost as if the strike was not on at all. Dealing with intimidation was a police job. The fact that the RUC

> didn't do too much about it was no concern of ours ... If Rees had ordered us
> to move against the barricades we would have said 'With great respect, this is a
> job for the Police. We will assist them if you wish, but its not terrorism. (cited in
> McKittrick and McVea, 2001 103–4)

Interestingly, the division of roles between the Army and police remains a problem to this day, particularly in relation to counter-terrorism, as does the co-ordination of actors with differing agendas, roles and responsibilities within a 'comprehensive approach'. In this case, the problems were primarily at an inter-agency level, rather than also at the wider political level, as has been the case in Afghanistan, for example. In Northern Ireland, there was a particular complexity in relation to the development of the RUC, which evolved into a 'formidable, militarised security force', an example of 'hard' policing. According to Weitzer, 'paramilitary policing and internal security duties have become the *core features* of police work ... shaping virtually every aspect of the RUC's activity'(emphasis in original) (Weitzer, 1985, 41–2, 48). In effect, the military had an additional challenge in adapting to a police force that appeared to do military roles.

Learning

Not all of this historical revisiting is about identifying errors and mistakes made, even if some of them suggest that history has repeated itself, although in a different context. There is also evidence of lessons being learned, of foundations being built upon. While it was difficult at times, between 1968 and 1997, to discern a long term vision and strategic plan for Northern Ireland, underlying principles were identified that could be built on, and, with a long-term and wider commitment from all those involved, made to work. Not only that, but, as is often the case, timing is a key consideration. Solutions that were proposed prematurely were destined to fail, only to be dusted off again for a second outing, with a more positive outcome as a result. For example, there had been a long-standing political problem for generations across the communities – namely the widespread perception that violence ultimately works. It would take a generation – and significant blood shed on both sides – for the major political parties to realise that, for security and peace to be secured and entrenched, they all needed to move on from a zero-sum situation. Until the Major and Blair administrations, the majorities within both camps – both Loyalist and Unionist on one side and Nationalist and Republican on the other – believed that, if the other side made gains, it had to be at their expense. Slowly, but particularly during the 1990s, more of the key participants came to view Northern Ireland differently, as a 'variable-sum' game, where ultimately everyone could win, at least part of their agenda. Although there had been other declarations which implied the same thing, John Major regarded the Downing Street Declaration of 1993 as particularly important because it reassured Unionists that a united Ireland would not be imposed on them, while guaranteeing to the wider Nationalist and Republican communities that, if it was the expressed will of the Northern Irish people, the UK would not stand in the way of Irish unity. Tony Blair took the same view and was able to build on the work of Major between 1990 and 1997.

This was combined with a wider sense of war weariness, within the wider public, but also within certain aspects of the main terrorist groups, most of which have decommissioned or demilitarised. This was certainly the official view of the Army, in its formal assessment of the end of 'Operation Banner':

> It should be recognised that the Army did not 'win' in any recognisable way; rather it achieved its desired end-state, which allowed a political process to be established without unacceptable levels of intimidation. Security force operations suppressed the level of violence to a level which the population could live with … The violence was reduced to an extent which made it clear to the Provisional Irish Republican Army (PIRA) that they could not win through violence … (Ministry of Defence, 2006, 8–15)

It took some time, but the underlying lesson identified was that the UK needed to address the conditions that had fostered the conflict, rather than simply tackle the symptoms (although some critics would argue that that lesson did not translate into thinking about Iraq and Afghanistan). In 1969, there was a view that the UK was involved in a counter-insurgency (COIN) campaign which, by 1972, had evolved into to a counter terrorist operation (a division that the Obama administration has been publicly debating with regard to Afghanistan, which centres around the desire to focus primarily on eliminating the terrorist threat or, with COIN, to placing far greater emphasis on securing the home population and winning wider 'hearts and minds'). At the outset, there was a belief that such an insurgency could be defeated militarily; yet, the failure to appreciate that military campaigns that were initially expected to be brief and economical could easily became protracted and costly is hardly restricted to the planning for Northern Ireland. It took a while to appreciate that efforts to achieve a military solution yielded not security and peace but could just as easily lead to escalating levels of violence. Northern Ireland was unwinnable in strictly military terms, so the emphasis had to shift from defeating insurgents to protecting the population, maintaining society and preventing wider fragmentation. As General Sir Mike Jackson noted:

> We have seen a pattern in the way campaigns have evolved: often starting with a short intense decisive campaign … followed by long, sometimes very long, periods of peace support operations, nation building, post-conflict operations, call them what you will. (Jackson, 2006)

Yet, this does pose the obvious question – if that was one of the lessons learnt from Northern Ireland, why was the same mistake ultimately made after 11 September and specifically in the planning and presentation of the 2003 intervention in Iraq?

Another contemporary lesson to be learned – or at least identified – from the development of the conflict in Northern Ireland is the need to talk. Despite public utterances throughout the period that the British would never negotiate with terrorists, there were a number of occasions when talks did take place, often through back channels. This pattern of secret, informal talks continued for over a quarter of century, and played a key part leading up to the Belfast Agreement in 1998. Jonathan Powell, Tony Blair's Chief of Staff, had many encounters with PIRA representatives in safe houses along the border and elsewhere. As a result of his – and the wider political-experiences – he has become an advocate of the process of constructive negotiation, even with the most obdurate of enemies. At the end of his exhaustive personal narrative of the GFA peace process, both in its initiation and extensive maintenance, he comes to this potentially significant conclusion:

> ... there is every reason to think that the search for peace can succeed in other places where the process has encountered problems – in Spain, in Turkey, in Sri Lanka, in the Middle East, in Afghanistan and even, in the longer term, with Islamic terrorism, if people are prepared to talk. (Powell, 2008, 322)

There is an issue in terms of how far to extrapolate from the experiences of Northern Ireland, particularly given that the nature of the threat, as well as the wider security environment, has altered substantially (hence why the formulation is lessons identified, rather than lessons learned). While there have been some signs in Afghanistan that local arrangements and negotiations with aspects of the wider Taliban movement is being given more active consideration, to take the next step, as Powell advocates, towards Islamist terrorism more generally is a step that not even President Obama seems prepared to make, as part of his wider outreach policy.

Another useful lesson to learn from the wider political behaviour during the Northern Ireland 'Troubles', is the requirement, as much as possible, for the main political parties within the UK to maintain a united front. Despite the odd setback, such as the 'troops out' campaign in the late 1970s and the Conservative Party's regular complaint about a group of Labour MPs refusing to support the annual review of the Prevention of Terrorism Act (PTA), British political parties and the public have managed to exhibit and maintain a degree of cross-party support on Northern Ireland, defined as 'a general agreement ... on the principles of the constitutional approach towards the conflict in Northern Ireland', which 'has extended beyond the constitutional sphere to other areas of policy, including security, social and economic policy ... agreement between the parties on the basic principle of consent if there is to be change' (Dixon, 1995, 148). One reason for this continued support – which was not evident in the heated debates over Iraq, although has been the case with regard to the underlying reasons, if not always the resourcing of, the Afghan campaign – was that Northern Ireland is an integral part of the UK, and therefore is part of British territory and sovereignty. The further an armed force strays from that domain, the more problematic bipartisanship and public acceptance becomes. In your own back yard, people will tacitly accept the pain, as it is their fellow citizens that are being assisted or protected; it is a conflict of necessity, that even noted sceptics of military intervention, such as Paul Robinson, can agree to, rather than an intervention of choice (Robinson, 2005). When one goes into a fractured society, this becomes even more problematic.

There is another linkage that needs to be made, between the experience in Northern Ireland and the wider defence policy of the Labour government. As Freedman has noted, it should never be forgotten that the UK is 'a smallish country with a limited capacity and when we are totally preoccupied … in one or two countries there will always be a problem somewhere else' (Freedman cited in House of Commons, 2006). In some senses the Labour government were lucky. It seems unlikely that Her Majesty's Government could have committed to Afghanistan or Iraq if the situation in Northern Ireland had not improved substantially. In 1972, statistically the worst year for violence – after Bloody Friday, when bombs were planted in Belfast and Londonderry, and a decision was taken to end the so-called 'No Go' areas, with 28,000 soldiers involved in Operation Motorman – about 15 per cent of the British Army were committed to Northern Ireland. It should also be remembered that this was still at the height of the Cold War. In that sense, and relating back to an earlier point regarding timing, it should be noted that the SDR, published in July 1998, came out after the Belfast Agreement, suggesting that a more expeditionary approach was only really possible with a much more secure home base. This point is confirmed in the SDR:

> The government believes that the Belfast Agreement provides the basis for a lasting political settlement. The Armed Forces have already responded flexibly in their deployment following the various ceasefires since 1994. The government hopes that the level of threat from terrorism will reduce further and allow for reductions in the numbers of troops required to assist the civil authorities consistent with the level of threat, while maintaining normal garrisons as elsewhere in the United Kingdom. (Ministry of Defence, 1998)

This is not to suggest that Northern Ireland was unimportant. The SDR's 'scales of effort' – which, as of 2009, have been broken for the last seven years – accepted the need to provide continued, if more limited, support to Northern Ireland, with the planning guidelines adding the rider that this should be 'in addition to providing whatever military support is required to continuing commitments such as Northern Ireland' (Ministry of Defence, 1998). The SDR also made clear that part of the mission and military tasks would continue to provide Military Aid to the Civil Power in Northern Ireland, to support the police in maintaining law and order and to combat terrorism through the conduct of operations to deter terrorist activity (Ministry of Defence, 1998).

Ernest May noted that care must be taken that the right lessons from history are learned, so that we do not misapply lessons from the past (May, 1973). The lessons to be identified from Northern Ireland are summarised thus:

- There is a need to be prepared – and to prepare the general public – for a longer military campaign, rather than a quick result.
- For success to be achieved, the key players have to be willing to have patience in negotiating and an ability to weather the twists and turns of the end game of a protracted conflict. Arguably, Blair was better suited to this role than some of his predecessors.
- There needs to be a holistic approach to 'hearts and minds' and a movement away from seeing things as a 'zero sum game'. In Northern Ireland, while providing reassurance to the Unionists by focusing on consent and a referendum, the Nationalist community was encouraged by bringing in external support, notably US President Clinton, to reassure them about their longer term future.
- Soldiers need to be flexible in their approach, able to move from warriors to peace-builders – the so-called 'Three Block War' concept (Krulak, 1999) – through wide-scale training.
- Part of what is necessary is the realisation that military power can set the framework for politics, diplomacy and potentially talks, but is rarely, if ever, a solution in its own right.
- Making sure that you have joined up administration in *all* areas, as early as is possible to achieve it, both between agencies on the ground, as in the case with the Army and the RUC in Northern Ireland, and between government departments, and, within the wider diplomatic dimension, between governments. Such an approach is difficult to achieve and maintain, but is crucial to overall success.
- Being aware, as the RUC was not in 1968–1969 (and arguably beyond) that your actions, more and more, are taking place before a 24-hour, international media, with all that that entails in terms of media management – an area where New Labour seemed to have grasped the importance, if not always the most effective, skill set.
- That soldiers need to strike up relationships within the local populace, so that they can become the eyes and ears of intelligence – 'with the general population, familiarity with what is normal in an area provides the basis for detecting anomalous behaviour that might indicate insurgent activity … this strategy leverages an individual's ability to learn what baseline activity is in his area of responsibility and then apply his own human processing power to identify activities of concern' (Jackson, 2007, 77).
- Finally, perhaps the most important lesson, is to establish what 'victory' means, in a clear and expressed manner, to know when the best that can be achieved is to contain the problem and to respond accordingly.

The issue of what constitutes victory – which in Northern Ireland terms relates to the issue of 'normalisation' – will now be considered, as it is here where there may be the most significant lessons for the future of British defence and foreign policy and of military contributions to post-conflict stabilisation operations more generally.

Normalisation?

One of the major concerns relates to what normalisation meant, to all parties. All negotiations and agreements are, to some extent, built on constructive ambiguity. Jonathan Powell is very clear that such ambiguity is crucial in maintaining some sense of momentum, even if, eventually, the ambiguity has to be resolved one way or another (Powell, 2008, 314–15). He claims, for example, that it was essential in the context of decommissioning.

What is normalisation? For the Republicans, it had a definite meaning and was also used in their propaganda war with the British (Gormally, McEvoy and Wall, 1993, 57). For many Republicans, 'normalisation' ultimately means British de-militarisation, firstly by a less prominent position on the streets of Northern Ireland (which effectively has been achieved) before a final withdrawal from the island of Ireland, so that the wishes of those involved in 1916 or the elections of 1918 could be ratified, validated, re-legitimised and enforced. Having portrayed their overall struggle as a 'war of liberation', normalisation would be about national self-determination. For others, 'normalisation' could mean what Merlyn Rees called 'an acceptable level of violence' (cited in Gormally, McEvoy and Wall, 1993, 87), although it is a matter of dispute what such a level would look like – the minimisation of violence per se, the greater prominence of organised crime rather than the politically inspired violence that was so abnormal to the rest of the UK? In the GFA, rather than specify an end state – which would have strained the limits of 'constructive ambiguity' to its limits – it was noted that 'the development of a peaceful environment … can and should mean a normalisation of security arrangements and practices', bringing Northern Ireland more in line with the rest of the UK. It offered some specific indices for greater normalisation, including 'the reduction of the numbers and role of the Armed Forces deployed in Northern Ireland to levels compatible with a normal peaceful society', 'the removal of security installations', 'the removal of emergency powers in Northern Ireland' and the most vague and non-military specific commitment, namely a commitment to 'other measures appropriate to and compatible with a normal peaceful society' (Northern Ireland Office, 1998).

There were also specific commitments on policing – of which part of 'normalisation' would be a rebranding of the RUC as the new Police Service of Northern Ireland (PSNI), as part of wider measures to ensure 'policing structures are … professional, effective and efficient, fair and impartial, free from partisan political control, accountable, both under the law for its actions and to the community it serves; representative of the society it polices' (Northern Ireland Office, 1998). There was a more explicit statement regarding what normalisation would mean here, with the emphasis being placed on 'a substantial reduction in the current numbers, type and style of police stations … Fortifications would be removed from police stations. Police would patrol in normal police vehicles, on foot, on bicycles and as single officer beat patrols, without army support'. As the process steadied itself, further moves could be made with regard to the key issue of accountability, where 'decisions are made with the support of the community and of District Policing partnerships, of the Policing Board and of the Northern Ireland Executive once responsibility for the police has been devolved' (Northern Ireland Office, 2003). For another five years this continued to be a particular problem, with considerable reluctance to change, in part due to the chequered history, the lack of mutual trust and the continued disagreement over what was required for normalisation to work. It was only in November 2008 that Peter Robinson – Ian Paisley's successor as First Minister and DUP leader – and Martin McGuinness, Northern Ireland's Deputy First Minister, were able to announce that they had agreed a deal on devolving policing and justice. This broke an ongoing dispute which had led to a five-month deadlock, which had stopped the Executive meeting. The real impasse was over when policing and judicial powers would be transferred from London to Belfast. Given the continued sensitivity of such matters, it was expected that the Alliance Party will be given the new policing and justice ministry at Stormont. In recognition of continuing issues regarding trust, the DUP and Sinn Féin accepted that neither party would hold the post under arrangements initially intended to last until May 2012. This remains a very politically sensitive issue.

Some sense of optimism may be engendered from considering the other major stumbling block of the Blair era, the issue of decommissioning. While also emphasising the problem of producing agreed, but ambiguous, statements of intent, in order to keep negotiations going, it would ultimately have a more successful outcome, particularly in relation to PIRA. As part of the GFA, 'all participants … reaffirm their commitment to the total disarmament of all paramilitary organisations. They also confirm their intention to continue to work constructively and in good faith with the Independent Commission, and to use any influence they may have, to achieve the decommissioning of all paramilitary arms within two years … in the context of the implementation of the overall settlement'. Sinn Féin, in particular, argued that, in order for there to be genuine disarmament – and therefore normalisation – the desire to take the 'gun out of Northern Ireland politics' had to apply to all parties, including the British Army (despite obvious differences in terms of the legitimacy of the parties involved). They would also make significant use of the caveat 'in the context of the implementation of the overall settlement'. It would take almost seven years after the GFA for the Independent International Commission on Decommissioning (IICD) to finally announce 'that we have observed and verified events to put beyond use very large quantities of arms which the representatives has informed us includes all the arms in the IRA's possession … In summary, we have determined that the IRA has met its commitment to put its arms beyond use in a manner called for by the legislation' (IICD, 2005).

More generally one could argue that normalisation requires a society where the authority of the institutions is acceptable to an overwhelming majority and that those institutions are accountable to an electorate which had the real possibility of bringing about a change of government. The gun must be taken out – and kept out – of politics, and the government should have a legitimate monopoly over the use of force within its given territory. Citizens should feel secure and safe in their everyday living, emphasising the human aspect of security. They should also feel that there is a genuine sense of and demonstration of equality of opportunity for all and that there are effective inclusive human and minority rights with a shared sense of justice (Clark, 2008; Jackson, 2007; McAleese, 2008; Tuck, 2007).

In Northern Ireland in particular this means:

- a cessation of all paramilitary activity, whether it be attacks, intelligence gathering, intimidation or exiling of 'victims';
- an end to summary justice, knee-capping, disappearances/kidnapping, robberies and criminality;
- a decommissioning of all non-state arms;
- a professional and politically neutral police force, concentrating on enforcing criminal law in a proportionate and non-discriminatory way;
- the vast majority of military support in Northern Ireland will be broadly comparable to the assistance that is currently provided in Great Britain, tailored to the particular circumstances in Northern Ireland.

In some senses, maybe normalisation is when 'normal politics' returns, and other cleavages take centre stage, issues of social class, rural-urban division, gender, the generations gap (McAleese, 2008). Northern Ireland has not yet reached that stage, but the process has clearly begun under the Major, Blair and Brown administrations.

Conclusion

Ten years after the signing of the Good Friday Agreement, and after some of the moves towards normalisation, there might be grounds for optimism. Yet, it would have to be cautious optimism. In November 2008, the Twentieth Report of the Independent Monitoring Commission overview said:

> Three things are clear. First, in the six months under review ... dissidents – mainly Continuity Irish Republican Army (CIRA) and the Real Irish Republican Army (RIRA) – have been especially active ... they have also been undertaking planning and preparation for other attacks. Second, if it were not for the fact that the police ... have been successful in disrupting dissidents operations and arresting suspects, the number of reported incidents would have been higher. Thirdly, dissidents have turned their efforts more directly to trying to kill PSNI officers, using a variety of tactics and methods. (IMC, 2008)

These dissident groups, although small in number, continue to pose a threat and are capable of serious violence, as was noted in a number of incidents throughout the latter part of 2009. As such, one of the underlying concepts of normalisation has not yet been met, although politically inspired violence has been pushed more to the periphery. More reassuringly, the Commission said the PIRA had maintained an 'exclusively political path'. The Loyalist Volunteer Force was engaged in 'crimes ... for personal gain' – a not abnormal occurrence – while the leadership of the Ulster Defence Association (UDA) 'has continued to show what we believe is a genuine desire for change and has worked for it', with the proceeds of crime going to individuals and not to the organisation. In general, there are grounds for cautious optimism although there may be further bloodshed before 'victory' for the people of Northern Ireland can conclusively be declared. As such, even as the UK's horizons have widened significantly, with an ever greater internationalist perspective adopted, there needs to be continued vigilance on this key part of the home turf. Yet, as Ahern has summarised, in 2008, ten years after the GFA was put in place, hope remains – 'After decades of what has been described as the "great, icy silence", we can look back on a great thaw' (Ahern, 2008).

Bibliography

Ahern, B (2008), *Implementing the Agreement – Speech by the Taoiseach Bertie Ahern to the Institute for British-Irish Studies on 3 April 2008* (Dublin: UCD) – http://www.ucd.ie/news/2008/04APR08/030408_bertie_ahern_speeches.html

Aylwin-Foster, N (2005), 'Changing Army for counter-insurgency', *Military Review* November–December

Clark, J (2008), 'Northern Ireland: A balanced approach to amnesty, reconciliation, and reintegration', *Military Review* January–February

Cox, M, Guelke, A and Stephen, F (2006), *Farewell to Arms? Beyond the Good Friday Agreement* (Manchester: Manchester University Press)

Cunningham, M (2001), *British Government Policy in Northern Ireland 1969–2000* (Manchester: Manchester University Press)

Dixon, P (1995), '"A house divided cannot stand": Britain, bipartisanship and Northern Ireland', *Contemporary Record* 9/1, 147–87

Fitzduff, M (2002), *Beyond Violence: Conflict Resolution Process in Northern Ireland* (New York: United Nations Press)

Gormally, B, McEvoy, K and Wall, D (1993), *Criminal Justice in a Divided Society: Northern Ireland Prisons* (Chicago: University of Chicago)

House of Commons (1998), *Northern Ireland: Political Developments Since 1972 – Research Paper 98/57* (London: HMSO)

House of Commons (2007), *Testimony of Professor Lawrence Freedman Regarding UK Defence: Commitments and resources to the Defence Select Committee on 13 March 2007* (London: HMSO)

Independent International Commission on Decommissioning (2005), *Report of the Independent International Commission on Decommissioning on 25 September 2005* (Belfast: IICD)

Independent Monitoring Commission (2008), *Twentieth Report of the Independent Monitoring Commission on 10 November 2008* (London: HMSO)

Jackson, B (2007), 'Counter-insurgency intelligence in a "long war": The British experience in Northern Ireland', *Military Review* January–February

Krulak, C (1999), 'The strategic corporal: Leadership in the three block war', *Marines Magazine* January

Maginnis, J (2004), *The Belfast Agreement 1998 – A Sunningdale for Slow Learners – submitted for the M.Litt at the University of Aberdeen* (Aberdeen: University of Aberdeen)

May, E (1973), *Lessons of the Past: The Use and Misuse of History in American Foreign Policy* (Oxford: Oxford University Press)

McAleese, M (2008), *Peace at Last? The 'Normalization' of Politics in Northern Ireland Since the Good Friday Agreement – Speech by the President of Ireland at the International Studies Association 49th Annual Conference on 26–28 March 2008* (San Francisco: ISA)

McKittrick, D and McVea, D (2001), *Making Sense of the Troubles* (London: Penguin)

Ministry of Defence (1998), *The Strategic Defence Review: Modern Forces for a Modern World* (London: HMSO)

Ministry of Defence (2006), *Operation Banner: An Analysis of Military Operations in Northern Ireland* (London: HMSO)

Northern Ireland Office (1998), *The Good Friday Agreement of 10 April 1998* – http://www.nio.gov.uk/agreement.pdf (London: HMSO)

Northern Ireland Office (2003), *Joint Declaration by the British and Irish Governments* (London: HMSO)

Powell, J (2008), *Great Hatred, Little Room: Making Peace in Northern Ireland* (London: Bodley Head)

Sneddon, S (2007), 'Northern Ireland: A British Military Success or a Purely Political Outcome?', *Joint Services Command and General Staff College Defence Research Paper* 10

Tuck, C (2007), 'Northern Ireland and the British approach to counter-insurgency', *Defence & Security Analysis* 23/2, 165–83

Weitzer, R (1985), 'Policing a divided society: Obstacles to normalization in Northern Ireland', *Social Problems* 33/1, 41–55

Wyllie, J (2008), 'Force and security', in Salmon, T and Imber, M (eds), *Issues in International Relations* (London: Routledge)

Chapter 7

Defence Policy and the 'Joined Up Government' Agenda: Defining the Limits of the 'Comprehensive Approach'

Stuart Gordon[1]

Introduction

Since the end of the Cold War, the MoD has struggled to come to terms with the implications of a changed operational environment, particularly the challenges of defining the military responses to fragile, failing or fragmented states, globalisation and 'unconventional' arms bearers, increasingly termed 'irregular actors'. This struggle has manifested itself in two ways: firstly, the development of new doctrines, instruments and capabilities within the armed forces – focusing on developing doctrine for counter insurgency (COIN) and peace support operations (PSO), as well as enhancing information operations and civil-military co-operation capabilities – and secondly, the pursuit of new institutional arrangements and partnerships, both internationally and across government. In terms of the latter, the early post-Cold War period saw the focus of attention firmly on international partnerships, with a particular focus on the UN and the development of PSOs. However, the latter period, particularly after the invasion of Iraq in 2003, is characterised more by an increasing appetite within the MoD for partnerships *across* government, particularly with DFID. However, whilst it is easy to primarily focus on the changing operational environment as the cause of this process, this chapter situates its analysis within the broader trend of Labour's 'joined up government agenda'. Whilst recognising that the changing approach is undoubtedly a response to perceptions of an evolving operational environment, it is also a powerful aspect of broader attempts to reverse the 'departmentalism' that has characterised British governmental administration since the post-World War One Haldane reforms of the civil service. Whilst concluding that significant progress has been made in joining up defence, diplomacy and development activity, the chapter explores the British experience in Helmand, Afghanistan and suggests that there are very clear limits to these partnerships, highlighting significant outstanding problems in operationalising the 'comprehensive approach'.

---

1   The views contained within this chapter reflect solely those of the author, and are not representative of the views of the Royal Military Academy Sandhurst, the British Army, the Ministry of Defence or the British government more widely

The 'Joined Up Government' Agenda: Wider Context

From 1997, when Tony Blair first used the term 'joined-up government' at the launch of the Social Exclusion Unit (Mulgan, 2005), it has become a key motif of the two Labour administrations. However, unlike previous attempts at enhancing co-ordination within government, Labour has sought to elevate a policy of administrative 'coordination' from a simple driving principle of bureaucratic organisation to a radical political objective at the heart of a much broader agenda of government reform and renewal. Consequently, the 1997 Labour manifesto (Labour Party, 1997) set out a broad programme of change, involving enhancements to the accountability of institutions, their decentralisation and the elimination of bureaucratic secrecy. The strength of the emphasis placed on 'joining up' government lay partly in a sense that complex domestic, social problems, such as social exclusion, drug addiction and crime, could not be resolved by any single department of government, requiring instead a coordinated approach that harnessed all of the instruments available to central *and* local government, as well as non-traditional partners drawn from the private and voluntary sectors. However, before considering the broad range of factors that led to the imperative to 'join' being extended into other policy areas, principally defence, development and foreign policy, there is a need to explore this wider bureaucratic context.

The British Approach to Government: 'Departmentalism'?

The sense that, by emphasising 'joined up government', the Labour Party had embarked upon a radical policy departure reflects the strength with which the UK had originally opted for departmental arrangements, in which government Ministries were functionally very separate (Mulgan, 2005). In particular, the Haldane reforms of 1918 (Haldane, 1918) strengthened the organisation of departments into vertical and functionally differentiated silos, consolidating the existence of different departments with prerogatives over the management of specific functions such as finance, education, defence and housing. Such arrangements made sound organisational sense at the time: communication technology was in its infancy and the management of knowledge and horizontal coordination was extremely expensive. As a consequence, organising government within a framework of functionally differentiated, hierarchical and bounded institutions promised an efficient delivery of programmes, as evidenced by the creation of the NHS and the mass building programmes that followed both World Wars. The arrangements also had certain constitutional advantages within a democratic polity, with lines of accountability rising singly and sharply towards Ministers, whilst the principle of Cabinet responsibility and the sense of a common ethos and unity within the civil service as a whole fostered both a reasonable degree of coherence *across* government and were perceived as counteracting baronial impulses on the part of individual Ministers. The resulting arrangements tended to lead to the development of close working relationships with related professions (for example, health with doctors, education with teachers, the Home Office with the police), furthering Lord Haldane's belief that the 'knowledge base was the best determinant of how organisational boundaries should be defined' (Haldane cited in Mulgan, 2005). The result was a set of arrangements that strengthened the linkages between civil servants and Ministers and led to powerful and vertically organised departmental structures.

Problems of the Post-Haldane World

Whilst providing an appropriate governmental structure for addressing the issues of post-War Britain, Haldane's reforms created additional challenges. In particular, the arrangement of government in departmental 'silos' had a distorting effect on priorities, causing those issues which fitted less than perfectly within departmental frameworks or priorities to be downplayed or even ignored (Bogdanor, 2005; Mulgan, 2005). Government attention and money tended to flow down pre-existing departmental chains, following bureaucratic preferences and structures rather than addressing complex problems that fell across departmental boundaries, such as, for example, social exclusion. Furthermore, the faith in the cohesion of Cabinet government as an antidote to departmentalism was somewhat misplaced in the face of the tendency for the system to dissolve into a system of competing baronetcies (Foley, 2000). The principle of ministerial responsibility emphasised the necessity for success within departments rather than across government, leading commentators such as Vernon Bogdanor to argue that:

> Ministers gained credibility and won their political reputations, not so much by their skills at collective discussion and decision making in Cabinet, but through their success in managing their departments and in interdepartmental in-fighting.
> (Bogdanor, 2005)

Furthermore, the organisation of departments *vertically* militated against genuine cross Cabinet co-operation in more subtle ways: refocusing attention from those activities, such as prevention, which benefited another department or diverting attention from client groups 'whose needs cut across departmental lines' (Mulgan, 2005). At times, it incentivised 'departments and agencies to dump problems onto each other – like schools dumping unruly children onto the streets where they become a problem for the police ... Over time it reinforces the tendency common to all bureaucracies of devoting more energy to the protection of turf rather than serving the public' (Mulgan, 2005).

The pressures on Minsters to behave 'departmentally' also permeated the civil service, with senior civil servants being rewarded for advising *individual* Ministers rather than the *Cabinet* collectively, leading to perceptions of a certain departmental myopia. Such pressures were perhaps strongest when clear differences of policy existed amongst Cabinet Ministers. However, this is not, by any means, a new phenomenon. Bogdanor quotes Richard Crossman, a former Minister of Housing and Local Government in the 1960s, who stated that 'we come briefed by our Departments, to fight for our departmental budgets, not as Cabinet Minsters with a Cabinet view' (Crossman cited in Bogdanor, 2005). In effect, the system institutionalises the preservation of departmental autonomy, decision making 'space' and resources, creating a strong tension between the theoretical benefits of Cabinet government and the practice.

Reforming the Pathology

Reversing the excesses of departmentalism introduced by Haldane's reforms has been a recurring theme of the wider literature (see, for example, Perri et al., 2002), with previously significant reforms ranging from the creation of coordination bodies to the promotion of principles underpinning policy formulation. In that sense, New Labour was not attempting anything particularly different, at least not in terms of the identification of the wider problem. In the 1950s, Churchill attempted to establish an 'overlord' minister; Edward Heath developed super-ministries, such as the Department of Health and Social Security, whilst Wilson adopted the Joint Approach on Social Policy (JASP) (see Kein and Plowden, 2005). Lesser arrangements have included new Cabinet sub-committees, such as Margaret Thatcher's cross-departmental committee on inner cities, and John Major's attempt at underpinning institutional arrangements with a set of common principles, enshrined in the Citizen's Charter. However, the successive waves of initiatives reflected both the enthusiasm for the topic and the stubbornness of the underlying problems. Each encountered challenges, with super-ministries tending to overloaded the centre with information, requiring further 'super-ministers to make them work' whilst 'JASP failed because of the lack of political will, inadequate buy-in by departments, lack of clarity about goals and insufficient attention to the mechanisms for achieving greater integration' (Mulgan, 2005).

Given such a context it was perhaps surprising that Blair's administration sought new ways of balancing the necessities for vertical with a much stronger emphasis on horizontal integration. What is, perhaps, even more surprising is that they did this by enthusiastically recasting the policy as a radical political agenda, rather than an essentially bureaucratic reform. Arguably there were three principal factors that encouraged this reconsideration of the conventional wisdom: the complex nature of the Labour policy agenda; the perceived failure of the 'new public management reforms' of the 1980s and early 1990s; and the rise of new opportunities for horizontal coordination.

In terms of the first of these, the Blair agenda did not fit neatly within existing departmental frameworks. Not only did the issues appear to cross boundaries but increasingly the evidence regarding how they should be addressed demanded a much broader range of policy instruments than could be marshalled by individual departments. Issues high on Labour's domestic agenda, especially those relating to social exclusion (crime, poverty, housing, the family), industrial competitiveness and the environment, clearly fell outside both the formal departmental competences but also necessitated a reconsideration of the instruments with which to address them. Furthermore, there were a significant number of Labour Ministers who had experience of local government, where innovations in horizontal coordination had worked more effectively than their equivalents at national level. Mulgan, himself a former Whitehall policy maker with responsibilities for delivering the 'joined up' agenda, also argues that new Ministers were confronted with a:

> rapidly growing evidence base on the interconnectedness of problems. Social scientists had steadily accumulated evidence on, for example, the extent to which the avoidance of social exclusion is bound up with the balance of risk factors and protective factors in early life; or the extent to which crime is influenced by the economy, family and so on. Faced, for example, with evidence that barely a quarter of health improvements come from health services, Ministers wanted to know where else they might direct their attention to get better results. (Mulgan, 2005)

The second stimulus to the Labour approach derived from increasing discomfort with the 'new public management' reforms of the 1980s. Osborne and Gaebler's 'Reinventing Government' captured much of the spirit of these reforms, articulating a call for the application of a business model and the discipline of the market place to the problems of government (Osborne and Gaebler, 1992). However, the model's emphasis on isolating and simplifying problems and devolving responsibility for their resolution to 'business units' was at odds with the need to manage complex social problems 'holistically', both across government and more widely with partnerships spanning local government and civil society. Whilst not without some merit, as a panacea for the complex New Labour agenda it was perceived increasingly to be inappropriate.

Finally, new technologies made horizontal coordination both increasingly possible and desirable. Developments in communication technologies, such as e-mail and the Internet, dramatically reduced the costs of horizontal transactions, creating both new pressures for, and opportunities to develop, forms of working. In particular, they made possible much flatter project based structures, the development of formal and informal social networks that crossed departmental (as well as government/civil society) boundaries and real time and increasingly demanding forms of accountability to 'customers' and 'clients' within and outwith government. In effect, technology contributed to a sense that the transaction costs of managing the *complexity* of horizontal *collaboration* were now outweighed by the benefits.

Such pressures created a sense that Haldanesque 'departmentalism' was no longer inevitable or desirable, recasting perceptions of the old forms of organising activity in a new light – as a pathology that lead inevitably to departmental myopia, problem transference (or bypassing) and the defence of departmental interests. Whilst this led to a renewal of the search for 'joined up' government, there was no simple blueprint available. Consequently, the period since 1997 has been characterised by a broad range of experiments in cross departmental working that increasingly shaped the structures and processes of government (National Audit Office, 2001; Performance and Innovation Unit, 2000a–b; Treasury, 2001). For example, there has been greater emphasis on shared targets and objectives – particularly through the Public Service Agreements (PSA) – the introduction of cross departmental funding arrangements, new coordination structures and processes at various levels, as well as adaptations to traditional ministerial roles and responsibilities. Whilst organisational and procedural innovations abounded, so did the sense that the 'approach' had permeated the ethos of Whitehall.

Yet, it is easy to become carried away. 'Departmentalism' remained alive and well, with Ministers and civil servants continuing to behave 'departmentally' and the overwhelming proportion of government business still conducted through traditional departmentally based stovepipes. Furthermore, many of the new 'joined up' arrangements are still in their infancy and much of the work of government remains focused on embedding the arrangements and processes, rather than actually delivering through the mechanisms themselves. There is, nevertheless, a strong sense that the approach is more than a temporary change.

'Joining Up' Defence

In the area of defence and foreign policy, departments have also been subject to the 'joining up' agenda in different ways and have responded with differing degrees of enthusiasm. The MoD, alone in developing a conceptual framework in this area, has been particularly positive, noting that 'a conceptual framework' could be used to 'reinvigorate the existing, Cabinet Office-led, approach to coordinating the objectives and activities of government Departments in identifying, analysing, planning and executing national responses to complex situations. Post-operational analysis of situations and crises at home and abroad has demonstrated the value and effectiveness of a joined-up and cross-discipline approach if lasting and desirable outcomes are to be identified and achieved' (Ministry of Defence, 2007).

The MoD's enthusiasm for comprehensive working lies in a number of interrelated factors, particularly the changes in its understanding of the complex nature of conflict and perceptions of its roots in poverty and its experiences of working alongside civilian organisations and agencies in Bosnia and Kosovo during the 1990s and subsequently during the 'war on terror'. These experiences have also impacted on debates relating to the transformation of the military itself, in particular regarding the 'Effects Based Approach' (EBA), defined as 'the way of thinking and specific processes that, together, enable the integration and effectiveness of the military contribution within a Comprehensive Approach' (Ministry of Defence, 2007). The UN's 'human security' agenda has also helped shape both the understanding of conflict causality and the MoD's appetite for harnessing the capacity of other actors to address root causes (United Nations, 1994).

The level at which 'joined up working' was sought has also changed. The UK's experience with the UN Protection Force (UNPROFOR) mission in Bosnia (1992–1995) led to an initial focus on comprehensive working at a tactical level, particularly between low level Army commanders and the field staff of non governmental and UN humanitarian agencies. The scale of the Kosovo refugee crisis (1998/1999) and the subsequent stabilisation operation encouraged a sense that the Bosnian model was insufficient, requiring the elevation of co-operation to the 'operational' level – initially with the establishment of (limited) DFID and FCO representation in the UK Defence Crisis Management Organisation (DCMO). Subsequent experiences in both Sierra Leone (2000) and particularly during the 2003 invasion of Iraq highlighted the necessity for co-ordinating machinery at the strategic level, resulting, in 2004, in the creation of the cross-Whitehall Post Conflict Reconstruction Unit (PCRU).

The MoD initially placed considerable faith in the PCRU's ability to deliver the 'comprehensive approach' and continually reinforced its declaratory commitments to the holy grail of cross governmental working in the form of its own doctrinal publications – 'The Military Contribution to Peace Support Operations' (Joint Doctrine and Concepts Centre, 2004) and the 'Comprehensive Approach' (Ministry of Defence, 2007). However, whilst the MoD made much of the need for a 'comprehensive approach', it made little progress in enhancing its own capacity to deliver what were increasingly termed 'stabilisation effects'. There was even a degree of stagnation in its 'Civil-Military Co-operation' capabilities, as these were afforded insufficient influence in MoD planning structures and processes at all levels and neither attracted the appropriate numbers or calibre of staff. The MoD's almost evangelical approach to comprehensive working also stimulated opposition in the other departments.

MoD 'evangelism' was reinforced by what became known as the 'transformation agenda' (Farrell, 2008). Originating in the US DoD, this approach sought to leverage stealth, sensor, information technology and communication technologies to transform military capabilities through what was termed the 'effects based approach'. This was rooted in two fundamental notions:

> firstly, that of understanding the enemy as a complex, adaptive system of systems and, secondly, identifying and then concentrating action against the key nodes and links that comprised that system. Such an approach resonated strongly in the UK; offering both a means for addressing the complexity of the contemporary battlefield and for offsetting the deleterious impact of budgetary pressures on capabilities. (Farrell and Gordon, 2009)

The UK approach to transformation was somewhat different from that of the US. In addition to being less well resourced the approach was embedded within a different policy context – the pursuit of an 'ethical dimension to foreign policy', a stronger preference for 'softer' effects, such as leveraging diplomatic, information and development actors and a much greater willingness to countenance less hierarchical forms of cooperation between the defence and foreign ministries' (Farrell and Gordon, 2009). The consequences of this were twofold. It strengthened the Army's expectations that the FCO and DFID had the capacity to 'transform' conflict through rapid diplomatic and development interventions and that this would make possible the consolidation of tactical military victories. However, little thought was given to the mechanics of this process and the implications for the MoD in terms of operational level decision making or the conditions that would make possible the activities of the other departments.

Limited Partnerships?

Whilst the MoD's appetite for comprehensive working grew, the ability and willingness of other departments to engage in such a process showed marked variations, particularly within DFID and the FCO. Neither department was structured for working in what the MoD termed 'expeditionary environments', lacking both flexibility in funding arrangements (neither department was able to access the Treasury Reserve in the same way that the MoD was) and career incentives for staff to deploy to 'non-traditional' environments such as Iraq and Afghanistan. Within DFID the problems were even more fundamental. From its creation in 1997, New Labour had constructed a department that was no longer configured around a traditional 'national interest' agenda. Rather, directed by the 2002 International Development Act (IDA), it focused on poverty reduction and the delivery of the UN's Millennium Development Goals (for details, see United Nations, 2008). The approach to development also reflected the Organisation for Economic Co-operation and Development, Development Assistance Committee (OECD-DAC) debates on 'aid effectiveness', where the emphasis was increasingly placed on country ownership and donor alignment, delivery through effective national institutions and minimal aid conditionality (Biggs, 2005). Whilst many Army officers within Helmand anticipated the direct delivery of projects by DFID staff and their implementing partners, in reality they were confronted with a development department that focused on institutional capacity building at Afghanistan's centre and used unfamiliar aid instruments, such as Poverty Reduction Budget Support, that poured money through national level ministries rather than managing projects directly at village level. Consequently, DFID's focus tended to be Kabul rather than Helmand. Frustrated with the DFID approach, several high ranking Army officers began to talk in terms echoing the American use of 'money as a weapon system' seeking to use development to buy influence amongst the Helmandis. DFID officials increasingly warned against this, highlighting the risks associated with 'backing winners' rather than 'institutions' and 'processes' and drawing attention to the potential of the Army's preferred approach to undermine both the peace-building process and the beneficiary state (Anderson, 1999; Anderson, 2000). DFID staff also expressed privately significant (and well founded) concerns that the Army had been unable to create the security conditions in which development could reasonably take place; arguing consistently for a security first model of development (Interviews, 2008). Furthermore, DFID staff tended to argue, again with considerable justification, that, since 2004, they had invested heavily in the PCRU as a more appropriate mechanism for delivering conflict stabilisation work and this was rooted in a fundamentally different set of norms from those of development practice (Interviews, 2008).

Whilst the development literature reinforced the DFID position (see Biggs, 2005; Browne, 2007; Leader and Colenso, 2005; Menocal et al., 2008), the MoD was able to voice its assumptions more powerfully, often seeking to use the lure of development money to buy security and force protection and pushing for the simultaneous delivery of security and development activities even in highly dangerous environments. The FCO, itself struggling to define its 'diplomatic' role in Helmand, resurrected debates about the linkage between foreign policy, diplomatic leverage and the delivery mechanism formerly provided by the Overseas Development Administration (ODA) – a part of the FCO until 1997 when it was hived off to form DFID. These debates tended to emphasise the differences between them, in terms of culture and approach, and led to significant frictions between the departments, which, in turn, hindered effective collaboration.

Theatre Level Challenges

Engagement in Iraq and Afghanistan both encouraged deeper collaboration and challenged the UK's capacity to deliver a comprehensive approach. From 2006, as the Iraq theatre became an experience of managing drawdown, Afghanistan increased in significance, particularly with the UK's commitment to assume responsibility for Helmand. However, it was clear from the outset that Afghanistan was an enormous challenge to any state building strategy. It effectively represented an attempt to affect a 'triple transition' in the security, political and socio-economic spheres (Boyce, 2002) in 'the context of vast physical distances between urban areas, unforgiving terrain, a paucity of established infrastructure, a tribally fragmented and xenophobic population', with little experience of central government and where the idea of a strong, central state was contested and lacked legitimacy (Farrell and Gordon, 2009). As described in more depth in previous works by this author, Helmand was hardly the most conducive ground to test the effectiveness of the 'comprehensive approach', with the Helmandi economy 'mobilised around criminality, corruption and networks of narcotics traffickers' or 'simply absent from large areas' (Farrell and Gordon, 2009). Whether it be a lack of overall capacity, both in governmental or simply the human capacity of its people, or the exacerbation of 'significant military difficulties', including an inability to deny the home base of the insurgents' and 'an almost inexhaustible supply of foreign jihadist', the reality on the ground was always going to test – and ultimately find wanting – the paper concepts of 'comprehensiveness' (Farrell and Gordon, 2009).

The UK involvement in Helmand began seriously in October 2005, when the Cabinet Office tasked the PCRU to lead Whitehall's development of a strategic framework for both the civilian and military deployments, resulting in the UK Joint Plan for Helmand. Its authors sought consistency with a wide variety of policy frameworks: the Afghanistan Compact, the Interim Afghan National Development Strategy, the government of Afghanistan's National Drug Control Strategy, the UK Strategic Plan for Afghanistan, NATO's strategy and the emerging Afghan Development Zone concept. Whilst achieving coherence at the level of strategic plans and declaratory objectives was relatively straightforward, achieving 'internal coherence' between departments and also within them, particularly within the MoD, proved far more troubling. DFID never bought fully into the counter insurgency model articulated by the MoD (Interviews, 2008) and the counter narcotics (CN) strategy appeared orphaned from – and at times at odds with – the overall plan's emphasis on cultivating the support of the Helmandi population (many of who grew opium). Within the MoD, the military executors of the UK plan were largely relegated to the margins of the initial planning process and, consequently, did not buy fully into the result – a problem replicated over several subsequent deployments. Similarly, with Whitehall's attention and particularly its intelligence assets largely diverted towards the deteriorating situation in Iraq, the planners lacked much of the support that was necessary to develop a thorough understanding of Helmand's extremely complicated tribal dynamics (and particularly the poisonous relationships between leaders from the Ishakzai and Alizai communities) – resulting in an insufficiently detailed and resourced plan that became increasingly irrelevant as the security situation spiralled out of control in the summer of 2006. There is considerable evidence that, from the outset, the initial Helmand planners understood the striking incompatibility between the resource levels being committed to Helmand and the broad and unrealistic goals being sought by the UK. There is also evidence that this analysis was communicated to the Cabinet Office and rejected without explanation (Interviews, 2008).

The Absence of the Civilian 'Voice'?

The Helmand planning process sought to create an operational interdepartmental 'management' structure that would enable the military and civilian elements to interact and integrate effectively, creating a space for what could be described as a civilian 'voice' alongside or above that of the UK military 'voice'. The model chosen initially was to create a Provincial Reconstruction Team (PRT) led by a 'Triumvirate', a leadership committee comprising military, FCO and DFID representation. This approach was exported from the first British PRT in the Northern town of Mazar-E-Shariff and reflected the reasonably positive experiences with this structure, as well as the assumption that the military were deployed largely in support of a political and development effort. Whilst the planners had a clear understanding that the situation was different in Helmand, they initially concluded that consensual decision making between the MoD, the FCO and DFID staff at the operational level remained appropriate.

However, the scale of challenges posed by Helmand were of a fundamentally different order from those in the North – the scale and intensity of the insurgency, the impact of the counter narcotics agenda and the number of liaison tasks (with donors and political authorities) necessitated a much tighter and hierarchical mechanism for establishing priorities and delivering against objectives. In practice, from the outset, there were strong calls from within the MoD for a single empowered leader (predictably their preference was for a military leader) in country, who could actively coordinate MoD, FCO and DFID activities in support of a UK Joint Plan (Interviews NSID Team, 2008). Subsequently, the UK experimented with a range of alternatives, but even the deployment of an energetic and charismatic UK ambassador, Sir Sherard Cowper Coles, in 2007 and the creation of a two star, FCO led Civil-Military Headquarters in 2008 (in Helmand's provincial capital, Lashkargar) struggled to deliver genuinely 'comprehensive' working.

Perhaps the greatest obstacle to 'comprehensive' working related to the military perceptions of DFID's role. Several middle ranking military officers complained vocally that DFID's approach to state building resulted in an approach based on overtly long term results that were too physically distant to have a tangible impact in Helmand. Furthermore 'more senior military frequently conceptualised the civilian role in terms of delivering a form of development based 'backfill' designed to enable and improve military operations. In such a model the military defined the operational priorities and objectives and civilians were expected to provide a form of reconstruction 'follow on force' (Farrell and Gordon, 2009). Given the marked disparities in planning capabilities between the British civilians and the military in Helmand, operational level military decision making in Helmand proved largely impervious to civilian influence, until at least 2008. Understandably, the civilian staff and ministries chaffed against this situation 'arguing that this could not be further from the intention of a politically led, intelligence shaped counter insurgency campaign that characterised the military's own counter insurgency literature' (Farrell and Gordon, 2009). DFID staff in particular were critical of the way in which the military employed quick impact projects (notably between 2006 and 2007) as part of a 'hearts and minds' strategy, questioning the effectiveness of an approach 'that simplistically linked the construction of Afghan infrastructure by international donors (and military) and the consolidation of an Afghan state' (Farrell and Gordon, 2009). Other aspects of the military strategy were subject to criticism: the desperate paucity of troops and helicopters (which has not been fully resolved), the military's failure to take 'sufficient account of the interdependencies between security, political, reconstruction and development efforts at an operational level' (Farrell and Gordon, 2009) and the strategic inconsistency that characterised the overall military approach during the first two years – with significant changes in direction as each new Brigade deployed (Interviews MOD senior officials, 2009). Furthermore, there was a sense that every Brigade sought its own 'kinetic moment', rather than the steady consolidation of the state that was necessary to support the creation of a durable political settlement (Whaites, 2007; Farrell and Gordon, 2009).

Government Priority Setting

The challenges posed both by operations in Iraq and Afghanistan stimulated a series of changes in the way in which the UK approached such problems. Some progress was made in increasing strategic political leadership, with the establishment of a new Cabinet sub-committee in 2007, the 'National Security, International Relations and Development' sub-committee (NSID), tasked to 'consider issues relating to national security, and the Government's international, European and international development policies' (Cabinet Office, 2009). NSID was also augmented by a range of subordinate senior officials groups coordinated by the Cabinet Office, including the Iraq and Afghan Strategy and Senior Officials Groups.

Tony Blair's departure from office also created space for a policy refresh and enhancements to political leadership, but the continued division of responsibilities between different Cabinet Ministers remained problematic and the proliferation of different strategy groups risked reflecting rather than resolving the underlying departmentalism. The resulting plans, encapsulated in a range of NSID strategic documents in 2007 and the innovative Helmand Road Map in 2008, were unable to resolve all of the contradictory departmental preferences. The NSID strategy in particular never adequately resolved the question of what constituted an adequate balance of investment between top down national state capacity building approaches and more visible and immediate activities in Helmand Province. This directly reflected and added to considerable frictions between departments (Foreign and Commonwealth Office, 2008) and diverted attention away from the real problem of catastrophic underinvestment in the military resources necessary to effect meaningful change. Instead, Whitehall's strategy for delivering in a more 'joined up' way focused increasingly on supporting NSID decision making, rather than more wide ranging alternatives, such as empowering a particular Minister as the 'Afghan Tsar', with authority over the Afghan work of DFID, the MoD and the FCO. Whilst potentially useful, such technocratic solutions remained rooted in enhancing the quantity of information provided to Ministers – with information continuing to be passed by departments that, arguably, sought to preserve the autonomy of their own bureaucratic space – the very core of the problem (Interviews Cabinet Office, 2008).

The influence of 'departmentalism' was also apparent in the constitution of the PCRU (formed in 2004 and renamed the Stabilisation Unit – SU – in 2007). Its tri-departmental ownership (MoD, DFID and FCO) was designed partly to curb its power and deprived it of much of its potential to direct, rather than simply influence, individual departmental responses. Arguably, from the outset, the SU required a much firmer association with the Cabinet Office and more direct and high level political leadership if it was ever to realise fully its considerable potential. However, there are considerable dangers even with this approach – potentially adding yet another Whitehall voice to the pre-existing noise, leading other departments to disengage.

There was also increased recognition that the way in which the UK funded its conflict related policies encouraged 'departmentalism' and what could best be described as a 'multi-speed engagement'. Whilst the military costs of new operations (including military assistance with stabilisation) were met from the Treasury Central Reserve – enabling the MoD to react with a degree of speed and flexibility – DFID and FCO were required to fund the new commitments in Iraq and Afghanistan largely through reprioritising their existing budgets and making politically and bureaucratically challenging trade offs between new and old commitments. In each case budgets had already been committed, contracts let and bureaucracies were in place to supervise delivery – often developing interests in preserving the original arrangements. Such an approach raised the possibility of perverse incentives, with the simplicity and flexibility of the MoD's financial arrangements almost encouraging politicians to favour military rather than civilian solutions. It also created a complex set of arrangements for funding conflict work, reducing the ability of Ministers to obtain an overview of commitments and the level of financial investments made in support of the different elements of the strategy.

The tri-departmentally managed Global Conflict Prevention Pools (GCPP) were prime candidates for reform. 'Civilian' stabilisation activity in Iraq and Afghanistan was funded both from these and from Departments' own resources, creating a confusing array of funding sources spread amongst multiple departments. This made strategic prioritisation very difficult and reduced the ability of Minsters to shape or to develop a strategic overview of investments against the strategy as a whole. It is perhaps striking that it was not possible for Cabinet to have an overview of the (over) £220 million of UK expenditure against their own NSID strategy for Afghanistan, even as late as July 2008 (Foreign and Commonwealth Office, 2008). Furthermore, there were questions over why 'stabilisation' investments in Iraq and Afghanistan were being made from money earmarked for 'prevention', which led to commitments in Iraq and Afghanistan taking over 50 per cent of prevention resources previously earmarked for conflict prevention activities in Africa (Interviews Treasury, 2008).

A partial solution to these conundrums was found in 2007 – merging the Global and Africa Conflict Prevention Pools into a new single 'Conflict Prevention Pool' focused solely on 'prevention' work, whilst simultaneously establishing a new 'Stabilisation Aid Fund' to take on the role of funding stabilisation and reconstruction activity in 'hot' conflict zones, particularly Iraq and Afghanistan. Subsequent reforms also sought to establish new governance and programme management arrangements for these budgets in order to ensure that all activity was based on a common understanding of the overall strategy, with spending prioritised effectively against that and focused where it could best add value. The intention was for NSID to set the overall direction and prioritise between countries, whilst decision-making on how to spend in theatre was devolved as far as possible to the frontline. Whilst this represents a sensible adaptation, the challenge remains that of ensuring that the fund does not become a new arena for a devolved inter-departmental struggle for access to resources or a means for offloading unpopular financial 'responsibilities' from 'core' budgets (Interviews Treasury, 2008).

Conclusions

The MoD has, in many ways, captured the debate on comprehensive working and defined it in terms of 'harnessing DFID', which is potentially problematic, in and of itself. Perhaps the simplest solution to this would be to restore DFID to its former place as the ODA within the FCO, thereby consolidating budgets and reducing the level of co-ordination required. However, there is no indication that either Labour or the Conservative Party have an appetite for this, or have indeed given it any serious consideration. In fact, the Conservative Party have made clear that DFID will remain a separate Department of State, with a further commitment to ring fence DFID's overall budget (Interview, 2009). However, DFID remains subject to a range of strategic, financial and politico-bureaucratic pressures that threaten its current autonomy. The 2009 Institute for Public Policy Research (IPPR) report on national security makes clear the financial pressures on the UK's security strategy, concluding that this will necessitate more effective coordination and the exploitation of synergies 'across development and security spending' (IPPR, 2009). It also calls for legislation adapting the IDA to require DFID to 'promote development through poverty reduction and the promotion of conditions of safety and security in the developing world', arguing that such a 'change is necessary to remove any ambiguity that may exist over a DFID role in development activities not directly related to poverty reduction' (IPPR, 2009). Furthermore, it argues for DFID to make more money available for stabilisation activities in conflict affected areas and to develop enhanced linkages with the FCO (IPPR, 2009). Such calls resonate strongly within the Conservative Party, and also within the senior levels of the MoD and FCO. Additionally, given the straitened financial circumstances that the UK is in, there may also be support for this approach within the Treasury.

In practice the 'comprehensive approach' has involved a much less ambitious aim, that of cajoling a disparate flotilla of agencies, departments, units and professions to point in broadly the same direction – or, at the very least, not to undermine each other's work. The UK experience of operationalising this in Helmand is testimony to the difficulties involved and the limits that result, with real challenges in setting 'strategic' priorities rather than simply reconciling departmental interests; in agreeing, integrating and prioritising tasks, activities and objectives across departments; in aligning decision making structures with responsibility, authority and funding arrangements; and in creating cultures and career incentives that enable government to undertake tasks which cut across conventional organisational boundaries. In many ways, the solution to this can be reduced to a simple but problematic imperative, to develop a common sense of 'mission' that is shared widely and binds, in a real sense, the activities of the departments, providing a sense of common purpose sufficient to overcome contradictory departmental imperatives.

Much more can be done to facilitate the 'horizontal imperative'. In particular, departments should make more effort to agree on 'what works' and be more realistic about their objectives and assumptions. The military attachment to a particular conception of DFID's role and DFID's rejection of the dominant model of state building employed by the MoD is a major obstacle to 'joined up' working. Equally, the MoD's efforts in defining 'comprehensive working' in terms that look suspiciously like harnessing other government departments to an essentially 'military' plan are ultimately self defeating and run counter to the concept of a politically led counter insurgency. The MoD's attachment to the 'human security' agenda is also problematic in situations where resources are scarce – encouraging commanders to push for a broad front of social and economic reforms that outstrips the political will and resources that are necessary to deliver. There needs to be recognition that holistic security policies have the potential to frame a set of objectives for civilian departments that are both unrealistic for them to deliver and sufficiently broad as to prevent prioritisation, leading to strategic stalling as progress is pursued on too broad a front. The same criticism is possible with regard to the development community – who run the risk of loading country programmes with broad sets of objectives without necessarily prioritising core contributions to stability and the development of political settlements over the pursuit of broader development norms. They face similar challenges with principles such as 'do no harm' and the 'sustainability' imperative, with both often leading to a sense of paralysis rather than creativity and problem solving. Equally there needs to be a decision within government as to whether DFID discharges its conflict related work through the SU or is still expected to contribute in areas where it has genuine comparative advantage, such as in infrastructure programming.

If the 'comprehensive approach' is to work, there also needs to be greater investment in defining country strategies that go beyond stitching together departmental plans – requiring a difficult balance to be struck between a more assertive place in Whitehall for the SU, real Ministerial leadership and autonomy for those in the field. Funding arrangements should also, as a principle, follow tasks, problems and client groups rather than bureaucracies – and, whilst developments such as the transformation of the Conflict Prevention funds, are to be welcomed, more needs to be done to prevent their management structures from becoming hijacked by departmental imperatives. Finally career incentives for civil servants should be developed to take into greater account the setting out and delivery of cross departmental targets.

Referring to the failure of previous attempts to enhance joined up government Geoff Mulgan argues that many had failed to create a 'clear enough sense of the critical tasks; authority had often been dissipated rather than distributed; the sense of mission had not been widely shared, and was certainly not strong enough to counter the deep cultures of many departments; and at a local level there had rarely been sufficient autonomy to get things done' (Mulgan, 2005). In other words, cross governmental working is easiest when 'tasks are defined simply and clearly articulated, when the mission is defined without ambiguity and is recognised throughout the delivery organisations, when funding and organisation follow the demands of the tasks rather than pre-existing departmental structures, when those delivers have sufficient authority, autonomy and resources to address the tasks' (Mulgan, 2005). In this there is a striking paradox; the very complexity that makes joining up necessary is also the reason why it fails.

Bibliography

Anderson, M (1999), *Do No Harm: How Aid can Support Peace – or War* (Boulder: Lynne Rienner)

Anderson, M (2000), *Options for Aid in Conflict: Lessons from Field Experience* (Boulder: Lynne Rienner)

Biggs, D (2005), *Poverty Reduction Budget Support – Presentation by the Senior Governance Adviser DFID Asia Directorate to the Chartered Institute of Public Finance and Accountancy conference on 16 June 2005*, – http://www. cipfa.org.uk/international/download/david_biggs16jun05.ppt

Boyce, J (2002), 'Unpacking Aid', *Development and Change*, 33/2, 239–46

Browne, S (2007), *Aid to Fragile States: Do Donors Help or Hinder? How Should Donors Engage in Fragile States?* (Helsinki: World Institute for Development Economics Research) – http://www.eldis.org/go/topics/dossiers/health-and-fragile-states/aid-effectiveness-in-fragile-states/aid-instruments&id=32670&type=Document

Cabinet Office (2009), *Details, Roles and Responsibilities of the National Security, International Relations and Development* (London: HMSO) – http://www. cabinetoffice.gov.uk/secretariats/committees/nsid.aspx

Crossman, R (1975), *The Diaries of a Cabinet Minster* (London: Jonathan Cape and Hamish Hamilton)

Department for International Development (2008), *Guidance on Aid Instruments – A DFID Practice Paper* (London: HMSO) – http://www.dfid.gov.uk/ Documents/publications/aid-instruments-guidance.pdf

Farrell, T (2008), 'The Dynamics of British Military Transformation', *International Affairs*, 84/4, 777–807

Farrell, T and Gordon, DS (2009), 'COIN Machine: The British Military in Afghanistan', *Royal United Services Journal*, 154/3, 18–25

Foley, M (2000), *The British Presidency* (Manchester: Manchester University Press)

Foreign and Commonwealth Office (2008), *Afghanistan Portfolio Review* (London: Foreign and Commonwealth Office – unpublished)

Gordon, DS (2009), 'Civil Society, the "New Humanitarianism" and the Stabilisation Debate: Judging the Impact of the Afghan War', in Howell, J (ed.) *Civil Society Under Strain* (London: Kumarian Press)

Haldane, RB (1918), *The Haldane Report – Report of the Machinery of Government Committee Under the Chairmanship of Viscount Haldane of Cloan* (London: HMSO)

Hood, C (2005), 'The Idea of Joined Up Government: A Historical Perspective', in Bogdanor, V (ed.), *Joined up Government* (Oxford: Oxford University Press)

Institute for Public Policy Research (2009), *Shared Responsibilities: A National Security Strategy for the United Kingdom. The Final Report of the IPPR Commission on National Security in the 21st Century* (London: Institute for Public Policy Research) – http://www.ippr.org/publicationsandreports/publication.asp?id=308

Joint Doctrine and Concepts Centre (2004), *The Military Contribution to Peace Support Operations: Joint Warfare Publication 3–50* (London: JDCS)

Kein, R and Plowden, W (2005), 'JASP meets JUG: Lessons of the 1975 Joint Approach to Social Policy for Joined Up Government' in Bogdanor, V (ed.), *Joined up Government* (Oxford: Oxford University Press)

Labour Party (1997), *Labour Party Manifesto for the 1997 General Election* (London: Labour Party) – http://www.psr.keele.ac.uk/area/uk/man/lab97.htm

Leader, N and Colenso, P (2005), *Aid Instruments in Fragile States: Making the Right Choices – Poverty Reduction in Difficult Environments Working Paper 5* (London: Department for International Development) – http://www.globalpolicy.org/component/content/article/211-development/45064-aid-instruments-in-fragile-states-making-the-right-choices.html

Macrae, J (2002), *Uncertain Power: The Changing Role of Official Donors in Humanitarian Action – Humanitarian Practice Group Report 12* (London: Humanitarian Practice Group) – http://www.odi.org.uk/hpg/papers/hpgreport12_screen.pdf

Menocal, AR, Othieno, T and Evans, A (2008), *The World Bank in Fragile Situations: An Issues Paper delivered at the 'Eye on the Future: the World Bank Group in a Changing World Conference in Amsterdam on 12–13 July* – http://www.congrexnetwork

Ministry of Defence (2007), *The Comprehensive Approach – Joint Discussion Note 4/05* (London: Ministry of Defence)

Mulgan, G (2005), 'Joined Up Government: Past Present and Future', in Bogdanor, V (ed.), *Joined Up Government* (Oxford: Oxford University Press)

National Audit Office (2001), *Joining Up to Improve Public Services* (London: National Audit Office) – http://www.nao.org.uk/publications/nao_reports/01-02/0102383.pdf

Osborne, D and Gaebler, T (1992), *Reinventing Government: How the Entrepreneurial Spirit is Transforming America* (New Jersey: Addison-Wesley)

Performance and Innovation Unit (2000), *Wiring it Up – Whitehall's Management of Cross-cutting Policies and Services* (London: HMSO)

Performance and Innovation Unit (2000), *Adding it Up – Improving Analysis and Modelling in Central Government* (London: HMSO)

Perri, 6, Leat, D, Seltzer, K and Stoker, G (2002), *Towards Holistic Governance: The New Reform Agenda* (Basingstoke: Macmillan Palgrave)

Richards, DE (1997), *The Civil Service under the Conservatives, 1979 – 1997 Whitehall's Political Poodles* (Brighton: Sussex Academic Press)

Smith, R (2005), *The Utility of Force: The Art of War in the Modern* (London: Allen Lane)

Stabilisation Unit (2009), *Details and Activities of the Stabilisation Unit* – http://www.stabilisationunit.gov.uk/

Treasury (2001), *Improving Performance Information* (London: HMSO) – http://archive.treasury.gov.uk/performance_info/strategy.html#_ftn1

United Nations Development Programme (1994), *New Dimensions of Human Security: Human Development Report 1994* (New York: United Nations) – http://hdr.undp.org/en/reports/global/hdr1994/

United Nations (2008), *Millennium Development Goals* (New York: United Nations) – for details, both of the goals, and subsequent reports and analyses, see – http://www.un.org/millenniumgoals/

Whaites, A (2007), *States in Development: Understanding State-building – A DFID Working Paper from the Governance and Social Development Group* (London: Department for International Development) – http://www.dfid.gov.uk/pubs/files/State-in-Development-Wkg-Paper.pdf

Chapter 8

MoD PLC: New Labour, Managerialism, Marketisation and the Privatisation of British Defence Policy

Stephen Deakin[1]

Introduction

In recent decades, the MoD has increasingly adopted a more business-like approach to the management of its activities. An important strand in this approach has been the adoption of what the MoD refers to as partnerships with the private business sector and what others see as amounting to the privatisation of defence functions. This chapter examines some of the main forms of this phenomenon and evaluates them, with particular reference to the military's ethics and ethos.

In the UK, the line that separates what the public sector military has done in defence and what the private business sector has done has fluctuated over the centuries. British military activities have often relied on locally recruited soldiers and contractors. Some early military units were privately raised ones and monarchs relied on wealthy subjects to provide private armies. Private firms supplied logistical support to British troops in operational theatres, for example in the Crimea in the 1850s. From these early Victorian times, policy moved in the direction of defence being a public sector activity. Indeed, by the 1960s and 1970s, the Labour governments of Wilson and Callaghan had nationalised many of the industries that supported Britain's defence, such as shipbuilding and the British Aircraft Corporation. The MoD was a government department given general policy aims and civil servants and the military was trusted to achieve these to the best of their abilities. The military was a 'total institution' in which everyone was committed to the set goals (Edmonds, 1999). Britain's defence was a state function and self sufficiency and unity in defence were viewed as vital strengths.

All this began to change following the election of the Thatcher government in 1979. This administration and subsequent ones emphasised the role of the market place and private sector managerial ideals to provide public services, in areas such

---

1   I am grateful for the helpful comments of David Brown, Bjorn Muller-Wille, Donette Murray and Alan Ward. The views contained within this chapter reflect solely those of the author, and are not representative of the views of the Royal Military Academy Sandhurst, the British Army, the Ministry of Defence or the British government more widely.

as transport, education and health. The same thinking was applied to defence and, since the early 1980s, private sector ideals have played an increasingly important role in providing Britain's security. Once it was common to think of British defence as a public sector activity; now it has become increasingly accepted to think of defence as a business that should be largely managed according to private sector business principles.

When New Labour came to power in 1997, it developed further the earlier Conservative administrations' policies of bringing private sector principles into the delivery of public services. In the area of defence, New Labour adopted two principles that were potentially in conflict with each other. The first was to reduce the amount of resources expended on defence by making efficiency savings, such as reducing military personnel numbers, closing bases and reducing equipment and ammunition stock levels. The second principle was to adopt an expeditionary strategy, whereby UK military forces would go to crises around the world. The SDR sets out an ambitious defence police with an expeditionary global role for Britain, in co-operation with its allies. This would allow it to continue 'punching above its weight'. One of SDR's sentiments is about effectively getting 'more with less', itself an authentic summation of contemporary managerialism (Micklethwaite and Wooldridge, 1996 319). An expeditionary strategy requires highly trained military personnel and varied military equipment, able to be used in desert, jungle, mountains and other environments. To move and support the military on these expeditionary operations requires a powerful and very expensive logistic capability. New Labour, as the Conservatives had done before them, looked to private sector ideals to help them marry these two principles.

Managerialism

New Labour strongly embraced the ideology of managerialism, effectively the use of commercial private sector business techniques to provide public services. Blair may himself have been personally attracted to management ideals and to leading in the style of a private sector business leader (Owen, 2008, 257). Its first defence review, the SDR, was a glossy publication, mirroring the style of a business report and using the language and concepts of the market place and of private business practice. Then Defence Secretary George Robertson, in his introduction to the SDR, expressed exactly this ambition, noting that 'we must apply modern management methods to ensure that we deliver results as efficiently as possible for the taxpayer' (Ministry of Defence, 1998a, 3).

To this end, the MoD has adopted a wide range of modern managerial practices: benchmarking, human resource strategies, flatter management structures, balanced scorecards and many others. Private sector budgetary practice has been adopted; previously accounts had detailed the running costs of activities, whereas they now show the full cost, offering managers more information. A whole chapter of the SDR is dedicated to human resource management, exploring how to get the best out of the defence work force – something that earlier defence reviews had given little or no attention to. Activities that the three services had carried out separately were ultimately combined into one tri-service organisation. Such jointery saw, for example, a combined Naval and RAF Harrier aircraft force and the creation of the Defence Logistic Organisation (DLO) to manage the logistic needs of all the military. Changes in defence equipment procurement were labelled 'Smart Procurement', which the SDR claimed would lead to 'faster, cheaper, better' processes, through a co-ordinated approach to equipment purchase and development and strengthened customer supplier arrangements (Ministry of Defence, 1998b, 10). Just in Time (JIT) techniques, a management concept used by civilian manufacturers to ensure that stocks and raw materials are kept at a minimum to save money, were adopted. In line with the thinking of the wider business community, the rationale was that large supplies of ammunition and other equipment could be purchased just before a conflict or military operation began, thereby dramatically reducing the cost of capital, storage and depreciation that would otherwise accrue. As the SDR claimed, 'we should not hold stocks when industry can be relied upon to deliver within the warning time we judge would be available for a major conflict' (Ministry of Defence, 1998b, 49). The conflicts in Iraq and Afghanistan since 2003 have seriously tested this JIT policy, with several instances highlighted of equipment that was ordered too late to arrive before the conflicts began, leaving some personnel to enter combat without the necessary equipment, weaponry and personal protection. This remains a potent political issue, even after the UK's presence in Iraq has come to an end, as the discussions during the 2010 Chilcot Inquiry demonstrate all too clearly (Chilcot, 2010). As has become clear, the JIT principle also served a wider political purpose, as it aided political leaders in their wish not to signal that they had exhausted diplomatic means and were preparing for war. However, it also posed a wider managerial problem, given that the principle proved impossible to implement effectively in the time available.

The UK's Armed Forces, and the MoD, are expected to be modern, flexible, outward looking, opportunity seeking, mobile, agile and quick reacting, all of which will help the organisation value its employees. In effect, the challenge was to modernise and change many of the past ways of doing things. These qualities – inherent in the wider managerial movement – were presented as essential for success in modern armed conflicts. The SDR has had a great impact on the way that the MoD operates. Reviewing the past decade of activity, the MoD itself noted that 'it would be difficult to overstate the level of change the Department has delivered over this period. Its structure, its ways of working and its culture have all evolved radically' (Ministry of Defence, 2008, 129). The British military should be both effective and efficient; however, the adoption of a strong managerialist ethos alters somewhat the nature of thinking about British defence. It focuses attention on the efficient use of resources, on numbers and on planning, whilst simultaneously maintaining a softer side that values people as the most important asset of an organisation. It emphasises commitment and trust to the organisation, whilst adopting efficiency strategies that may ultimately cost workers their jobs. The SDR conveys an impression of efficiency, process, targets and outputs rather than one of military virtues, such as bravery, self sacrifice and patriotism (an issue that will be returned to at the end of this chapter).

The SDR also accelerated existing trends and led to new initiatives, whereby the MoD increasingly utilises a business model as it seeks better ways to do 'business'. At the same time, the MoD has spent many millions of pounds on private sector management consultants to provide advice on precisely such issues (Craig, 2006, 47). This is in no sense unique to the military arena. For example, the 1999 'Modernising Government' initiative was aimed at modernising all public services, by the adoption of contemporary management best practice. However, there remains a question-mark as to whether it is appropriate to extend such practices so wholeheartedly into the defence arena. Defence is a difficult activity to manage, not least because the figures involved are huge (at the time of writing, the MoD's budget for 2009–10 is £36.365bn (Ministry of Defence, 2010), and the activities complex and diverse. Moreover, defence is often a political activity that involves many relationships with others, both nationally and internationally, where efficiency and saving money may be only one of the goals in the relationship. Despite its best intention to behave like an efficient business, the MoD's management of UK defence has attracted criticism for inefficiency. For example, it is asserted that the MoD paid several tens of millions more for each of its Apache helicopters by deciding to build them in Britain, rather than to buy them directly from the US (Page and Evans, 2006, 79). Others have suggested that the MoD paid a top price to have its London headquarters modernised, only to then move many of its staff out of the building (Craig, 2008, 61). The Public Accounts Committee, the main Parliamentary scrutiny body, noted in 2007 that 'over the years, the Department has not made sufficient improvements to deliver major military equipments to time, budget and quality' (House of Commons, 2008, 5). In addition, it noted that 'there are a wide range of factors leading to cost and time overruns on defence projects, and, despite numerous reforms to working practices, the Department seems unable to bring about lasting improvements' (House of Commons, 2008, 8). Adding to the wider criticism, the National Audit Office specifically highlighted the MoD's procurement of eight new Chinook helicopters in 2001 as a problem, noting that, subsequently, they have been stored, unused, and will require an additional £500m to be spent on them to ready them for use (National Audit Office, 2008).

The Marketisation of Defence

New Labour enthusiastically continued the previous Conservative government's policies of involving the private sector in supplying defence resources, through what has been labelled as a 'public-private partnership'. These have taken a number of forms, but generally they involve outsourcing defence activities to private firms. Whilst previously such activities had been done 'in house', more and more they are being performed by the private sector. Outsourcing has become a common practice in the commercial world, although both here and in the public sector it can still be a controversial practice. Firms identify activities that are not their core business and which can be done more cheaply by other firms, for example, retaining an accountancy firm to examine the company accounts. It is argued that this allows a greater concentration on the firm's core business, whilst the outsourced contractor does the same, to the mutual benefit of all. This may ultimately save money, as each organisation is doing what it is specialised at doing and so has comparative advantage. The theory is simple; the practice less so.

Several problems exist. To begin with, once started, outsourcing can effectively develop a logic of its own and it can become more difficult to know when to stop. Organisations may also find it difficult to identify what constitutes their core activities and what does not. There is also a danger that the internal workforce's wider feelings of loyalty and commitment can be dissipated or weakened, with outsourced workers simply working to fulfil the letter of their contract. Control of the outsourced activity can prove to be more difficult than when such matters were held 'in house', particularly in the areas of drawing up and monitoring supplier contracts. Despite talk of partnership, ultimately the supplier of the outsourced activity is doing the work to make a profit. It has every incentive to provide the service at the lowest possible cost and therefore it is likely that it will adopt strategies to bring this about, such as, for example, off-shoring activities – namely the use of cheaper labour and production facilities in lower cost countries – or, by cutting difficult to measure intangibles, such as the wider quality of service.

Despite these concerns, the MoD has been particularly enthusiastic about outsourcing, which it began before New Labour came to power. The SDR stated that the MoD was already involved in 'the biggest market testing and contracting out programme in government' (Ministry of Defence, 1998b, 11). Huge areas of defence activity have been outsourced to the private sector, including provision of simulator training equipment, rapid deployment ferries and accommodation, management of property, cleaning of buildings, Information Technology systems, security guarding, training, logistic support and servicing of equipment. A visitor to a British military base today will likely find that most support services are provided by civilian contracting staff. In the past, these functions were carried out by members of the military or by MoD employed civil servants.

Public Finance Initiatives (PFI) take outsourcing a significant step further. Typically, defence PFIs are large capital projects, where a private sector firm agrees to build and to maintain for the length of the contract, which may be several decades long. At the same time, the MoD pays a charge to use the facility during the length of the contract. In some cases, the equipment is deployed into operational theatres. The Army has Tank Transporters procured by this method, while the Royal Navy has roll on roll off ships. PFIs are a form of borrowing and have the advantage that the capital costs of a project do not appear on balance sheets, thereby effectively disguising future financial obligations. The MoD has made extensive use of PFI initiatives. In 2008, it was estimated that it had spent a total of £8.9bn on PFI projects since 1996 (Ministry of Defence, 2008 139). This figure presumably does not include committed future expenditure on PFI contracts, for example, the life costs of its tanker aircraft PFI contract signed in 2008, estimated to be approximately £13bn. As Chancellor of the Exchequer, Gordon Brown set out New Labour's justification for PFI projects in 2003, claiming that PFI was in the public interest because the most cost effective public services were achieved through this method. He also argued that the private contractor took on the risk of the project, for example cost overruns, and that the public sector was effectively invigorated by the infusion of private sector best practice. He asserted that PFI was not privatisation, because the private sector was simply helping with public service delivery:

> PFI enables us to do this by binding the private sector into open and accountable long term relationships with the public sector aimed at a proper sharing of risk and access to private sector managerial expertise and innovative ideas, in order to secure better services. (Brown, 2003)

What is reputed to be the world's largest PFI contract (at the time of writing) was agreed in 2008, when the MoD signed an agreement with a private sector consortium to provide 14 multi-role air-to-air refuelling tanker aircraft for the RAF. The contract is for the supply of the aircraft and their through life support, for a period up until 2035. The MoD does not own these aircraft and, when it is not using them, they will be hired out to private firms, with the income generated shared between the contractor and the MoD. This is innovative, since traditionally the RAF procures aircraft, crews them, maintains them and ultimately sells them off at the end of their life. Under this PFI, the RAF will buy aircraft flight time from the commercial contractor providing the refuelling aircraft. The MoD's business rationale for this arrangement is an understandable one. The RAF's existing air-to-air tanker fleet is a vital defence asset, but it is old and unreliable and new planes are required. For much of the time, the aircraft are not in use, perhaps a few hours a week typically. Of course, if a conflict occurs, usage will increase and they will be flown more intensively. Also, new tankers are an enormous capital outlay, which will have an effect on an already stretched defence budget.

This tanker PFI illustrates important issues with regard to the role played by PFI contracts in the UK's defence. At the ceremony to sign the PFI, an RAF Air Marshal was reported as saying, 'if the aircraft don't fly, then the MoD doesn't pay' (Jennings, 2008). In doing so, he illustrated the MoD's commitment to saving money and to commercial business practice. However, in reality, whether the tankers fly or not cannot be a cost decision alone and this illustrates an important issue with PFI projects in the defence area. Tanker aircraft fulfil a vital role in Britain's defence. They are used to refuel combat aircraft and, if they are not there to refuel them, the combat aircraft will run out of fuel and crash, destroying the aircraft and possibly killing their crews. This eventuality would be hugely expensive, both in lives and equipment lost. The reality then is that the tanker aircraft must fly when the MoD requires them to do so, making any idea of withholding payment from the private service provider if they do not seem unrealistic.

What is happening here, as with other outsourcing, is, in effect, to make a private business a trustee of an important part of the UK's defence. The MoD transfers the risks of providing the service to the firm, but, if the firm gets into difficulty, it is inconceivable that it will be allowed to fail. When Britain's air traffic control, an area adjacent to defence, was partly privatised through a PFI, the new firm subsequently got into financial difficulty in 2002. Air traffic control could not be allowed to fail and the government stepped in with a financial rescue package for the firm (Young, 2002). In addition, as revealed in the 2008–9 financial crisis, major privately owned banks were also considered too important to be allowed to collapse and so they too were rescued by the government.

Private Military Companies

Private Military Companies (PMC) and Private Security Companies (PSC) are private profit making firms that perform a range of military functions, from guarding to training to providing wider strategic assistance and analysis, in support of the armed forces. The UK, US and many other states make extensive use of these companies. PMCs today are not the archetypal mercenaries of the past; rather they are sophisticated companies that often command considerable military and financial assets. They fall into two broad categories; by far the largest number is firms that supply logistical support to the military in the operational theatre. Smaller in number are firms that provide specific military and security services to support the military. Some firms provide both types of services. The growth of these firms became more noticeable during the first Gulf War in 1991 and continued in the Balkans and Sierra Leone in the 1990s. The conflicts in Iraq and Afghanistan since 2003 have seen a huge increase in the use of PMCs – particularly by the US (see Singer, 2007) – and they have become a more prominent feature of modern conflict. During military operations in Iraq, contractors have provided air transport for military personnel between the UK and Iraq, made and repaired military accommodation camps, maintained military equipment, provided food and water for troops, catering, communications and many other things. The MoD had agreed close to £1bn of contracts in Iraq by mid-2005 to provide support functions (Maynard, 2005). A senior British Army officer and logistician, discussing contractors deployed on operations, suggests that 'the reality today … is that these contractors have made such serious inroads into the military business that it is no exaggeration to say that we could not deploy, sustain or deliver military intent without them' (Cross, 2007). If so, this is a major change in defence policy and one that seems to have occurred without much public discussion, nor without similarly substantive efforts in the field of regulation and management of such entities.

PSCs provide a range of services, including training, intelligence, consultancy, security guarding, interrogation, escort duties, mine clearance and close protection of personnel such as diplomats, contractors and others. For example, British embassies world wide are guarded by private contractors. In Iraq since 2003 security contractors have performed numerous roles for the UK and for the coalition. As the reconstruction programme got underway, there were insufficient soldiers in Iraq to protect the infrastructure of roads, bridges, power plants, schools and the like. Private contractors were employed to fill the gap and to provide the required security. Official US figures show that, in the 1991 Gulf War, around 9,000 civilian contractors were deployed, giving a ratio of one contractor to 55 soldiers. In Iraq in 2008, there were 163,590 civilian contractors deployed against 160,000 US military, giving a ratio of 1:1 (Hodge, 2008). On these figures, the US military is only the second largest external security capability provider in Iraq in 2008 – the British military may be the third largest.

Private security contractors working in Iraq and Afghanistan can call for military assistance and they sometimes work to protect military personnel. They have both opened and returned fire. It is clear that Iraqi insurgents see private contractors as part of the enemy and that they attack them as such. Contractors have done some good, but inevitably their position is a politically, ethically and legally contested one. Critics argue that they are mercenaries who exist in a legal grey area and that they are not sufficiently accountable for their actions. There is some evidence to substantiate such concerns. It is doubtful whether most PSCs are good at the 'hearts and minds' approach that is such a key part to counter insurgency strategy (Scahill, 2007, 71). Contractors who were killed and mutilated at Fallujah in 2004 precipitated an intense and probably previously unplanned American military attack on the town (Scahill, 2007, 113). In addition, contractors were implicated in some of the abuse of prisoners at Abu Ghraib prison (Taguba, 2004). Contractors working for the US security firm Blackwater opened fire in 2007 in Nisour Square, Baghdad, in disputed circumstances, killing 17 civilians, including women and children (Hodge, 2008). Occasionally, Blackwater personnel have commanded US troops in fire fights (Scahill, 2007, 123).

The use by the UK – or by a coalition of which the UK is a part – of private security firms to outsource activities previously undertaken by military personnel raises many political, legal and ethical issues. First, it is the ultimate privatisation of security. In the UK, the 1870 Foreign Enlistment Act relates to mercenaries and forbids any Briton to enlist in a foreign military, although it has been found to be an unenforceable law. In any case, it is arguably not relevant to the current growth of PMCs who present themselves as legitimate firms acting at the bequest of government. A Green Paper on the subject of PMC activity and regulation was published by the Labour government in 2002 (Foreign and Commonwealth Office, 2002). The Foreign Secretary's Forward indicated support for the use of the private sector 'as a cost effective way of procuring services which would once have been the exclusive preserve of the military' and proposed some form of regulatory system (Foreign and Commonwealth Office, 2002, 4). Part of the difficulty here lies with defining a private military company without labelling them as mercenaries. The FCO's Green Paper tried to side-step this problem by describing what tasks private military companies undertake, but the issue of definition is not easily avoided. The FCO launched a further public consultation in 2009, before advocating its preferred policy, whereby private military companies draw up a code of conduct in consultation with government, as part of effective self-regulation (Miliband, 2009). Concerned organisations, such as Amnesty International, immediately raised issues with this policy and particularly its emphasis on self regulation, noting that 'there are a large number of British-based, private military and security companies operating in conflict zones … if the government does propose a self-regulatory system it would effectively grant them impunity to do whatever they like. This is not an ordinary industry; this is men with guns we're talking about' (Norton-Taylor, 2009). Again, the issue of defence as a different or even unique aspect of government activity – with a different set of morals, ethics and its own ethos – was at the forefront of concerns regarding the Labour government's activities in these areas.

Politics, Ethics and Ethos

The MoD's policy is to consider outsourcing an activity if there is a sound business case for doing so. It argues that private sector businesses are employed to contribute towards public services if it is clear that they provide significant cost savings and a product as least as good as the existing public sector one. In its defence, the MoD argues that its use of the private sector results in financial savings. A figure of around 18 per cent is quoted for defence support functions that are not deployed on operations (Uttley, 2005, 37). For PFI projects, a saving of 10 per cent is often claimed (Uttley, 2005, 38). In the case of deployed logistic support functions on operations, not enough information is available in the public domain to know whether they are cheaper than the military doing the work themselves (Uttley, 2005, 39). Until such data is released, it is impossible for a comprehensive independent financial assessment to be made. Some defence economists cast doubt on whether outsourcing defence does indeed save money, identifying many hidden costs in the process that are often ignored (Parker and Hartley, 2003). Intangible measures also matter; privatising military functions can be viewed as weakening military knowledge and investment in public institutions (Avant, 2002). The public sector union Unison argues that the British government is paying an extra £2.7bn extra annually for its PFI programme, compared to using direct public sector procurement (Gosling, 2008, 38). A leading work on the privatisation of the military concludes that, both in the private sector and in the military, 'the simple fact is that it is not clear that outsourcing always saves money' (Singer, 2007, 157).

Outsourcing military activity assumes that the military does the operational work and that a line can be drawn between operational and non-operational activities. This seems implausible. Even in civilian life companies have difficulty identifying their core activities. For example, the Hatfield rail crash in North London in 2000, which killed four and injured 70, was largely caused by outsourcing rail maintenance and then losing control of this activity (Office of Rail Regulation, 2006). Likewise, British Airways sold off its catering division, reasoning that it was an airline not a caterer, and then found itself unable to fly in 2005, when a strike by its caterers, Gate Gourmet, led to no meals being made. The reality is that, even if an organisation outsources an activity, it is still its problem and its responsibility (*The Economist*, 2005).

There has been a 'shift in world view' (Singer, 2007, 70) in the way that defence provision is thought of and the UK has been in the vanguard of this change. This transfer of formerly public sector defence responsibilities to the private sector in recent decades is best understood as a manifestation in Britain of the weakening of the nation state and the gradual emergence in its place of the 'market state' (Van Creveld, 1999, 420; Bobbitt, 2002, 230; Bobbitt, 2008, 85; Williams, 2002). In the 'market state', there does not seem to be as much need to enforce common identity, goals and morality, with the focus instead on being an efficient provider of public services. Whereas in the traditional model, the concern is the relationship between the state and citizen, in the 'market state' model attention is focused on the government as the provider for its clients. Accordingly, the state can withdraw from many of its traditional activities and franchise them out to others, such as private firms and regulatory bodies, who it believes can provide these services more efficiently than it can. A powerful example of this in the area of the UK's national defence was the 2008 decision to sell the government's stake in the production of nuclear weapons at the Atomic Weapons Establishment Aldermaston to a US company. Private firms will now produce and maintain Britain's independent nuclear deterrent – although the government maintains a special share that allows it to intervene if necessary (Russell, 2008). In a 'market state' model, politics becomes about management to achieve the greatest opportunities for all citizens, rather than about how to protect the identity, morality and history of the state. Political conflict about what constitutes the 'good life' is replaced by a concern for managerialism and management efficiency (Micklethwaite and Wooldridge, 1996, 21). This state is a 'hotel' where paying guests are provided with services by the hotel staff, but are otherwise left alone to live their lives (Sachs, 2002, 19). Ethically, this is an outworking of a vision of the morally neutral state, a 'demoralized society' (Himmelfarb, 1995).

Militarily, this vision raises many questions about Britain's defence policy. There are many intangibles that are difficult, perhaps impossible, to measure or cost. In the area of defence, these include concepts that the British military use routinely, such as fighting spirit, morale, unit cohesion and a wider military ethos. All of these are viewed as being vital to ensuring military success and yet they sometimes collide with managerialism and the ethos of the market place. The 'market state's' lack of concern with promoting its own identity and culture has an obvious impact on the military, for the military use traditional state concepts and symbols to justify and motivate themselves. Military qualities such as patriotism, loyalty and self sacrifice are not much encouraged in the 'market state' and therefore the military find it difficult to appeal to them. In the traditional state model, the military is a powerful expression of unifying power and purpose; in the 'market state', the military's place seems more uncertain. The military of the traditional British state defended a specific national culture and identity and embodied this in its symbols and commitments, such as the defence of territory, monarchy, the Union Jack and the Church of England. Classical military thinkers, such as Clausewitz, noted that a successful war is a social activity that unites the whole nation state. Patriotic passion and ideals of service help to lead to victory (Heuser, 2002, 80–1). In contrast, the 'market state' may have far greater difficulty persuading its members to join its military. As Bobbitt has argued, why would you fight for the 'market state' and risk your life for a state that no longer stands for your identity, but for opportunity for all (Bobbitt, 2002, 230).

As with any other organisation, the way that the MoD manages should model the qualities that it requires from its personnel. In any organisation, an ethical climate is created, which then influences the behaviour of employees. In this case, an ethical climate is defined as 'shared perceptions of what is ethically correct behaviour and how ethical issues should be handled in the organization' (Peterson, 2002, 50). The British military emphasises that its members belong to a moral community, bound together by military virtues. Military success relies on an ethos consisting of intangible factors such as morale, fighting spirit and trust. The Army's statement of personal ethics for all its members, known as Values and Standards (Ministry of Defence, 2000), is very clear about this. The Army's list of essential moral virtues is selfless commitment, courage, discipline, integrity, loyalty and respect for others (Ministry of Defence, 2000). The ethos of the market place and the ethos of the managerialist business model pursued by the Ministry of Defence are arguably in tension with these military virtues, as demonstrated below (see Table 8.1).

Table 8.1   Comparison of Values

British Army – Values and Standards	The Market Place
Selfless Commitment	Survival of the fittest
Courage	Entrepreneurship
Discipline	Rule obeying
Integrity	Competition
Loyalty	Individualism
Respect for others	Profit first

Source: British Army (2008), Values and Standards of the British Army, (London: MoD) – http://www.army.mod.uk/documents/general/v_s_of_the_british_army.pdf.

The ethics of the commercial world and those of the military do have similarities and overlap; comparisons can be drawn between the survival of the fittest in the world of cut throat business and success in war. However, there are obvious conflicts between the ethos of military virtue and the ethos involved in managerialism, outsourcing and privatising military functions. Being managerial can lead to accusations of not caring sufficiently about people, as the mother of a British soldier wounded in Iraq argued: 'they [the injured] are simply figures on a balance sheet. They do not have any role, any function and the MoD wants to dispose of them as cheaply as possible' (Rayment, 2007). This allegation reflects a broader issue in the British public sector, where trust and shared values seem, ever more, to have been supplanted by financial considerations (Micklethwaite and Wooldridge, 1996, 330). In modern managerial organisations, it has been claimed that there is a diminished place for service and self sacrifice (Sennett, 2002, 139). The ethos of managerialism and the ethos of military virtue may ultimately prove to be at odds with each other.

References

Avant, D (2002), 'Privatising Military Training', *Foreign Policy in Focus* 7/6 – http://findarticles.com/p/articles/mi_hb6426/is_17_5/ai_n28788058/

Bobbitt, P (2002), *The Shield of Achilles: War, Peace and the Course of History* (London: Allen Lane)

Bobbitt, P (2008), *Terror and Consent: The Wars for the Twenty-First Century* (London: Allen Lane)

Brown, G (2003), 'State and Market: Towards a Public Interest Test', *Political Quarterly* 74/3, 266–84

Chilcot, J (2010), *Testimony and Documentation of the Iraq Inquiry* – http://www.iraqinquiry.org.uk/ (accessed on 11 January 2010)

Cobbold, R (1998), 'The Outcome of the Strategic Defence Review', *Whitehall Paper* 44

Coker, C (1998), 'Selling the Regimental Silver', in Frost, G (ed.), *Not Fit to Fight* (London: Social Affairs Unit)

Craig, D (2006), *Plundering the Public Sector* (London: Constable and Robinson)

Craig, D (2008), *Squandered* (London: Constable and Robinson)

Cross, T (2007), 'The Humanitarian Community and the Private Sector', *British Army Review* 141, 53–56

Economist, The (2005), 'The Dangers of Outsourcing', 18 August

Edmonds, M (1999), 'Defence Privatization: From State Enterprise to Commercialism', *Cambridge Review of International Affairs* 13/1, 114–29

Elliot, M and Rotherham, L (2006), *The Bumper Book of Government Waste* (Petersfield: Harriman)

Foreign and Commonwealth Office (2002), *Private Military Companies: Options for Regulation* (London: HMSO)

Freeden, M (1999), 'The Ideology of New Labour', *Political Quarterly* 70/1, 42–51

Gosling, P (2008), *The Rise of the Public Service Industry* (London: Unison)

Heuser, B (2002), *Reading Clausewitz* (London: Pimlico)

Himmelfarb, G (1995), *The De-Moralization of Society* (London: Institute of Economic Affairs)

Himmelfarb, G (1996), *The De-Moralization of Society: From Victorian Virtues to Modern Values* (London: Vintage Books)

Hodge, N (2008), 'High Risk, High Return?', *Jane's Defence Weekly* 9 July

House of Commons (2008), *Ministry of Defence Major Projects 2007 – Thirty-Third report by the Public Accounts Committee on 22 July* (London: HMSO)

House of Commons (2009), *Written Ministerial Statement by the Foreign Secretary, David Miliband, to the House of Commons on 24 April* (London: Hansard)

Jennings, G (2008), 'UK Ministry of Defence Inks Long-awaited RAF Future Tanker Deal', *Jane's Defence Weekly* 28 March

Maples, J (1998), 'An Opposition View: The Outcome of the Strategic Defence Review', *Whitehall Paper* 44

Maynard, G (2005), 'Support to Deployed Operations', *Defence Management Journal* 28, 6–8

Micklethwaite, J and Wooldridge, A (1996), *The Witch Doctors: Making Sense of the Management Gurus* (London: Heinemann)

Ministry of Defence (1998a), *The Strategic Defence Review: Modern Forces for a Modern World* (London: HMSO)

Ministry of Defence (1998b), *The Strategic Defence Review: Modern Forces for a Modern World. Supplementary Essays* (London: HMSO)

Ministry of Defence (2008), *Ministry of Defence Annual Report and Accounts 2007–2008 Volume One* (London: HMSO)

Ministry of Defence (2010), *Defence Spending* – http://www.mod.uk/DefenceInternet/AboutDefence/Organisation/KeyFactsAboutDefence/DefenceSpending.htm (accessed 11 January 2010)

National Audit Office (2008), *Ministry of Defence: Chinook Mk3 Helicopters. Report by the Comptroller and Auditor General on 4 June* (London: National Audit Office)

Norton-Taylor, R (2009), 'Foreign Office to propose self regulation for private military companies', *The Guardian* 24 April

Office of Rail Regulation (2006), *Train Derailment at Hatfield: A Final Report by the Independent Investigation Board on 24 July* (London: HMSO)

Owen, D (2008), *In Sickness and in Power: Illness in Heads of Government During the Last Hundred Years* (London: Methuen)

Page, L and Evans, H (2006), *Lions, Donkeys and Dinosaurs: Waste and Blundering in the Military* (London: Heinemann)

Parker, D and Hartley, K (2003), 'Transaction Costs, Relational Contracting and Public Private Partnerships: A Case Study of UK Defence', *Journal of Purchasing and Supply* 9, 97–108

Peterson, D (2002), 'Deviant Workplace Behaviour and the Organisation's Ethical Climate', *Journal of Business and Psychology* 17/1, 42–51

Rayment, S (2007), 'Wounded Troops are Treated as Just Figures', *The Daily Telegraph* 15 October

Robinson, P (2005), *Doing Less with Less: Making Britain More Secure* (London: Academic Imprint)

Russell, B (2008), 'Secret Nuclear Sell-off Storm', *The Independent* 20 December

Sachs, J (2002), *The Dignity of Difference: How to avoid the Clash of Civilisations* (London: Continuum Books)

Scahill, J (2007), *Blackwater: The Rise of the World's Most Powerful Mercenary Army* (London: Serpents Tail)

Sennett, R (2002), *The Fall of Public Man* (London: Penguin)

Singer, PW (2004), *Corporate Warriors: The Rise of the Privatized Military Industry* (London: Cornell Studies in Security Affairs)

Taguba, A (2004), *Article 15–6 Investigation of the 800th Military Police Brigade* (Washington, DC: United States Army)

Uttley, M (2005), *Contractors on Deployed Military Operations: United Kingdom Policy and Doctrine* (Carlisle: Strategic Studies Institute)

Van Creveld, M (1999), *The Rise and Decline of the State* (Cambridge: Cambridge University Press)

Williams, R (2002), 'Text of the 2002 Dimbleby Lecture by the Archbishop of Canterbury on 19 December', *The Times* 19 December

Young, A (2008), 'It May be PPP or PFI but the Public Still Foots the Bill', *The Sunday Herald* 24 February

Chapter 9

New Labour's Governance
of the British Army

Anthony Forster[1]

Introduction

In a European post-Cold War context, it was reasonable to have considered that the UK was in a very limited category of a number of European states that had managed to re-connect legitimacy with the armed forces and their role – a situation in which there had been a successful adaptation of the support mechanisms through the twin processes of sustained legitimacy for old roles (the defence of the nation) and the creation of support for new roles – peacekeeping and peacemaking (Forster, 2006a 80; Ministry of Defence, 1998). Between 1990 and 1999, peacekeeping deployments in Bosnia and small 'expeditionary' conflicts, such as the liberation of Kuwait, Kosovo and Sierra Leone, had popular support and appeared to be sustainable, even if the force structure was designed for Cold War purposes. The 1998 SDR recognised this and set out to re-structure the armed forces to provide a military capability to support the UK's foreign policy goals (Ministry of Defence, 1998). What it did not do – perhaps because the government did not consider it a problem at the time – was pay any regard to the wider relationship between the armed forces and society.

Over the last decade, this oversight has led to a serious crisis in civil military relations. In turn, this has had a major impact on the roles of the military and indeed the capacity of the armed forces to carry out functions on behalf of the government and the nation. There are three critical relationships – between government and the armed forces; between the armed forces and service men and women and between society and the armed forces. The argument here is that, since 1997, there have been profound tensions that have emerged in all three areas; that developments within the three critical relationships are negatively impacting on each other and indeed magnifying their effect and the armed forces are in the grip of a crisis that challenges the traditional nature of civil-military relations and indeed the very governance of the military. In combination, the current challenges faced by the armed forces are the greatest since the ending of conscription in 1962. This chapter will conclude by exploring how this has come about, its consequences and the lasting legacy of the Blair and Brown governments.

---

1   This chapter uses and develops arguments in two previous publications (Forster, 2006a and Edmunds and Forster, 2007).

Between Government and the Armed Forces

Edmunds and Forster have argued that the impact of the expeditionary model on the UK armed forces has been consistently under-estimated (Edmunds and Forster, 2007, 15). In a rapidly changing strategic environment, Labour governments have invested a considerable amount of effort in reviewing and updating the strategy and policy documents that shape the roles and structure of British armed forces. The 1998 SDR re-focused the armed forces mission on preventing crises further away from the UK and, if necessary, deploying forces overseas. Following the 11 September attacks, in 2002, the government added a New Chapter to the SDR (explored in more depth in this volume by Brown). In 2003, it published a new Defence White Paper and set out proposals for the structure of the armed forces through the 2004 Future Capabilities initiative. An increase in the operational tempo, a wider geographic area of deployment, the restructuring of armed forces to make them expeditionary in nature and a reduction in the size of the armed forces were the four features that ran through all these initiatives.

However, from 2002, for seven consecutive years, the armed forces have operated above the overall level of concurrent operations for which they are resourced and structured (House of Commons, 2008b, 3). As a direct result of the reduction in the number of service personnel and the increase in missions, the operational tempo of British armed forces has increased dramatically, leading to a breach of the MoD's own 'Harmony Guidelines'. These establish a benchmark that no more than 20 per cent of army personnel are on operational tours of duty with no less than 24 months between deployments. In January 2007, all three services breached the guidelines (House of Commons, 2008b). In turn, this has led to specialist individuals and units facing severe overstretch, notably in trades that require specialist skills and where it takes time to recruit and train personnel, such as linguists, ammunition technicians and medical staff. Between 2004 and 2008, the numbers affected by this increased across all Services. In the Army, pinch-point trades increased by 15.4 per cent, in the RAF by 63 per cent, and in the Navy by 150 per cent, so that, by 2008, there were 30 pinch-point trades in the Army, 31 in the RAF and 25 in the Naval Service (House of Commons, 2008a). In 2006, the then CGS General Sir Richard Dannatt referred to the Army 'running hot', with troops stretched to capacity and just about coping (cited Norton-Taylor, 2006). By October 2008, the armed forces trained strength was 179,060, representing 96.8 per cent of the full time strength and an overall shortfall of 5,790 personnel, with none of the services in manning balance (Ministry of Defence, 2008a; House of Commons, 2007, 7). By 2009, the situation in the Army had become so acute that the CGS announced yet another restructuring of the Army to prevent overstretch, with the explicit purpose of delivering the 'Harmony Guidelines' (Evans, 2009b).

As with many European governments, the Labour Government has struggled to match the ambitions and roles they have set out for their armed forces with the amount of expenditure they are willing to provide. It is the case that 'the Defence budget has had the longest period of sustained growth since the 1980s ... and the

UK has the second-highest defence budget in the world in cash terms' (Cabinet Office, 2008a). Despite this, UK defence spending levels have not matched the strategic ambitions outlined in the government's policy. The SDR was not properly costed or funded. In particular, the cost of adapting the force structure towards expeditionary warfare – but keeping previously approved procurement programmes that did not meet current operational requirements – has been consistently underestimated (Heaven, 2008; Martin, 2008). Moreover, the financial cost of fighting in Afghanistan and Iraq has been very high, with the direct costs some £1.63bn in 2006–07, £2.65bn in 2007/08 and an estimate of £3.36bn for 2008/09 (House of Commons, 2008c, 8–16).

By 2006, the mismatch between commitments and resources became so stark that it drew the CGS into calling for a national debate on the proportion of resources that need to be spent on national defence. He argued that it was not for him to say whether the 5 per cent of public spending (about £30bn) earmarked for defence – a figure he compared with the 29 per cent spent on social security – was sufficient, believing that 'there is room for debate ... about whatever [is judged] enough' (cited Norton-Taylor, 2006).

The following year, the UK National Defence Association was launched with the support of three former CDS, to campaign for fully funded armed forces to defend the UK's vital interests and security at home and abroad. At the same time, five former CDS who held seats in the House of Lords led scathing attacks on the government for failing to provide appropriate defence expenditure for the missions it had set for the armed forces (Evans, 2007). In spring 2008, the Defence Select Committee took up this point, highlighting that there may be difficult decisions to be taken to produce a realistic and affordable equipment programme – 'this may well mean cutting whole equipment programme, rather than just delaying orders or making cuts to the number of platforms ordered across a range of equipment programmes. A realistic Equipment Programme will give confidence to our armed forces that the equipment programmes that remain will be delivered in the numbers and to the timescale required' (House of Commons, 2008a). In the winter of 2008, to fill a £2bn black hole in the defence budget, the government announced major delays, but only a handful of cancellations in the equipment programme, in order to 'ensure the highest priority be given to operations in Afghanistan and Iraq' (Evans, 2008). In addition, the service chiefs pressed for a 'comprehensive strategic defence review, setting out the aims for the British forces at home and abroad, with a matching defence industrial review to say what the forces can afford to buy' (Fox, 2008). All parties are now committed, in principle, to holding such a review after the 2010 General Election, although it remains to be seen whether such a review will meet the needs of the Service Chiefs.

The failure of the government appropriately to fund the armed forces has taken on a very human angle, as a consequence of the poor provision of equipment for service personnel on operations and the number of deaths directly attributed to this. For example, since 2001, there have been repeated examples of such failure in the provision of body armour, 'Snatch' Land Rovers and night vision goggles that have led to avoidable deaths (BBC, 2003). The MoD must shoulder its share of responsibility for getting the right equipment at the right time and cost to the right people. As General Sir Michael Jackson commented critically about the MoD 'large procurement cost overruns in the past have been rather meekly accepted to the detriment of spending on personnel and training'(Jackson, 2006). Over the last seven years, improvements have been put in place to speed up the provision of Urgent Operational Requirements (UOR) (House of Commons, 2008). However, it is the government that bears significant responsibility for the failure to provide adequate resources for what the armed forces are being asked to do (issues relating to technology and procurement are explored in more depth by Codner in this volume).

Perhaps as damaging to the relationship between the armed forces and government has been the failure to convincingly convey to the public the role of the organised use of violence in support of the national interest The NSS offered an opportunity to locate the armed forces in a broader strategic context and to provide impetus to the 'comprehensive approach', which requires cross-government cooperation to deliver security in the context of development (which is discussed in more depth by Gordon in this volume). Sadly, the launch of the NSS was overshadowed by other government business and was a lost opportunity to put this right. Perhaps this is unsurprising when the government itself has failed to move beyond merely talking about the need for an effect link between the work of other government departments, notably the FCO, DFD, the MoD and the Home Office, to deliver an integrated approach to conflict prevention (Jackson, 2006; Cabinet Office, 2008b). This failure to communicate effectively has been highlighted most starkly in Afghanistan. Launching the mission in April 2006, John Reid, the then Defence Secretary, hoped British soldiers would return home within three years 'without firing one shot because our job is to protect the reconstruction' (cited BBC, 2006). Between August 2006 and August 2007, nearly 4 million rounds were fired and, by March 2009, 150 armed forces personnel had been killed since 2001. The sense that the government did not fully understand the link between security and development was given further credence by Lord Ashdown, who was vocal in criticising Ministers for wasting the lives of servicemen and women, but without a plan to take advantage of any military successes (Brady, 2009).

Finally, there has been a discernible deterioration in the broader relationship within the wider chain of command, particularly between the senior representatives of the armed forces and the government. This relationship has been traced by prominent journalists, such as Matthew Parris, highlighting interventions made by General Jackson in support of government policy, which'pushed forward the boundaries of commentary beyond operational matters by publicly endorsing the moral and political purposes of defence and foreign policy' (Parris, 2006). While these supportive comments caused few problems for the government, Parris believed that General Dannatt crossed a Rubicon by directly challenging government policy towards Iraq, thereby undermining democratic civilian control.

He argued that such comments should have led to his removal, a view supported by prominent former Labour and Conservative Cabinet Ministers (Parris, 2006; Ananova, 2006).

What is also striking is the willingness of retired Service Chiefs to break confidences of advice they gave in private to Ministers in what appeared as a broader campaign to highlight the plight of the armed forces. For example Lord Guthrie and General Jackson both revealed that they had considered resigning – although ultimately did not – because of a failure of Ministers to listen to their advice (Heaven, 2008; Jackson, 2007a). Retired senior officers have also attacked serving officers for their failure to speak out in support of service men and women. Typical of this were the comments of General Sir Michael Rose, who commented that 'Army Generals have betrayed their own soldiers for the sake of their careers' and Lord Bramall, who believed that 'in the last few years, our leadership appears to have had their 'knighthood lobotomy' and then toed the political line' (Sands, 2007; Harding, 2006; Jackson, 2007b). Indeed, the public backlash to General Jackson's 2007 Dimbleby Lecture, in which he belatedly criticised the government within months of his retirement, was seen as too little too late and provided a fillip to the more professionally assertive role adopted by his successor (Jackson, 2007b; Black, 2006).

For some, such as Michael Rose, 'the politicisation of the military ... is one of the most damaging developments of the Blair years' (cited Sands, 2007). Tensions in this relationship are inevitable and the leadership of the armed forces have always been important political actors. What is striking is that serving Service Chiefs have felt obliged to adopt a more prominent and controversial profile in national debates concerning defence issues, in order to fill what they perceive as the vacuum created by political leaders and to prevent the gaps between the armed forces, state and society widening any further.

Over the last decade, the changing nature of the relationship between senior commanders and the government has also been marked by a breakdown in trust. In part, this is a consequence of the types of military missions where there is no direct attack on the UK and where participation in armed conflict appears to be one of choice, rather than necessity. This was highlighted by the 2003 request from the CDS for an unequivocal written assurance that the invasion of Iraq was legal under international law. There were also reports that, worried about the independence of the government legal advice, one service chief even sought independent legal advice (Sengupta, 2007). Whilst falling short of accepting the need for parliamentary approval for British forces to participate in any armed conflict, the Brown government made proposals to strengthen the powers of Parliament in relation to armed conflict and has begun to recognise at least some of the problems raised by the Iraq war and the need to be clearer about how to legitimise wars of choice (BBC, 2007).

Between the Armed Forces and Individual Servicemen and Women

A second critical relationship, which has been the subject of fundamental change, has been the relationship between the armed forces itself and individual servicemen and women. In large part, senior commanders have been able to protect the self-regulation of the armed forces, which, in the past, has provided stability to the relationship between individual servicemen and women. However, in the face of a wide range of challenges, traditional structures of military authority – characterised as hierarchical, paternalistic and ageist – have been challenged. Increasingly penetrated by legal interventions and newly articulated individual demands, some service personnel are no longer willing to completely subordinate their own interests to the collective interests of the group.

In the area of equality and human rights, legal landmark rulings from the European Court of Justice (ECJ), European Court of Human Rights (ECHR), British courts and the work of the Equality and Human Rights Commission (EHRC) have dramatically transformed the landscape in which the armed forces and service personnel operate. Developments in this area have affected the MoD's approach to ethnicity, disability, gender, religion and belief and sexual orientation. For example, in 1999, the MoD sought exclusion from EU disability legislation to protect its approach to the recruitment of able bodied people, which remains fiercely contested by groups representing the disabled (*The Independent*, 2000; Guthrie, 2000). A decade later, in 2009, the EHRC informed the MoD that – in its view – the current ban was discriminatory and that the disabled should be allowed to serve, in order to meet the UK government's requirement to implement the UN Convention on the Rights of a Person with Disabilities (Rayment, 2009).

In 2000, the MoD was forced to lift the formal exclusion from the armed forces of people on grounds of their sexual orientation. In turn, this has led to a review of preferential treatment for heterosexual married couples, leading to new rules to provide equal treatment to service personnel in civil partnerships and partners living together. It also led to the 2000 Armed Forces Code of Social Conduct, which sets out policies on behaviour without a distinction being made on the basis of gender or sexual orientation. The MoD has also had to extend its faith provision for a wider range of religions. In 1999, initially through an industrial tribunal case and then the ECJ, Angela Maria Sirdar challenged the exclusion of women from combat units. Whilst the ruling upheld the right of the government to exclude women from combat roles, the MoD's approach has subsequently been challenged as a result of a blurring of the lines of combat, especially in Iraq and Afghanistan, deaths of women on operational duty and the number of gallantry awards awarded to women. As the head of the Army's Operational Law Branch commented 'Although the "Sirdar" operational effectiveness exemption still applies, there must be a real chance of further challenge' (cited Rayment, 2008). In 2005, the Equal Opportunities Commission initiated a Formal Investigation (FI) and subsequently signed a three-year agreement to address sexual harassment in the armed forces, which was resolved satisfactorily in 2008.

Another area of concern has focused on racial discrimination within the armed forces. Following a separate FI into racial discrimination in recruitment and selection, in 1998 the Commission for Racial Equality entered into an eight-year Partnership Agreement with the MoD to address these issues. Of particular interest however was the treatment of serving and retired Gurkhas soldiers. In a series of cases, the courts have upheld the right of Gurkhas to have equivalent treatment to UK nationals. Three challenges have been concerned with eligibility to the Prisoner of War (PoW) gratuity and entitlement to pension payments. In a class action estimated to affect 36,000 veterans in 2008, the High Court ruled that denying Gurkhas who had served before 1997 the automatic right to live in Britain was not only discriminatory but breached the Military Covenant (Evans, 2009c–d). Despite some significant steps forward in diversity and equality – and a prominent publicity campaign over treatment towards the Gurkhas led by the actress Joanna Lumley – there remain significant challenges. Commonwealth soldiers continue to feel vulnerable and have even established their own union for victims of racist bullying and abuse (Gillan, 2007).

The nature of the relationship of individual service personnel with their commanders accepting sole source of authority is also changing. There are several dimensions to this. On the issue of lawful orders, we have seen distrust between senior commanders and politicians concerning wars of choice, but this now reaches further down into the organisation, based on a general concern about the legality of missions. Decline in deference has affected members of the armed forces in the same way as it has wider society, leading to an increased unwillingness to accept without question the authority of the MoD. Service personnel are themselves less willing to keep quiet and are more willing to challenge authority through test cases. For example, Flight Lieutenant Kendall-Smith, who opposed the war in Iraq, could have claimed conscientious objection status and sought a discharge, but chose instead to take his case through the courts. Despite senior commanders and the current CGS repeatedly emphasising the moral component of soldiering, it is clear that the authority of commanders within the armed forces is more contested than ever before and that – in a hierarchical organisation like that of the armed forces – this is particularly challenging to handle (Ritchie, 2006).

Distrust between individuals, regiments and the MoD has also emerged as a real tension. For example, there has been a concern that individual service men and women will not be protected and supported by senior commanders for decisions they take in good faith – often in difficult circumstances. In this regard, the handing of military prosecutions in Iraq has become an important touchstone issues. Since 2003 – at the time of writing – there have been 184 complaints of illegal behaviour in Iraq, over 100 of them relating to troops in fire fights with insurgents. Of the total, 162 were dismissed, with the remaining 22 leading to prosecution or dismissal. Richard Holmes has argued that the combination of prescriptive rules of engagement and the perceived over-zealous nature of the Royal Military Police (RMP), requiring soldiers to prove they operated within the rules of engagement, has had a detrimental effect on morale (Holmes, 2006). In addition, troops have often had to wait two or three years before their cases have been heard. The delay between an allegation and the case being tried or dismissed has been unacceptably long. In a number of well-publicised instances, charges have had to be dropped because of a lack of evidence. In the interregnum, army regulations prevent those accused from publicly defending themselves and yet the MoD refuses to comment on any ongoing investigation, even to clarify the facts. In other cases, the problem has been compounded by the fact that the stigma of being under investigation has effectively set back or ended careers.

There is a growing feeling that service personnel are being placed in ever more difficult circumstances without sufficient care for their well-being, with justice not being well served by such long delays between accusation, investigation and trial. There has also been a concern that prosecutions have been politically motivated. Even though there is little evidence to this effect, it has caused real consternation and fed into a general feeling of a gap within the chain of command. In a series of the MoD's own Continuous Attitudes Survey, some 60 per cent of service personnel were either 'fairly dissatisfied' or 'very dissatisfied' with how grievances were handled. Whilst some steps have been taken to address this, it is eroding the Military Covenant that sets out mutual obligations underpinned by a principle of fair treatment. There is also one further problem that, in a complex international legal regime, service personnel can be acquitted in the UK, only for that decision to be followed by a prosecution in a civilian court or at the International Criminal Court (ICC) in The Hague (of which the UK became a signatory in 1998). Even with the best of intentions, there are thus limits on the UK government, in terms of the protection it can provide to its service personnel. Perhaps reflecting these concerns, in January 2009 the MoD, appointed Bruce Houlder QC to be the first independent Director of Service Prosecutions (DSP) for all three armed services. The appointment was made following several high profile failures of the current system of military investigation and prosecution. The cases referred to were the acquittal of all those charged in connection with the beating and death of Baha Musa, an Iraqi prisoner in Basra in 2003, and the failure to convict concerning the death of an Iraqi civilian in 2005 (Evans, 2009a). It remains to be seen whether the appointment of an independent DSP will reassure service personnel as well as society at large.

Another dimension to the changing relationship between the armed forces and servicemen and women is a much clearer sense of their individual rights and obligations. As the wars in Afghanistan and Iraq have run on, campaign groups like that of the Royal British Legion, 'Help for Heroes' and the newsprint media – notably the *Independent on Sunday* – have all become more interested in the duty of care we owe service personnel who are placed in danger. The debate crystallised around the Military Covenant, an Army doctrine launched in 2000 that was an implicit response to the Labour government's lack of understanding of the culture and values of the armed forces. It explicitly sets out the rights and responsibilities of government and society to soldiers and service families, stating that:

Soldiers will be called upon to make personal sacrifices – including the ultimate sacrifice – in the service of the Nation. In putting the needs of the nation and the Army before their own, they forgo some of the rights enjoyed by those outside the Armed Forces. In return, British soldiers must always be able to expect fair treatment, to be valued and respected as individuals, and that they (and their families) will be sustained and rewarded by commensurate terms and conditions of service. (Ministry of Defence, 2000)

Reports undertaken by the main political parties around the Military Covenant and the government's own commitment to this issue have therefore raised awareness not only of the obligations, but also the rights of service personnel (Conservative Party, 2008; Liberal Democrats, 2007; TSO, 2008a–b). In turn, this has highlighted the poor terms and conditions of service, specifically in areas such as pay, welfare support, housing, personal injury whilst serving in the armed forces and medical care. For example, in 2005, the government introduced the Armed Forces Compensation Scheme, but the Royal British Legion continued to highlight the poor treatment for ex-servicemen offered by the scheme, singling out the case of a young soldier injured in battle, who was awarded £152,150 for care for the rest of his life, whilst an RAF civilian typist received £484,000 after injuring her thumb (Royal British Legion, 2008). Despite significant investment in military health services, the Legion has criticised the practice of treating soldiers in wards alongside civilian patients, poor mental health provision and levels of support for bereaved families (Mostrous and Macintyre, 2009). In this way, whilst the senior commanders have been willing to use the Military Covenant to seek more resources from government and to remind society of its obligations, it has perhaps had an even greater impact in reminding senior commanders of their own duty of care to those under their command (Gillan, 2007).

By no means have all service personnel lost faith in traditional forms of raising issues and seeking resolution of them. However, a sufficient number have been willing to take alternative forms of action outside the chain of command. The Internet provides an opportunity for service personnel to raise issues anonymously and to network and collectively campaign for action. Anonymity provides a safe and risk-free means of rapidly raising issues. For example, the creation of the British Army Rumour Service and Royal Navy and RAF equivalents are now well established social and campaigning networks. Likewise, the use of mobile phones has allowed service personnel to communicate more easily. For example, the campaign for better service accommodation was triggered by the release of mobile phone footage of service quarters, forcing senior officers to publicly respond to complaints. To address the general problem of leaks to the media, the MoD responded by introducing a ban on any form of communication by military personnel without permission of a superior and accompanied this with a rider that communications must 'maintain, and where possible enhances the reputation of the organisation' (Ministry of Defence, 2007, 5). The launching of the British Armed Forces Federation in 2006 highlights the scale of unease and discontent with the effectiveness of the chain of command across a whole range of issues, such as terms and conditions of service, the realities of service life in terms of equality and diversity rights, injury and the need for legal support. Despite support from the Defence Select Committee and the reality that the MoD cannot stop the work of the Armed Forces Federation, it continues to assert that a Federation is not consistent with the ethos and traditions of the British Armed Forces (Ministry of Defence, 2008b).

A final source of contention is the MoD itself. Within the MoD, tensions exist in three major areas: between commanders of field forces and MoD senior commanders; between the three services within the MoD and between the uniformed officers and defence civil servants. In the first area, as the Hall report has clearly shown in relation to the investigation into the media handling of an incident in March 2007, even on issues within a single service, it has proved impossible to identify who was responsible for key decisions whether in London or in the field command (Hall, 2007). In the second area, the erosion of single service lines of responsibility has created confused lines of accountability, with senior commanders unable to provide a single voice of authority on many key issues. In addition, with some validity, service chiefs have complained that 'they possess astonishingly little real power to choose how cash is spent' (Jackson, 2006). In the third area, commentators have called for a better balance between the number of civil servants and uniformed officers – an issue that may form a central element of the next SDR process – and more effective political and military leadership (Wilson, 2007, 3–4; Hastings, 2007). Whilst these tensions are a perennial problem, the stakes have become much higher when the armed forces are deployed in major combat operations.

Between Armed Forces and Civil Society

The third critical relationship is between society and the armed forces. The latter are rooted in and part of British civil society and are profoundly affected by it. Over the period of the Labour government, as a direct result of the erosion of self government of the armed forces, the impact of changes in civil society has been more pronounced, perhaps than at any other time over the last 60 years.

The ability to recruit enough men and women is crucial to the future of armed forces and has been referred to above. Experienced service personnel are leaving at the fastest rate for years, while the services are struggling to recruit enough people attracted by a career in the armed forces (although the situation has ironically been improved slightly by the economic downturn during 2009). In part, this reflects unpopular or little understood wars, but also widespread socio-economic changes. These include changing attitudes to careers, a decline in the armed services traditional social bases for recruitment and competition from the private sector. Not without criticism, the armed forces have looked for new opportunities through contact with school children and promotion of the life style of the armed forces (Gee, 2007). They have also turned to new groups, by recruiting a greater number of women than ever before – now some 10 per cent of the armed forces – ethnic minorities and targeting areas of high unemployment. In the case of recruitment from the Commonwealth, this has increased from 360 in 1998 to more than 6,600 a decade later, with predictions that it will rise from 10 per cent by 2012 to 20 per cent by 2020 (Norton-Taylor, 2008). Yet, if insufficient numbers of UK citizens have any interest in joining up – a 'without me feeling' – there is clearly a danger of significantly weakening the connection between the armed forces and society (Haltiner and Hirt, 2000).

It is also striking that, over the last decade, the role of activist and campaign groups has changed. They have become more assertive, new groups have emerged and their profile and influence has become more significant. The Royal British Legion, for many years the epitome of an establishment charity of the MoD, in 2008 launched its highly successful 'Honour the Covenant Campaign'. The aim was to 'address the growing sense of disillusionment among service personnel and veterans about their treatment by the state'(Gillan, 2007). Prominent new military charities have been launched, notably 'Help for Heroes', and others – such as Combat Stress founded in 1919 – have found a renewed purpose. The MoD has become a partner with Stonewall – a group that was at the forefront of campaigning against the MoD's ban on gays and lesbians – and the MoD is now a Stonewall 'Diversity Champion', promoting lesbian, gay and bisexual (LGB) equality in the workplace. In turn, Stonewall has strong links with Proud2Serve, an LGB internet forum run by service personnel and partners for the benefit of the military community. This network of interconnected and independent charities and groups have created a new political and social milieu in which the British armed forces have to operate – one unrecognisable from a decade earlier in terms of the partnerships that have been forged and the new challenges of consultation and engagement that this requires.

The legal dimension of civil-society has also led to a number of developments that are striking. One of the issues that has emerged over the past four years has been the role of coroners, who have been very critical of the armed forces. Following an inquest into the death of anyone killed or dying in suspicious circumstances, the 1984 Coroners' Rules give discretion to coroners to report to 'the appropriate agency' any circumstances in which the coroner perceives that future deaths could occur if appropriate remedial action is not taken. Since all service personnel killed overseas are normally repatriated to the UK through RAF Brize Norton in Oxfordshire and RAF Lyneham in Wilshire, two coroners – Andrew Walker and David Masters – have played a key role in bringing to public attention the duty of care of the chain of command for service personnel. Since 2006, Andrew Walker has been particularly critical of the MoD, describing its conduct as 'inexcusable', 'a breach of trust', 'penny-pinching' and 'unforgivable' (cited Hines, 2008). Seen as someone independent of the armed forces, capable of asking difficult questions and uncovering unpalatable truths, Andrew Walker has widely been seen as the champion of bereaved service families.

In 2008, the government became so concerned by the impact of Walker's conduct and comments that it brought a failed High Court case to prevent narrative verdicts that attributed blame. The Coroners and Justice Bill going through Parliament in 2009 may well prove to be an opportunity for the government to try and change the law in its favour, though others want to strengthen coroners' powers, making submission of a report and a response mandatory, stating what remedial action has been taken or – if no action has been proposed – the reasons why.[2] In March 2009, the Head of the UK EHRC claimed that members of the armed forces have a right to life and the MoD had a duty of care to protect them. This intervention will add further pressure on the MoD to be accountable for its duty of care (Salkeld, 2009).

The role of military families has also become ever more important. Despite 17 investigations into recruit deaths at Deepcut, the families of the young people who died continue, with the support of Amnesty International, to press for a public inquiry where a judge can call witnesses and question them. Another example concerns the death of six military police at al-Majar in 2003. Following a ruling of unlawful killing by a UK coroner, the families requested an independent investigation by the Commissioner of the Metropolitan Police, expressed a willingness to bring a criminal case and to seek damages, arguing that it was a failure of specific individuals in the chain of command that led to the death of the RMPs. These examples indicate that there is declining trust in the capacity of the services to investigate themselves; that the appropriateness of military decisions is no longer considered above question and that service families are themselves willing to use whatever legal redress they can to get satisfaction, largely immune from the contrary pressures exercised by the MoD. In 2008 Dr Susan Atkins (formerly the police complaints commissioner) took up the government appointed post as Service Complaints Commissioner for the Armed Forces, with the power to investigate complaints and make recommendations. However, with fewer powers than set out through the Blake report, many still feel uncertain this will be sufficient to restore trust and public confidence.

Conclusions

Looking back on this period, we can see the impact of developments from three interconnected areas – between government and the armed forces; between the armed forces and service men and women; and between society and the armed forces. Projecting forward there are at least four lasting legacies. First, the fragmentation of military authority and, through necessity, the sharing of influence amongst different types of actors and across levels of governance. In the future, it is not just the case that the authority of the armed forces is being repositioned in

---

2   I am grateful to Don Carrick, Institute of Applied Ethics, University of Hull for this information.

a more complex milieu, but that military authority is in itself being transformed. There is no doubt that the armed forces will have to become more effective (and expert) at negotiating with other actors; the armed forces will have to engage across formal and to an increasing degree informal structures; and pay more attention to extra-territorially based influences, especially international legal reference points. This will pose very significant questions, not just about the ability of future governments to consider deploying military force in support of foreign policy goals. It will also test the political skills and organisational capacity of senior commanders to operate in this new environment.

Second, a lasting legacy of the three Labour terms is the increased politicisation of the armed forces. The period has been marked by a change to traditional patterns of defence public policy-making. Having condoned the intervention of senior commanders in support of Labour policies in the early period of government, it became difficult for the government to rein back on the public interventions of senior commanders, notably General Sir Richard Dannatt. Despite the government's decision not to promote Dannatt to the post of CDS, it remains an open question whether a new generation of service chiefs will – if not as overtly challenging as Dannatt – continue to be 'professionally assertive' in the discharge of their duties. The nature of the conflict in Afghanistan and the broader changes discussed above make this more likely than not.

Third, it is axiomatic that there is a very significant challenge of under-funding for the armed forces in relation to the roles they are asked to undertake. Over the last 13 years, defence planners have been preoccupied with the acquisition of expensive, high technology military equipment, which has diverted resources away from where they are really needed in the defence structure – specifically in areas such as pay and terms and conditions of service, training, recruitment and the welfare support (including housing) of the armed forces. Whilst equipment remains an issue, to sustain the armed forces, senior commanders need to recognise that – without service men and women who are well trained, highly motivated and willing to serve – there is no future for our armed forces, however well equipped it might be.

Fourth, of all the military deployments of the Labour government, it is likely to be the war in Afghanistan that has the most impact on British armed forces. It picked up significant momentum following the deployment and withdrawal from Iraq and thus brings its own challenges, on top of all the conflicts that have gone before it. It is also a conflict with its own intensity, with the casualty rate in parts of the country approaching 10 per cent. There are also those within government and the armed forces that believe that the conflict is also likely to last a generation (Harding, 2008; Kirkup, 2008). Whilst Afghanistan is a less unpopular intervention than the Iraq war, from the vantage point of 2009 and with the withdrawal from Iraq now confirmed, it looks unlikely that the armed forces will be broken by the long term and cumulative pressures of fighting two wars. However, the Military Covenant – the key stone on which the relationship between the government, the armed forces and society rest – may yet be broken in Afghanistan.

Bibilography

Ananova (2006), 'Army Chief accused of interfering' *Ananova* 16 October 2006 – http:www.ananova.com/news/story/sm_2036486.html

BBC (2003), 'Soldiers "having to buy own kit"', *BBCNewsonline* 16 January

BBC (2006), 'UK troops to "target terrorists"', *BBCNewsonline* 24 April

BBC (2007), 'MPs support war-powers proposals', *BBCNewsonline* 15 May

Black, C (2006), 'Sir Mike Jackson: The armchair general', *The Independent* 10 December

Brady, B (2009), 'Britain is wasting the lives of its soldiers, warns Ashdown', *The Independent* 25 January

Cabinet Office (2008a), *The National Security Strategy of the United Kingdom Security in an Interdependent World* (London: HMSO)

Cabinet Office (2008b), *The Comprehensive Approach* (London: HMSO)

Conservative Party (2008), *Restoring the Covenant: The Military Covenant Commission's Report to the Leader of the Conservative Party* (London: The Conservative Party)

Daily Telegraph (2007), 'What are your experiences of Army accommodation?', *The Daily Telegraph online* 10 August

Edmunds, T and Forster, A (2007), *Out of Step: The Case for Change in the British Armed Forces* (London: Demos)

Evans, M (2007), 'Coup? What coup? It was sheer coincidence, say defence chiefs', *The Times* 24 November

Evans, M (2008), 'Armed Services take first big hit in public spending', *The Times* 12 December

Evans, M (2009a), 'Accused troops will face more robust courts martial, says prosecutions chief', *The Times* 2 January

Evans, M (2009b), 'Troops get longer breaks to save marriages', *The Times* 27 January

Evans, M (2009c), 'Britain opens door to 36,000 Gurkha veterans after policy U-turn', *The Times* 29 January

Forster, A (2006a), *Armed Forces and Society in Europe* (Basingstoke: Palgrave)

Forster, A (2006b), 'Breaking the Military Covenant: Governance and the British army in the twenty-first century', *International Affairs* 82:6, 1043–57

Fox, R (2008), 'Hutton slashes defence spending across the forces', *Evening Standard* 11 December

Gee, D (2007), *Informed Choice: Armed Forces Recruitment Practice in the UK* (London: Joseph Rowntree Charitable Trust).

Gillan, A (2007), 'Commonwealth soldier sets up union for victims of racist attacks', *The Guardian* 8 March

Guthrie, C (2000), *Be on Guard and the Disabled Joining the Army – Speech by the Chief of the Defence Staff given at the Royal United Services Institute on 19 December* – http://www.knittingcircle.org.uk/armedservices.html# charles%20Guthrie

Hall, T (2007), *Review of Media Access to Personnel – Report by Tony Hall to the Ministry of Defence* – http://www.mod.uk/NR/rdonlyres/B6BBBA4B-02ED-45AC-84EF-A4AD4AB7DAA1/0/HallReport.pdf

Haltiner, K and Hirt, E (2000), 'Switzerland: Between Tradition and Modernity', in Moskos, C, Williams, J and Segal, D (eds), *The Post Modern Military: Armed Forces After the Cold War* (Oxford: Oxford University Press)

Harding, T (2006), 'Honesty of "a soldier's soldier" will lift morale, say Army officers', *The Daily Telegraph* 14 October

Harding, T (2008), 'Afghan casualty rate "at level of last war"', *The Daily Telegraph* 12 April

Hastings, M (2007), 'Our armed forces must now confront their greatest enemy: The MoD', *The Guardian* 30 April

Heaven, W (2008), 'Lord Guthrie attacks government for severe under-funding in defence sector', *Nouse.co.uk* 13 March

Hine, N (2008), 'Andrew Walker: The coroner the MoD couldn't gag', *The Times* 11 April

Holmes, R (2006), *Soldiers and Society – Speech by Professor Richard Holmes to the Liddell Hart Annual Lecture at King's College London on 10 May* (London: KCL)

House of Commons (2007), *Recruitment and Retention in the Armed Forces – Thirty Fourth Report by the Committee of Public Accounts Committee on 18 June 2007* (London: HMSO)

House of Commons (2008a), *Defence Equipment 2008: Tenth Report by the Defence Select Committee on 27 March 2008* (London: HMSO)

House of Commons (2008b), *Recruiting and Retaining Armed Forces Personnel: Eleventh Special Report detailing the Government response to the Committee's Fourteenth Report on 3 November 2008* (London: HMSO)

House of Commons (2008c) *Winter Supplementary Estimates 2008–09: First Report by the Defence Select Committee on 15 December 2008* (London: HMSO)

Independent, The (2000), 'Disabled people have every right to serve in the armed forces, Sir Charles', *The Independent* 21 December

Jackson, M (2006), *Defence of the Realm in the 21st Century – The Richard Dimbleby Lecture Speech on 7 December 2006* – http://www.bbc.co.uk/pressoffice/pressreleases/stories/2006/12_december/07/dimbleby.shtml

Jackson, M (2007a), *Soldier: The Autobiography* (Bantam: London).

Jackson, M (2007b), 'General Sir Mike Jackson: Last stand of the armchair general', *The Independent* 9 September

Kirkup, J (2008), 'Des Browne warns Afghanistan struggle will last a "generation"', *The Daily Telegraph* 18 July

Liberal Democrats (2007), *Our Nation's Duty – Proposals for Armed Forces Welfare* (London: Liberal Democrats).

Martin, I (2008), 'Britain's defence spending is a disgrace', *The Daily Telegraph* 22 February

Ministry of Defence (1998), *The Strategic Defence Review: Modern Forces for a Modern World* (London: HMSO)

Ministry of Defence (2000), *Soldiering – The Military Covenant* (London: HMSO)

Ministry of Defence (2006), 'MoD responds to Blake Review of trainee welfare', *Defence News* 13 June

Ministry of Defence (2007), *Contact with the Media and Communicating in Public – Defence Instructions and Notices* (London: HMSO)

Ministry of Defence (2008a), *UK Armed Forces Quarterly Manning Report* (London: HMSO)

Ministry of Defence (2008b), 'Forces manning issues being addressed – Twigg', *Defence News* 30 July

Mostrous, A and Macintyre, B (2009), 'British soldiers' victims of a mental conflict without end', *The Times* 28 March

Norton-Taylor, R (2006), 'Britain's new top soldier: "Can the military cope?" I say – just', *The Guardian* 4 September

Norton-Taylor, R (2008), 'MoD may halt surge in Commonwealth recruits to army', *The Guardian* 5 April

Norton-Taylor, R and Williams, R (2008), 'Snatch Land Rovers to be phased out from combat areas', *The Guardian* 17 December

Parris, M (2006), 'I agree with every word that Dannatt said. But he has got to be sacked', *The Times* 14 October

Rayment, S (2008), 'Army warned by own lawyers over ban on women serving in combat units', *The Daily Telegraph* 2 October

Rayment, S (2009), 'Disabled should be able to join armed forces', *The Daily Telegraph* 17 January

Ritchie, A (2006), 'The Army is a moral force. It's a force for good in the world. That's why people join', *The Daily Telegraph* 3 June

Royal British Legion (2008), 'Honour the Covenant' – www.britishlegion.org.uk

Salkeld, L (2009), 'Trevor Phillips in High Court battle against MoD for failing to protect human rights of soldiers on battlefield', *The Daily Mail* 9 March

Sands, S (2007), 'J'Accuse! Top General lambasts "moral cowardice" of government and military chiefs', *The Daily Mail* 13 April

Sengupta, K (2007), 'Ex-Navy chief "took private legal advice on Iraq"', *The Independent* 11 June

The Stationery Office (2008a), *Report of Inquiry into National Recognition of our Armed Forces.*(London: HMSO).

The Stationery Office (2008b), *The Nation's Commitment: Cross-Government Support to our Armed Forces, their Families and Veterans* (London: HMSO)

Wilson, J (2007), 'Editorial', *British Army Review* 142, 3–4

Chapter 10

The UK and Nuclear Weapons

Martin A Smith[1]

This chapter will examine the state and evolution of British nuclear weapon strategy and policy within a framework suggested by the concept of existential nuclear deterrence. This, it is contended here, offers a fruitful means of aiding our understanding as to why successive British governments – both Conservative and Labour – have decided to not only retain, but also update a strategic nuclear weapons capability in the years and decades since the ending of the Cold War.

In the first section, the main premises of existential deterrence thinking are outlined and discussed. Attention then turns to a brief examination of the evolution of the UK's nuclear posture during the Cold War years. It will be argued that, as this evolved, it came increasingly to be based on a recognisable existential foundation. It will subsequently be contended that this has substantially endured despite both changes of government in the UK and also the dramatic changes in the international strategic environment that have occurred since the late 1980s. With this in mind, the heart of the discussions in this chapter will focus on the extent and ways in which British nuclear policy has been affected by two seminal events: firstly, the ending of the Cold War in 1989–91 and secondly, the impact of the events of 11 September 2001. The latter ushered in a security environment in which the predominant threat was judged – at least by the Blair government in the UK – to come from international terrorism.

Existential Nuclear Deterrence

Following on from the above point, it should be borne in mind at the outset of the discussions here that the concept of existential nuclear deterrence was defined and developed during the Cold War years, with the focus on deterring *states* and not actors such as terrorists. The intellectual father of the concept was the late US presidential advisor McGeorge Bundy. His starting point was that nuclear weapons are recognised as being qualitatively different from all other weapon types and are treated with extreme caution by political and military leaders as a result. This

1   I would like to thank Nick Ritchie for his helpful and perceptive comments on an earlier draft of this chapter. The views expressed here are of course my own and should not be taken to represent the policy or views of the British government, Ministry of Defence or the Royal Military Academy Sandhurst.

applies just as much to those seeking to deter with nuclear weapons as to those that are supposed to be deterred.

In one of the earliest published outlines of his concept of existentialism in 1969, Bundy argued that:

> Think-tank analysts can set levels of 'acceptable' damage well up in the tens of millions of lives. They can assume that the loss of dozens of great cities is somehow a real choice for sane men. They are in an unreal world. In the real world of real political leaders – whether here [in the US] or in the Soviet Union – a decision that would bring even one hydrogen bomb on one city of one's own country would be recognised in advance as a catastrophic blunder; ten bombs on ten cities would be a disaster beyond history; and a hundred bombs on a hundred cities are unthinkable (Bundy, 1969, 10).

Deterrence, Bundy suggested, is thus an inherent property of nuclear weapons, given their unsurpassed destructive power and the consequent awe in which leaders and decision makers hold them. Their very existence in a state's arsenal is sufficient to deter potential aggressors – hence the term 'existential' deterrence. Deterrence need not depend on elaborate targeting plans, nor on force mixes or a virtually continuous process of force modernisation. Those seeking to deter do not have to convince a potential aggressor that they have firm plans to actually use nuclear weapons if attacked. The burden of proof lies with the would-be aggressor. It has to be certain that there is absolutely no prospect of nuclear retaliation. If nuclear weapons are present, complete certainty on this score is, by definition, impossible. Bundy summed up this strand of his argument in 1982: 'the certainty of this uncertainty is what deters the men of sanity on both sides' (Bundy, 1982, 26).

This proposition begs the question as to what might happen if an actor seeking to deter was to be confronted by an irrational opponent. Responding to this concern, Kenneth Waltz has argued that any decision to use nuclear weapons would almost certainly involve a significant number of political and military leaders, rather than a single individual. This would be likely to form an effective hedge against precipitate actions on the part of a single 'mad leader'. Waltz also argues that 'rulers like to continue to rule' and any supposition that they would risk even the remotest prospect of nuclear retaliation 'by questing militarily for uncertain gains is [therefore] fanciful' (Waltz, 1990, 737). Waltz, in common with the vast majority of nuclear theorists, assumed that the actors being deterred would be states. His logic might not of course apply in the case of terrorists in possession, for example, of a radiological or primitive nuclear device, although by no means all observers are convinced that terrorist groups are likely to be able to acquire such weapons.

In the existentialist view, the maintenance of adequate nuclear deterrence, particularly in a region where there are no overt or pressing threats, is relatively straightforward – indeed it has been called the 'easy' school of deterrence thought (Booth, 1991, 363–4). So long as some nuclear weapons are held by states in – or with an identified vital interest in – the region or issue in question, this should be sufficient to deter others from major aggression and thus help underpin strategic stability. Furthermore, because existential deterrence does not depend on the pre-targeting of specified potential aggressors, or the maintenance of Cold War numbers of missiles, bombs and warheads in the high hundreds or thousands, it should be relatively unproblematic politically to maintain *some* nuclear weapons, even in times when major overt threats are not generally evident. This could therefore be the case even when the UK government publicly asserts that the country faces no current threat from a hostile state or coalition of states. In the post-Cold War context, such confident assertions have been made by both the Blair and Brown governments. In Blair's case, the 1998 SDR stated clearly that 'there is today no direct military threat to the United Kingdom or Western Europe. Nor do we foresee the re-emergence of such a threat' (Ministry of Defence, 1998a, 5). Ten years later, the Brown government's National Security Strategy essentially repeated this: 'no state threatens the United Kingdom directly' (Cabinet Office, 2008, 3).

As Bundy evolved and refined his concept of existential deterrence during the Cold War years, it became clear that he was dubious about the core nuclear doctrine that underpinned the NATO alliance. This was based on 'extended' nuclear deterrence, which rested on the notion of the leading NATO power (the US) providing a nuclear guarantee of the security of its allies. In plain language, the US was committed – doctrinally at least – to using its nuclear weapons *in extremis* in response to an attack on an ally and thus exposing its own territory and population to the possibility of nuclear retaliation. Bundy was evidently particularly discomfited by the deployment of American nuclear weapons in Western Europe, which most European leaders viewed as an essential tangible demonstration of the strength of the US commitment to extended deterrence. In 1984, at the height of the great controversy over the prospective deployment of new medium range US missiles in Europe, he asserted that 'existential deterrence has been strong in every decade since 1945, and … it would still be strong if the entire plan for new medium-range missiles … were unilaterally cancelled by NATO tomorrow' (Bundy, 1984, 43). Whilst Bundy did accept that a conventional American military presence in Europe was an important underpinning to NATO, he never explicitly endorsed the specific deployment of US nuclear weapons there (Bundy, 1990, 598–602).

Those of an existentialist persuasion – including Bundy – were also at the forefront of calls for NATO to adopt a posture of no first use of nuclear weapons during the 1980s (Bundy et al., 1982). This call was based on the view that nuclear weapons should not be seen as having any operational military utility, apart from deterring the use of nuclear weapons by other state actors. They are essentially *political* instruments of deterrence. During the Cold War this view was perhaps most clearly expressed by former US Defense Secretary Robert McNamara – a colleague of McGeorge Bundy in the Kennedy administration. In 1983, McNamara wrote that:

> I do not believe we can avoid serious and unacceptable risk of nuclear war until we recognise – and until we base all our military plans, defense budgets, weapon

deployments, and arms negotiations on the recognition – that *nuclear weapons serve no military purpose whatsoever. They are totally useless – except only to deter one's opponent from using them.* This is my view today. It was my view in the early 1960s [emphasis in the original] (McNamara, 1983, 79).

As the intellectual founder of the nuclear existentialist movement, Bundy subscribed to the same basic view. In 1991, for example, he argued that: 'in the final analysis of strategy, politics and morals we are better off keeping this weapon unused except in deterrence of – and considered response to – a genuinely parallel ferocity by others' (Bundy, 1991, 86–7).

British Nuclear Policy and Strategy in the Cold War

The substantial literature that exists on the origins of British nuclear strategy and policy making since the Second World War suggests that these contained elements resembling the existentialist concept long before McGeorge Bundy began to develop his own ideas publicly. Margaret Gowing, author of the official history of the early years of the UK's nuclear weapons programme, reflected something of this in her summary of the Attlee government's motives for inaugurating this programme in 1947:

> This decision was not the result of careful strategic calculation but rather the reflex action of a still great power with great military commitments. The atomic bomb was the last word in weapons so Britain must have it, the more so since the only defence anyone could see against an enemy's bombs was the threat to retaliate in kind. At the time the decision was taken ... there was ... no real fear of war in the next decade at least, and the British government did not believe that Russia was necessarily a potential enemy. Moreover at the time the decision was taken it seemed enough simply to have a small supply of the primitive type of bomb dropped on Japan (Gowing, 1974, 209).

In a detailed study based on previously classified official documents, Ian Clark and Nicholas Wheeler have developed the argument that early British nuclear strategy was based on what subsequently came to be called a 'counterforce' approach. In other words, the targeting of the UK's nuclear weapons was primarily focused on Soviet military assets and forces (Clark and Wheeler, 1989). Such an approach would have been at variance with the ideas underpinning existential deterrence. John Baylis, however, has challenged the hypothesis of Clark and Wheeler and argued that British strategy was, at least to begin with, based on the notion of what is sometimes called 'deterrence through punishment'. This was based in turn on 'countervalue' targeting of major Soviet population centres, with the idea being to deter an attack by the credible threat of nuclear retaliation against assets of significant value to the Soviet state and society (Baylis, 1995, 87). Baylis does accept that there was an apparent shift towards counterforce targeting in the early 1950s – under the impetus of the RAF – but it is apparent from his analysis that this never became definitive or permanent (Baylis, 1995, 111).

In any event, from the second half of the 1950s, a clear shift towards a posture based on existentialist notions became evident. The catalyst for this seems to have been the advent of a strategic situation known at the time as the 'thermonuclear stalemate'. This followed the successful testing of variants of thermonuclear weapons by the US and the USSR and increasing acceptance of the view that neither side in the Cold War could realistically contemplate a disarming first strike on the other. In this situation therefore, the main – if not sole – purpose of continued possession of nuclear weapons was to deter a major attack and ensure underlying strategic stability. It may be recalled that Robert McNamara, who served as US Defense Secretary from 1961–68, later claimed that he adhered to this view throughout his time in office.

A brace of articles 'of some theoretical importance' (Groom, 1974, 232) in this context was published in *The Times* in October 1958. These set out one of the first public expositions in the UK of existential deterrence ideas, although the term itself was not used at the time. Instead, the paper's defence correspondent distinguished between 'active' and 'passive' nuclear deterrence. The former corresponded to what was subsequently called – in the NATO context – extended deterrence. This was criticised in *The Times* as having become 'incredible' in the age of thermonuclear stalemate (*The Times*, 1958a). In his second piece, the defence correspondent argued that passive deterrence from henceforth was the only viable nuclear strategy for the UK to follow.

The principles of passive deterrence as outlined in *The Times* in 1958 were strikingly similar to those of the existential deterrence which McGeorge Bundy began to publicly formulate a decade later. According to the former:

> The only point in having a nuclear deterrent … is to deter a direct attack. Deterrence of this kind is passive, in that the nuclear armoury deters simply by existing, and only a direct attack by the enemy can bring it into action. Passive deterrence is much simpler to achieve than active deterrence … Nor does it require the same standards of effectiveness as active deterrence. There is no need to guarantee the destruction of the enemy's war-making capability. The ability to inflict more damage than the enemy is willing to suffer is enough … there is no need for certainty, for the enemy cannot take risks if the penalty for miscalculation is thermonuclear destruction (*The Times*, 1958b).

Such ideas evidently were not confined to the commentariat. It is known from analysis of declassified official documents that comparable notions had been debated within government circles too (Baylis, 1995, 188–91, 220). In 1958, the notion of passive deterrence was also given an official imprimatur in the government's annual defence White Paper. This stated that 'there is … no military reason why a world conflagration should not be prevented for another generation or more through the balancing fears of mutual annihilation. In fact, there is no reason why all this should not go on almost indefinitely' (Ministry of Defence, 1958, 1).

The effective official approval of passive or existential deterrence was reflected in the progressive move away from interest in counterforce targeting from the mid-1950s. Instead, the focus was increasingly on developing the capacity to strike a (progressively smaller) number of major population centres in the USSR (Freedman, 1985; Baylis, 1995; Twigge and Macmillan, 1996, 270). Eventually this became focused on causing unacceptable damage to the Soviet capital and hence was widely known as the 'Moscow criterion'. Moves in this direction gathered pace during the 1960s, when Denis Healey was Secretary of State for Defence. Healey had devoted considerable thought to nuclear strategy and policy before coming to office and was basically sympathetic to passive deterrence thinking (Healey, 1989). As a politician he was, however, realistic enough to accept that Cold War realities rendered the maintenance of US extended deterrence through NATO a political necessity. He pithily expressed the central dilemma through a formulation which he termed 'the Healey Theorem'. In this formulation, it took 'only 5 percent credibility of American retaliation to deter the Russians, but 95 percent credibility to reassure the Europeans' (Healey, 1989, 243). Hence the political requirement for extended deterrence.

After 1962, the UK's strategic nuclear force at least nominally became a part of extended NATO deterrence too. As part of the deal that year, under which the Kennedy administration agreed to sell the British government the *Polaris* missile system, it had been agreed that the UK's strategic nuclear weapons would become part of NATO's (that is the US's) integrated nuclear operations plan. This was qualified however by inclusion in the agreement of a clause that enabled the British Prime Minister to use *Polaris* independently when supreme national interests were judged to be at stake. By the late 1960s, when *Polaris* entered service, the basic premises and parameters of the UK's nuclear posture had been formally and firmly established.

The argument developed here points to the conclusion that, once a situation of thermonuclear stalemate had been reached in the second half of the 1950s, the UK's nuclear strategy and policy effectively came to rest on the kind of ideas which were later formalised by McGeorge Bundy as the existential deterrence concept. The discussions in the sections which follow will consider whether this posture has essentially been maintained in the period since the ending of the Cold War.

British Nuclear Policy and Strategy Since the Cold War

The Major Government

Taking stock of the UK's nuclear posture in the first four years after the Cold War, Nicholas Witney, who was then a senior MoD official on secondment to the RAND Corporation in the US, argued that it had been characterised by 'a notable reluctance to embrace new policy or doctrinal innovation' (Witney, 1994–95, 96).

If that posture did indeed rest on basic existential deterrence assumptions, then this should not have been considered overly surprising or indeed concerning. As Bundy had suggested in developing the concept, if deterrence was an inherent product of the possession of nuclear weapons, then political or doctrinal reformulation was hardly necessary, even in response to dramatic changes in a strategic environment.

In reality, however, the situation during this period was not as marked by inertia as Witney's analysis suggested. There were two reasons for this. To begin with, the 1990s saw the progressive rolling out of the new *Trident* submarine fleet, to replace *Polaris* – a development which began under John Major and was completed under Tony Blair. The acquisition of this state of the art missile system and associated submarines seemed significantly at variance with the idea of the necessary minimum, as suggested by existential deterrence thinking. It was not a new departure however. A similar situation had pertained at the time of the acquisition of *Polaris* during the 1960s. The *Polaris* and *Trident* acquisitions can probably best be explained in substantial part by reference to Anglo-American relations and the tendency of successive British governments to view the UK's strategic nuclear weapons capability as an essential component of that bilateral relationship. This had been evident from the earliest days of official British interest in a nuclear weapons programme (Gowing, 1974). It has been argued in particular that British leaders and policy makers have seen the close nuclear links which have existed between the two states since the 1950s as an essential means of trying to secure some discernable UK leverage over the Americans' core military strategies (Baylis, 1995).

Existentialism Challenged?

A second important reason for casting doubt on Witney's assertion that the early 1990s were essentially characterised by policy inertia can be found in the Major government's interest in the question of a so called 'sub strategic' role for its new *Trident* system. This was first mooted in 1993 and the rationale for it was outlined in the following year's Defence White Paper:

> Trident was conceived as a replacement for our strategic nuclear capability. But the ability to undertake a massive nuclear strike is not enough to ensure deterrence. An aggressor might, in certain circumstances, gamble on a lack of will ultimately to resort to such a strike. We also need the capability to undertake nuclear action on a more limited scale in order to demonstrate our willingness to defend our vital interests to the utmost, and so induce a political decision to halt aggression without inevitably triggering strategic nuclear exchanges (Ministry of Defence, 1994, 19).

At first sight, this could be seen as a move towards adopting a limited nuclear use strategy, making the potential military use of nuclear weapons more likely. This was certainly how some of the government's critics chose to see the declaratory moves towards a sub strategic role for *Trident* (Rogers, 1996).

Given the importance of this issue, it is worth considering it in a little more detail here. Official statements of the time suggest that the government did *not* have in mind a move towards a more militarily usable nuclear strategy and it was at pains to stress this. One of the clearest statements to this effect had been made in November 1993 in a major address on the UK's nuclear posture by then Defence Secretary Malcolm Rifkind. Rifkind stated that:

> There is sometimes speculation that more so-called 'usable' nuclear weapons – very low-yield devices which could be used to carry out what are euphemistically called 'surgical' strikes – would allow nuclear deterrence to be effective in circumstances where existing weapons would be self-deterring. I am thoroughly opposed to this view. The implications of such a development of [a] new war-fighting role for nuclear weapons would be seriously damaging to our approach to maintaining stability in the European context, quite apart from the impact it would have on our efforts to encourage non-proliferation and greater confidence outside Europe. This is not a route that I would wish any nuclear power to go down (Rifkind, 1994, 29).

The shift to a sub strategic role for *Trident* was essentially a political move, albeit one probably induced partly by financial considerations. The government announced during 1993 the cancellation of a project to develop a short-range missile to replace the UK's only other extant nuclear system: air launched freefall bombs. This decision, paralleled by the announcement of the sub strategic *Trident* role, can be seen to have served three useful purposes at that time. Firstly, it enabled the government to cancel a new weapons programme and thus save money at a time when the defence budget was under severe pressure. Secondly, the government could claim political credit for taking a disarmament initiative, because the weapons systems the new short-range missile would have replaced were still going to be phased out. Finally, the government could make an attempt to provide a more appropriate justification for its new *Trident* system in an era of 'smaller' threats.

An essentially political rationale can be inferred from a closer examination of the text of the 1994 Defence White Paper. It may be recalled that this stated that 'we ... need the capability to undertake nuclear action on a more limited scale in order to *demonstrate our willingness* to defend our vital interests to the utmost, and so *induce a political decision to halt aggression without inevitably triggering strategic nuclear exchanges*' [emphasis added]. The highlighted portions of this statement suggest that the government's thinking was focused on the UK considering at most a capacity to threaten a nuclear demonstration strike – or put more colloquially, fire a warning shot – in order to persuade a potential aggressor to cease and desist before it became necessary to consider employing nuclear weapons more widely.

The idea of nuclear weapons as an 'essentially political' instrument had found favour in official circles in NATO in the late 1980s (Smith, 2000, 43). Contemporary British government statements closely paralleled agreed NATO positions on this issue (Rogers, 1996, 8–9). In the strategic context of the time, this emphasis was judged necessary by Western governments as a means of decoupling NATO's nuclear weapons from a traditional Cold War emphasis on them being necessary in substantial part to compensate for imbalances in conventional forces between NATO and the Warsaw Pact. Once Soviet leader Mikhail Gorbachev had signalled his willingness to contemplate substantial reductions in Soviet conventional forces, this rationale became increasingly tenuous. The position adopted in the late 1980s remains essentially the NATO position today – that the much reduced residual stockpiles of US nuclear bombs in Western Europe are necessary to ensure that there are no circumstances in which a potential aggressor could be certain that an act of aggression against a NATO member state would not invoke a nuclear response. Thus the emphasis is very much on deterrence rather than potential nuclear war fighting.

The view that, far from contemplating usable nuclear options, the Major government in the early 1990s in fact envisaged the UK's nuclear capability as being essentially a political means of last resort deterrence is actually reinforced by considering its hardware decisions. The Major government made a series of decisions to phase out the UK's existing operational sub strategic nuclear capability. This had consisted of nuclear tipped artillery shells, various naval systems and the freefall bombs for the RAF. Taken together, these decisions ensured that, by the time Tony Blair's Labour government came to power in May 1997, *Trident* would effectively be the UK's sole extant nuclear weapons capability. Complementing this, government Ministers stressed the limited and essentially non operational role which their strategic thinking accorded to the UK's residual nuclear capability. This was especially apparent in statements made by Malcolm Rifkind, the minister who appeared to give most thought to the matter, at least in public. Rifkind's statements suggested that nuclear deterrence only really had a continuing role in the European context, in contributing to the strategic stability necessary to ensure that Russia and the other post-Soviet states could be successfully integrated into an emerging post-Cold War security order (Rifkind, 1994, 25–30; Witney, 1994–95, 103).

In Nicholas Witney's view, the official reticence about the extension of British nuclear deterrence outside of the European context reflected official concerns about the burgeoning threat of nuclear proliferation:

> Reluctance to redefine the point and purpose of the UK deterrent by reference to all-too-palpable new threats emerging in the post-Cold War world might seem almost perverse. But it was probably rendered inevitable by the mutual reinforcement of intellectual honesty and political calculation – the latter turning on the importance of denying any proliferators the chance to argue that if the British were entitled to nuclear weapons to face new regional threats then so, too, should it be (Witney, 1994–95, 103–4).

In summary, it may be said that perceptions of an apparent move away from an essentially existentialist concept of the utility of British nuclear weapons during the early post-Cold War years are not really sustainable on closer examination. As discussed here, the Major government's 'sub strategic' idea was much more of a political construct than an operational one. This impression is reinforced when it is noted that this government also took the decision to cancel a proposed tactical air to surface nuclear tipped missile. This would, if deployed, have offered a more militarily credible – and therefore potentially usable – sub strategic option than the plainly strategic *Trident* system (notwithstanding government protestations to the contrary). The existential underpinnings of the UK's nuclear posture thus remained effectively in place when the Blair government came to power in 1997.

The Blair and Brown Governments

Much political fanfare attended the New Labour government's SDR of 1997–98. It was announced as a root and branch review of all aspects of British defence policy which, unlike previous efforts, would be both foreign policy (rather than Treasury) driven and significantly more open and consultative. With specific regard to the UK's nuclear posture, there are grounds for doubting whether the SDR lived up to its 'root and branch' billing. The published review documents trumpeted an allegedly 'rigorous re-examination of our deterrence requirements' (Ministry of Defence, 1998a 17). However, the future of *Trident* was specifically off limits as a subject of genuine questioning and debate (McInnes, 1998, 831). This would account for the fact that many of the 'changes' announced in the SDR were essentially cosmetic and simply continued the process of nuclear build down initiated by the previous government.

Indeed, the charges of inertia laid at the door of the Major government by Nicholas Witney could have been directed more fairly at its successor. Much was made, for example, of the announcement of lower warhead requirements for *Trident* under the new government (Ministry of Defence, 1998a 18–19). Yet, even a sympathetic observer such as Malcolm Chalmers noted that 'because the production programme was not completed, implementation of the SDR will not require the decommissioning of any warheads' (Chalmers, 1999 64). More significant changes, such as taking warheads off the *Trident* missiles and storing them separately or ending the requirement to have at least one submarine on patrol at all times, were explicitly rejected (Ministry of Defence, 1998b, 5). The notion of a sub strategic role for *Trident* was retained (Ministry of Defence, 1998a, 18), in spite of the fact that this appeared no more credible to many than under the previous government.

It is not difficult to work out one important reason for the official reluctance to expose the UK's nuclear posture to a more searching review. The Labour Party had been woundingly defeated in two successive general elections – in 1983 and 1987 – in large part because of its then commitment to pursuing a policy of unilateral nuclear disarmament if elected. Most of the party's leadership in 1997 had lived through those barren times and politically, therefore, felt that they had every incentive to ensure that the issue of British nuclear weapons was not reopened as a subject of serious debate and discussion.

This party political requirement was not the only – or even the decisive – factor however and it can be argued that *any* incoming government would probably have maintained the existing basis of the UK's nuclear posture in any event. In analysis bearing a clear existential hallmark, retired naval commodore Tim Hare argued that the policy outlined in the SDR made clear that 'the role of nuclear weapons is fundamentally political and ... therefore any rationale for their retention is political. The UK does not possess nuclear weapons as part of the military inventory, they have no function as warfighting weapons or to achieve lesser military objectives' (Hare, 2005, 30). Hare's views are of interest here because he served as the MoD's Director of Nuclear Policy from 1999–2002. In this role, he was responsible for overseeing the nuclear element of the new government's defence policy.

There were a number of important public statements from the Blair and Brown governments stressing essential continuity in nuclear posture and policy. In a January 2007 address, for example, then Defence Secretary Des Browne referred back to Malcolm Rifkind's 1993 speech, discussed earlier, and noted that he was 'struck by the continuity of approach' between the government of John Major and that of Tony Blair, of which he was a part (Browne, 2007). In the previous month, the Blair government had published a White Paper outlining its intention to proceed towards a new submarine launched ballistic missile system to eventually replace *Trident*. This paper argued that 'the fundamental principles relevant to nuclear deterrence have not changed since the end of the Cold War and are unlikely to change in future'. The government's basic stated rationale in this paper was – again – existentialist:

> Nuclear weapons pose a uniquely terrible threat and consequently have a capability to deter acts of aggression that is of a completely different scale to any other form of deterrence. Nuclear weapons remain a necessary element of the capability we need to deter threats from others possessing nuclear weapons (Ministry of Defence, 2006, 17).

Both reflecting and reinforcing these political statements about the role of nuclear weapons, current British defence doctrine distinguishes clearly between 'deterrence' and 'coercion', although it accepts that the two approaches are closely related and can be complementary. The doctrine also makes clear that the UK's nuclear capability is a deterrent rather than coercive force. It states that:

> Deterrence is at the heart of UK Defence Policy; its purpose at all levels of warfare is to dissuade a potential opponent from adopting a course of action that threatens national interests ... The British Armed Forces in their entirety serve to deter, with strategic deterrence ultimately underpinned by a nuclear capability. Deployable nuclear weapons provide an effective means of deterring other states' use of the most destructive weapons and indicate absolute national resolve (Development, Concepts and Doctrine Centre, 2008, 1–12).

Strategic uncertainty is also highlighted in the defence doctrine as a positive asset in influencing a potential aggressor's calculations:

> Whereas the purpose of deterrence is to dissuade an opponent from taking a course of action, coercion induces behaviour that he would not otherwise choose. In reality, it is useful that a potential opponent cannot easily distinguish between deterrence and coercion; most situations are likely to require a combination of the threat of force, reassurance and encouragement to prevent undesirable consequences and to induce desirable behaviour in an adversary (Development, Concepts and Doctrine Centre, 2008, 1–12, 1–13).

It is also apparent that nuclear weapons are not envisaged as being the only deterrence asset in the UK's armoury. As quoted above, the country's armed forces 'in their entirety' are viewed in deterrence terms. Moreover, the military instrument is viewed as being just one of three component parts of UK 'national power'. The others are diplomacy and the economic instrument (Development, Concepts and Doctrine Centre, 2008, 1–4, 1–6). In this context, Sir Michael Quinlan, former Permanent Secretary at the MoD, told the House of Commons Select Committee on Defence in March 2006 that:

> Deterrence is an extremely broad concept. It refers to a whole range of instruments, some of which may not even be military. We may be trying to discourage Iran by economic or political pressure, for example. That is deterrence. I never liked the phrase 'the deterrent', as though it meant just this [nuclear weapons]. This is one of many instruments (House of Commons, 2006).

Existentialism Challenged Again?

Notwithstanding what has been argued above, at times during the period following the 11 September terrorist attacks on the US it appeared as if British nuclear policy was being reformulated in the direction of contemplating more usable nuclear options, as part of a full spectrum of possible responses to terrorist and terrorist related threats The MoD's first post-11 September White Paper, published in July 2002, could be read as opening the door to the possible limited use of nuclear weapons as one part of a package of responses. It stated that:

> The UK's nuclear weapons have a continuing use as a means of deterring major strategic military threats, and they have a continuing role in guaranteeing the ultimate security of the UK. But we also want it to be clear, particularly to the leaders of states of concern and terrorist organisations, that all our forces play a part in deterrence and that we have a broad range of responses available. We must influence leaderships by showing that we are prepared to take all necessary measures to defend ourselves. Where necessary, military and other action will be taken to disrupt the political, economic, military and technical means by

which aggression is pursued. We want it to be clear that the UK, along with our partners, can reach into the way they operate, and that they could lose their power, and see their organisations closed down ... the only certainty we should offer is that we shall respond appropriately if we need to, using any of the wide range of options open to us (Ministry of Defence, 2002, 12).

Four years later, the Blair government's White Paper on the *Trident* follow on presented three rationales for the retention of a British nuclear capability under the general heading of 'insuring against an uncertain future'. The first of these envisaged the UK retaining nuclear weapons as a hedge against the possible re-emergence of a major hostile state with a nuclear capability of its own. This fitted fairly comfortably within existentialist thinking. The second focused on 'emerging nuclear states' and it was suggested that a continuing British nuclear weapons capability would help to ensure that 'we cannot be subjected in future to nuclear blackmail or a level of threat which would put at risk our vital interests or fundamentally constrain our foreign and security policy options'. The third and final rationale was focused on 'state-sponsored terrorism'. In this context, the White Paper stated that British nuclear weapons 'should influence the decision-making of any state that might consider transferring nuclear weapons or nuclear technology to terrorists' (Ministry of Defence, 2006, 18–19).

These last two suggested that the rationalisation for the UK's nuclear capability that had been attempted was not solely on the basis of the existentialist premise that nuclear weapons should exist to deter the possible use of their own kind by other nuclear armed states. In the 2006 White Paper, it seemed to be clearly suggested that the UK's nuclear capability might have a role to play when 'vital interests' or important 'foreign and security policy options' were perceived to be at risk more generally. This sounded like active rather than passive deterrence. It also seemed to open the door to the maintenance of an extended deterrence posture for the UK, a posture which existentialists have often been dubious about.

In this context, it is worth recalling that British strategic nuclear forces have been designated as a part of NATO extended deterrence since the early 1960s. Since the end of the Cold War, not only has this commitment been formally maintained, but, on occasion, it has also been played up. In February 2009, for example, the FCO released a discussion document which stated that:

> Including states which come under a 'nuclear umbrella', such as NATO allies, well over half of the world's population is covered by a nuclear deterrent. The impression that only a small minority benefit from nuclear weapons is misleading (Foreign and Commonwealth Office, 2009, 5).

Elsewhere the report claimed that:

> One of the most effective ways of persuading a state that it does not need to acquire nuclear weapons has been to ensure that it does not face threats which it feels

could only be deterred by possession of its own nuclear weapons. A key means of doing so is termed 'extended deterrence'. This involves the extension of nuclear deterrence to some Non–Nuclear Weapons States such as South Korea, Japan, Australia and NATO allies (Foreign and Commonwealth Office, 2009, 11).

On the other hand, British planning assumptions have apparently remained based on the premise that 'the UK must have the ability to destroy key Russian centres of military and political power, many of which are located in and around Moscow' (Chalmers, 1999, 64). There is little evidence to suggest that any detailed planning and targeting strategies have been developed for other possible contingencies around the world. At first sight, the continuing focus on Russia might seem rather bizarre, especially in the context of the late 1990s and the SDR. UK and Western policy was then very supportive of the Yeltsin government in Russia. That country was, in any event, in a severely weakened condition and was thus unlikely to militarily threaten any other major state. Deterring a reviving Russia might in fairness seem somewhat more credible in light of Russian nuclear threats made after the conflict with Georgia in August 2008 (*The Times*, 2008). Some, such as Colin Gray, were indeed arguing for this even before that crisis erupted (House of Commons, 2006). Thus far, this position has remained the preserve of a minority, and the mainstream view of Russia's military strength sees it as still bearing the characteristics of a 'paper tiger' (International Institute for Strategic Studies, 2009, 207–16; *The Times*, 2009).

British governments' continuing focus on Russia deep into the post-Cold War era becomes more understandable if the policy is viewed as deterrence planning based on the worst possible case. If the UK remains able to credibly threaten unacceptable damage to a potential adversary of Russia's size (measured both in geographical terms and the size of Russia's nuclear holdings), then logic suggests it could do so against any lesser state. This helps to explain the consistent refusal of all British governments since the end of the Cold War to consider measures such as ending continuous at sea deterrence patrols or separating missiles from their nuclear warheads. It also explains why, in 2006, the Blair government attempted to sweeten the pill for opponents of its decision to proceed with a follow on to *Trident* by announcing a cut in the UK's warhead stockpile – but only from about 200 to about 160 (Ministry of Defence, 2006, 8). This remains substantially in excess of the number of nuclear weapons which many existentialists consider necessary to maintain adequate minimum deterrence. Even in the late Cold War context, Robert McNamara was arguing that NATO and the Warsaw Pact *collectively* would require no more than 500 nuclear warheads each to ensure adequate deterrence and 'very possibly it would be far less, perhaps in the tens' (McNamara, 1989, 177).

All told, it is noteworthy what little impact the events of 11 September seem to have had on the UK's nuclear policy and posture. These have remained state based and the planning template has continued to be Russia. The impression of continuity – indeed perhaps inertia – which surrounded them in the early Blair years has been noted earlier. Even the shock of 11 September does not seem to have jolted things. The Blair government continued to take pains to distance itself from any impression that it wished to change the UK's established nuclear posture and to enhance potential usability options. In October 2005, for example, in a statement much quoted by the British anti nuclear lobby, the Prime Minister publicly averred that 'I do not think that anyone pretends that the independent nuclear deterrent is a defence against terrorism' (House of Commons, 2005). The 2006 Defence White Paper on the *Trident* follow on did, as noted, argue that British nuclear weapons could deter potential state sponsors of terrorism. This can be seen as primarily a political rather than operational formulation, designed to justify the decision for the UK to remain a nuclear weapons state in the foreseeable future. In its overview the 2006 White Paper accurately asserted, as noted earlier, that the 'fundamental principles' of nuclear deterrence were – as far as the government was concerned – unaltered since the end of the Cold War. For the Blair and Brown governments, the events of 11 September reinforced the perception that the international security arena was characterised above all else by – as McGeorge Bundy might put it – the certainty of uncertainty.

There was one significant change in the British nuclear posture under New Labour. In his January 2007 speech, Des Browne announced that the government had formally abandoned the notion of a sub strategic role for *Trident*, which it had inherited from the Major government in 1997 and maintained hitherto. Browne declared that 'our weapons [are not] intended or designed for military use during conflict. Indeed, we have deliberately chosen to stop using the term "sub–strategic Trident", applied previously to a possible limited use of our weapons' (Browne, 2007). This statement moved British declaratory policy in an existential direction in the sense that it suggested that from henceforth the UK's nuclear weapons would serve a sole function as a last resort deterrent, focused on deterring their own kind. The 2009 Foreign Office discussion paper was clear in asserting that 'the UK believes that the use of any nuclear weapon would be strategic in nature and has consequently stopped using the terms 'sub-strategic', 'tactical', 'non-strategic' or 'battlefield' nuclear weapon' (Foreign and Commonwealth Office, 2009, 28).

On the matter of extended deterrence, McGeorge Bundy was, as noted, uncomfortable with this notion in the Cold War context. This therefore raises a valid question about the extent to which the British nuclear posture can be judged to be significantly existential so long as it embraces an extended deterrence element. However, it can be argued that, although the formal assigning of *Polaris* and *Trident* to NATO has been maintained since the Cold War's end, the actual prospect of nuclear use in response to an attack on a NATO ally has receded substantially, notwithstanding periodic deteriorations in relations with Russia. Despite speculative formulations about the possible utility of nuclear weapons in deterring or threatening rogue states or terrorists (including in the 2006 Defence White Paper), it is worth recalling that, on the one occasion to date when NATO members agreed to invoke the organisation's Article Five mutual defence clause, there was no serious discussion about nuclear weapons playing any role in the response. The occasion was of course in reaction to the terrorist attacks of 11 September 2001.

Taking these considerations into account – and also the Blair and Brown governments' public and clear hedging about the circumstances in which the UK's nuclear weapons might actually be used – it can fairly be concluded that, *de facto*, the UK's nuclear capability continued to rest on essentially – though not perfect – existentialist premises. It is instructive here to briefly consider a key difference between the UK's nuclear posture and that of France. During the Chirac era there had been a number of statements from or on behalf of the President to the effect that French strategy and policy should allow for the possibility of nuclear use against 'rogue' states threatening to use chemical or biological weapons (Independent, 2003; *The Times*, 2003). Chirac's successor, Nicolas Sarkozy, did not alter this basic premise and was notably hawkish in his statements about the possibility of Iran acquiring a nuclear weapons capability (*The Times*, 2007). France, unlike the UK, has maintained a nuclear 'dyad' consisting not only of a submarine launched ballistic missile fleet akin to *Trident*, but also shorter range air to surface missiles, more obviously suited to a sub strategic (or 'pre strategic' in French parlance) role. Although post-11 September official rhetoric sometimes suggested an interest in limited nuclear use options, the UK has developed no capability comparable to the latter. This hardware divergence reflects, as John Simpson has astutely noted, the position that 'while the UK seems content to have a military *deterrent capability*, France continues to seek a *deterrent relationship* with potentially hostile states by seeking to elucidate how its forces would be used, even if only in generic terms' [emphasis in the original] (Simpson, 2004, 150). A crucial difference in the histories of the British and French nuclear weapons capabilities helps to explain this enduring and important conceptual divergence and thus also helps us to understand why the UK has maintained a markedly more existential posture than France.

The key difference has been the UK's nuclear 'special relationship' with the US, which has endured in its current form since 1962. The UK's role as junior partner in this unique *de facto* nuclear alliance has freed it from a perceived political or military requirement to develop an all–embracing nuclear capability of its own. During the Cold War, France maintained capabilities in all three legs of the strategic nuclear 'triad' – submarine launched missiles, land based missiles and long range nuclear capable strike aircraft. The UK, on the other hand, effectively maintained just one strategic system: first the V-Bomber force in the 1950s, then *Polaris* and then *Trident*. Its other nuclear weapons systems were essentially tactical in the Cold War context.

The historical record suggests that states that choose to maintain a multifaceted strategic nuclear capability are more likely to justify and underpin it on the basis of counterforce notions about nuclear use. Counterforce came to be associated during the Cold War years with the view that nuclear weapons had a potential operational utility and were not essentially a last resort deterrent. Earlier discussions in this chapter suggested that, but for a relatively brief period in the 1950s, counterforce ideas have never taken a firm or enduring hold on official British thinking about nuclear weapons. Notwithstanding some initial suggestions of new thinking in this regard under the impetus of the events of 11 September, this has not had sufficient discernable impact on actual policy to allow the conclusion to be drawn that the traditional existential basis of the UK's nuclear weapons capability has been significantly changed or eroded.

Considerations of political expediency have also been important. This has been most especially the case since the demise of the Soviet Union and Warsaw Pact in 1989–91 removed the traditional rationale for the development and maintenance of British nuclear weapons. Maintaining a deterrent posture based upon the existentialist 'certainty of uncertainty' is a politically essential means of ensuring that it is likely to endure. As noted earlier, both the Blair and Brown governments averred publicly that the UK faced no direct security threat from other states. Yet, the doctrinal premises of British nuclear policy remained state based. Both governments thus played up arguments about strategic uncertainty. Ken Booth tells us why:

> Retaining nuclear weapons as a hedge against uncertainty is a powerful argument – and a very convenient one. As a rationale for nuclear weapons, 'uncertainty' is timeless in a way the Soviet Union was not; this rationale offers a permanent case for retention, one that transcends the threat posed by any particular enemy (Booth and Barnaby, 2006, 79).

Conclusion

The overall conclusion suggested by the analysis in this chapter is that the existential deterrence premises upon which the UK's nuclear posture has rested since at least the late 1950s have given it a marked stability and have also proved enduring. These characteristics have spanned the Cold War and the period of Conservative government from 1991–97, as well as the Blair and Brown eras. In the post-Cold War period, there have been, as noted, two occasions when the existentialist underpinnings of UK nuclear policy and posture appeared to be under challenge. On both occasions however, declaratory or political adjustments did not result in significant changes to the underlying substance. During their period in opposition from 1997, Shadow Defence Ministers from the Conservative Party gave no real indication of deviating seriously from arguments favouring the retention of a British nuclear weapons capability based on the existentialist premise of a last resort deterrent hedge against current and future uncertainty (Fox, 2006; Lewis, 2006). It is therefore unlikely that the next change of government will usher in any significant re-evaluation of nuclear policy and doctrine. All things considered therefore, the situation at the time of writing bears comparison with that described in the Defence White Paper of 1958. To paraphrase that document, the UK's nuclear deterrent posture and policy have demonstrated essential long term stability. And there seems to be no reason why this should not go on almost indefinitely.

Bibliography

Baylis, J (1995), *Ambiguity and Deterrence – British Nuclear Strategy 1945–1964* (Oxford: Clarendon Press)

Booth, K (1991), 'War, Security and Strategy: Towards a Doctrine for Stable Peace', in Booth, K (ed.), *New Thinking about Strategy and International Security* (London: Harper Collins Academic)

Booth, K and Barnaby, F (eds) (2006), *The Future of Britain's Nuclear Weapons – Experts Reframe the Debate* (Oxford: Oxford Research Group).

Browne, D (2007), *The United Kingdom's Nuclear Deterrent in the 21st Century – Speech by the Defence Secretary on 25 January* – http://www.mod. uk/DefenceInternet/AboutDefence/People/Speeches/SofS/20070125The UnitedKingdomsNuclearDeterrentInThe21stCentury.htm

Bundy, McG (1969), 'To Cap the Volcano', *Foreign Affairs* 48/1, 1–20

Bundy, McG (1982), 'America in the 1980s: Reframing Relations with our Friends and Among our Allies', *Survival* 24/1, 24–8

Bundy, McG (1984), 'The Unimpressive Record of Atomic Diplomacy', in Prins, G (ed.), *The Choice – Nuclear Weapons Versus Security* (London: Chatto and Windus)

Bundy, McG (1990), *Danger and Survival – Choices about the Bomb in the First Fifty Years* (New York: Vintage)

Bundy, McG (1991), 'Nuclear Weapons and the Gulf', *Foreign Affairs* 70/4, 8–94

Bundy, McG, Kennan, GF, McNamara, RS and Smith G (1982), 'Nuclear Weapons and the Atlantic Alliance', *Foreign Affairs* 60/4, 753–68

Cabinet Office (2008), *The National Security Strategy of the United Kingdom: Security in an Interdependent World* (London: HMSO)

Chalmers, M (1999), '"Bombs Away"? Britain and Nuclear Weapons under New Labour', *Security Dialogue* 30/1, 61–74

Clark, I and Wheeler, N (1989), *The British Origins of Nuclear Strategy 1945–1955* (Oxford: Clarendon Press)

Development, Concepts and Doctrine Centre (2008), *British Defence Doctrine: Third Edition JP 0-01* (Shrivenham: Development, Concepts and Doctrine Centre)

Foreign and Commonwealth Office (2009), *Lifting the Nuclear Shadow: Creating the Conditions for Abolishing Nuclear Weapons* (London: HMSO)

House of Commons (2005), *Official Report of the debate in the House of Commons 19 October 2005* (London: HMSO)

House of Commons (2006), *The Future of the UK's Strategic Nuclear Deterrent – the Strategic Context. Eighth Report by the Defence Select Committee on 20 June* (London: HMSO)

Fox, L (2006), 'Is There a Sound Political Rationale for the UK Retaining its Nuclear Weapons?' in Booth, K and Barnaby, F (eds), *The Future of Britain's Nuclear Weapons* (Oxford: Oxford Research Group)

Freedman, L (1985), 'British Nuclear Targeting', *Defense Analysis* 1/2, 81–99

Gowing, M (1974), *Independence and Deterrence – Britain and Atomic Energy 1945–1952. Volume 1: Policy Making* (Basingstoke: Macmillan)

Groom, AJR (1974), *British Thinking About Nuclear Weapons* (London: Frances Pinter)

Hare, T (2005), 'What Next for Trident?', *RUSI Journal* 150/2

Healey, D (1989), *The Time of My Life* (London: Penguin)

Independent, The (1993), 'Scaled-down Trident to Replace New Missile', *The Independent* 15 April

Independent, The (2003), 'France May Allow "First Strikes" on Rogue States in Policy Shift', *The Independent* 28 October

International Institute for Strategic Studies (2009), *The Military Balance 2009* (London: Routledge/IISS)

Lewis, J (2006), 'Can the Retention of British Nuclear Weapons be Justified Ethically in Today's World?', in Booth, K and Barnaby, F (eds), *The Future of Britain's Nuclear Weapons* (Oxford: Oxford Research Group)

McInnes, C (1998), 'Labour's Strategic Defence Review', *International Affairs* 74/4

McNamara, R (1983), 'The Military Role of Nuclear Weapons: Perceptions and Misperceptions', *Foreign Affairs* 62/1, 59–80

McNamara, R (1989), *Out of the Cold* (New York: Simon and Schuster)

Ministry of Defence (1958), *Britain's Contribution to Peace and Security: Defence White Paper* (London: HMSO)

Ministry of Defence (1994), *Statement on the Defence Estimates 1994: Defence White Paper* (London: HMSO)

Ministry of Defence (1998a), *The Strategic Defence Review: Modern Forces for a Modern World* (London: HMSO)

Ministry of Defence (1998b), *The Strategic Defence Review – Supporting Essays* (London: HMSO)

Ministry of Defence (2002), *The Strategic Defence Review – A New Chapter* (London: HMSO)

Ministry of Defence (2006), *The Future of the United Kingdom's Nuclear Deterrent: Defence White Paper* (London: HMSO)

Rifkind, M (1994), 'The Role of Nuclear Weapons in UK Defence Strategy', *Brassey's Defence Yearbook 1994* (London: Brassey's)

Rogers, P (1996), *Sub-Strategic Trident – A Slow Burning Fuse* (London: Brassey's/Centre for Defence Studies)

Simpson, J (2004), 'France, the United Kingdom and Deterrence in the Twenty-first Century', *Contemporary Security Policy* 25/1, 136–51

Smith, MA (2000), *NATO in the First Decade after the Cold War* (Dordrecht: Kluwer Academic)

Times, The (1958a), 'Thermonuclear Stalemate', *The Times* 15 October

Times, The (1958b), 'The Necessary Minimum', *The Times* 16 October

Times, The (2003), 'Chirac Sets New Terms for Nuclear Weapon Use', *The Times* 28 October

Times, The (2007), 'Sarkozy Talks of Bombing if Iran Gets Nuclear Arms', *The Times* 28 August

Times, The (2008), 'Russia in Nuclear Threat to Poland', *The Times* 16 August

Times, The (2009), 'Why a Mighty Military is Now Just a "Paper Tiger"', *The Times* 28 January

Twigge, S and Macmillan, A (1996), 'Britain, the United States, and the Development of NATO Strategy 1950–1964', *Journal of Strategic Studies* 19/2, 260–81

Waltz, K (1990), 'Nuclear Myths and Political Realities', *American Political Science Review* 84/3, 24–8

Witney, N (1994–95), 'British Nuclear Policy after the Cold War', *Survival* 36/4, 96–112

Chapter 11

An Instrument of Honour?
Britain's Military Strategy and the
Impact of New Technologies

Michael Codner

The UK government under New Labour has faced perceived strategic challenges that can be roughly grouped into three periods. In the first, beginning in 1997, the primary issues were instability in Eastern Europe following the end of the Cold War, uncertainty as to outcomes and the problems of a trans-Atlantic approach to engagement in the former Yugoslavia. NATO's future was particularly unsure and the UK's dilemma was the need to continue a close military association with the US while building its status in an expanding EU, where defence was regarded as a 'strong suit'. The St Malo Accord was something of a triumph for Tony Blair in this respect. The June 1999 outcome of the Kosovo War was a surprising success at the time and one that, to some extent, confirmed an expeditionary role for NATO, albeit exposing vast inadequacies in execution. The second period began when George W. Bush came into power, bringing in an administration characterised by unilateralism and a belief that the military instrument could directly shape the security environment. The terrorist attacks on the US of 11 September 2001 were a defining event, following which Britain led the international community in supporting the so-called 'Global War on Terror' and in committing to fight alongside the US in the wars in Afghanistan and Iraq. The third period – following the successful overthrow of Saddam Hussein in 2003 – is one of military embroilment in the consequences of enforced regime change in Afghanistan and Iraq, as the principal supporter of the US. The problems of occupation, stabilisation and counter-insurgency have been of a different order to the 'wider peacekeeping' challenges of the former Yugoslavia and the comparatively elegant interventions, in retrospect at least, in Sierra Leone and East Timor.

The significance of military technology has also changed throughout this period. In the latter part of the Cold War, the emphasis was on dominating the Soviet Union in a technology race which is described later in this chapter. Since the end of the Cold War, the extreme aspects of technological competition have dwindled for the UK, although it has needed the information and communications technology to hang onto the coat tails of the US. At the same time, there has been a perceived need for Britain to retain and develop sufficient assured access to technology to maintain operational autonomy. Advanced technology was one element of the 'operational sovereignty' issue addressed among others in the 2005 Defence Industrial Strategy (DIS) (Ministry of Defence, 2005). Finally, there is the need for specific technologies to counter irregular operations and to cope with the weapons of insurgents and terrorists in difficult environments, such as built-up areas, as has been most prevalent in the third phase.

Technology as an Instrument of Power

There are several aspects to the relationship between technology and military strategy. One must, of course, understand the use of the military instrument in the context of security more generally, alongside the other instruments of a state security and indeed that of an alliance or coalition. Classically, these instruments are defined as economic, diplomatic, and military. More recently, 'information' has been identified in some doctrinal analyses as an instrument in itself. For example, US military doctrine employs the DIME (diplomatic, informational, military and economic) analysis of instruments of power. In this chapter, the author accepts the proposition, which is not new, that technology in the widest sense should also be considered as a discrete category of power in itself. It can furnish economic capacity as well as military capability. It can contribute to security by enhancing human well-being, as well as destructive power. And it can assist in protecting against non-human threats to security, such as natural disasters, resource shortages and disease. Access to technology and control of critical technologies, through ownership and limits to proliferation, should be a fundamental element of any security strategy.

There are two facets to the relationship between the military instrument and technology. First, technology is a principal contributor to military threats. Indeed, in developing military concepts for the future, technological trends are among the more predictable features of the future security environment. At the time of writing, there is considerable uncertainty as to the future global economic condition and with regard to political change. However, there can be more confidence in predictions of the development of advanced technologies. The second facet is technology as a military enabler. Technological development has a symbiotic relationship with operational concepts, in that it can, on the one hand, provide the solutions to capability needs or open the door for new concepts, which can, in turn, generate new capability needs. And, because the defining feature of the military instrument is the ability to dominate in the organised use of violence, there is still an inherent competition in access to military and dual-use technologies and their control and exploitation.

Technological Competition

The issue of technological competition had its heyday in the Cold War. Its relationship to the economic instrument was expressed most clearly in the US'

Competitive Strategies Initiative (CSI) in the 1980s, conceived to force the Soviet Union into a technology race that would destroy its economy (Weinberger, 1987). The UK was, of course, a relatively minor player in this. However, capabilities such as submarine detection by sonar and underwater weaponry were very important to specific UK contributions in anti-submarine warfare and to the survivability of the independent nuclear deterrent. Although anti-submarine warfare has been a low priority since the end of the Cold War, sea control expressed as safe access to safe waters is as important as ever to nuclear deterrence.

While the US has continued to pursue technological dominance, it has been less important for medium Western powers in the recent past. For the UK, there was an emphasis directly after the Cold War on a 'capability' rather than 'threat' based approach to operational concepts.[1] This approach reflected, on the one hand, uncertainty with regard to the evolving security situation and, on the other, the diversity and complexity of emerging threats and the need for a 'toolbox' of capabilities from which the appropriate means could be drawn for any particular crisis. In the 1990s, the 'toolbox' approach lessened the emphasis on technological competition for the UK, in favour of having the appropriate enabling technologies that would allow capabilities to be fit for purpose, rather than able to overmatch any specific threat. However, technological competition had not gone away completely. After the 11 September 2001 attacks, a new field of competition emerged in developing counter-terrorist weapons and in their detection and management of the consequences of terrorist attack. One enduring aspect of competition – which is as relevant to traditional warfare as to countering irregular operations and terrorism – is operational and tactical agility and the demands this places on information superiority provided by C4ISTAR capabilities.[2]

Technology and Defence Inflation

The issue of affordability relates technology with both the military and economic instruments. Military competition is a contributor to defence inflation, the factor denoting that defence spending must be increased above the annual Gross Domestic Product (GDP) deflator before there is any 'real' increase in defence spending. Professor David Kirkpatrick has placed UK defence inflation at approximately 3 per cent (Kirkpatrick, 2008). A large proportion of defence inflation can be attributed to inflation in acquisition costs, with the further pursuit of excellence in a competitive environment – however limited – considered to be one of the contributing factors. There is debate as to whether defence inflation is a necessary feature of defence spending or reflects poor acquisition practice (Chalmers,

---

1 'Concepts' is here used in the military technical sense of the methods or ways whereby the military will execute strategy.

2 Command, control, communications, computers, intelligence, surveillance (target acquisition) and reconnaissance. The similar US acronym, C4ISR, omits 'target acquisition'.

2009). One inflator, which could be interpreted as bad practice, is the aspiration to achieve '100 per cent' system solutions to operational requirements where a slightly lower capability could be greatly more cost effective. Nonetheless, the premium of procuring advanced technology is clearly an important factor in these additional costs.

The matter of defence inflation illustrates an important point about British use of the most advanced technology. It may not only be military competition that promotes its use in military systems. Another factor may be instilled acquisition practices that do not allow for cost-effective concessions in delivering requirements. Furthermore, there is not sufficient empirical evidence for defence budgets to be adjusted in the short term on the assumption that defence inflation will dwindle because of greater efficiency in acquisition. Intended improvements in acquisition practice, such as those implemented in the 'Smart Acquisition' initiative launched by the MoD in 1998 (Ministry of Defence, 1998), failed to deliver the planned savings in acquisition costs that were needed to make the ambitious equipment plan of the 1998 SDR affordable. It also bears mention that advanced technology is not only expensive because of the costs of development on the open market but also because states will pay premiums to generate their own technologies for reasons of operational sovereignty and guarantee of supply. So the perceived need for cutting edge technology enhances costs, which in turn reduces the number of platforms if defence budgets do not increase significantly above general levels of inflation. Additionally, numbers are important whatever the individual capability for most operations short of full scale combat, because there is very often a need to disperse capability geographically, whether it is ships, troops, vehicles or aircraft.

Britain's Military Strategy Under New Labour

Having considered some general issues regarding the relationship between technology and defence, it is now worth considering the more specific relationship between technology and British military strategy. In definitional terms, 'strategy' is meant to refer to how, in broad terms, the UK has planned to use the military instrument in the product of SDR, how these plans, such as they have been, have evolved and what plans will be drawn up for the future (Ministry of Defence, 1998). What are the objectives, the concepts and the resources – the ends, the ways and the means? Strategic theory would mandate a military strategy as the substance of defence policy that can be actually applied to deliver effect. To use a business neologism, it is the 'operationalising' of the vision, aspirations and objectives of defence policy. And, because military capability can take many years to develop, a useful military strategic concept needs to project a good 20 years ahead.

There is one view that the UK does not really 'do strategy' in the sense of designing an enduring concept that addresses a route to the longer term. The argument is well made by Sir John Coles, a former Permanent Under Secretary of

State at the FCO, who suggests that the so-called pragmatic British official approach is to create policy devoid of a vision of the future, without any overarching long term objectives (Coles, 2000). For British policy makers, existing policy, such as it is, must form the basis for long term planning. As this policy is adjusted to meet changing circumstances, long-term plans can be similarly adjusted. If we transfer this model to defence policy planning, the expectation of government would be that the expeditionary capacity defined in SDR, the 'toolbox' for use overseas as and when government chooses, would be sustained into the foreseeable future but would be modified to address emerging needs for greater homeland protection, garrison operations abroad, affordability and other factors that may emerge. In effect, the pattern of policy White Papers since SDR confirms this model (Ministry of Defence, 2002, 2003, 2004).

The British pragmatic approach is not necessarily wrong. Expression of a vision of a preferred future implies that a particular states's defence policy has something to do with shaping the future security environment in a predictable way. Only a superpower can have the necessary instruments of power to have global influence in such a way that there might be predictable outcomes. As recent experience has shown, even a superpower can lack the intellectual capacity to deal with the vast challenge of complexity that the future imposes. There is a metaphysical gulf between divine inspiration and divine capacity. There is another problem with 'the vision thing' and it is one not only for medium powers. If it is declared as national public policy, it may attract an adverse response internationally, even from erstwhile friends. By way of historical example, a 'place in the sun' requires a route map across territory and implies obstacles to be dealt with remorselessly.

In the view of this author, Britain does indeed have a military strategy which explains how an expeditionary Joint Rapid Reaction Force (JRRF), with its land, naval and air components, is intended to make the UK a safer place for its people through operations of choice overseas. This strategy deals with the vision free future through an argument of reputation, continuity and consistency. However, this strategy is not presented in so many words in public policy. Paul Cornish and Andrew Dorman have addressed the issue of the relationship between declaratory policy and military strategy in their excellent paper, 'Blair's wars and Brown's budgets' (Cornish and Dorman, 2009). Their focus is on the inadequacies of government process and the ongoing debate between supporters of 'war amongst the people' and the return of inter-state conflict. They identify Rupert Smith and Colin Gray respectively as the champions of each (Smith, 2005; Gray, 2002).

One can, however, derive a number of more fundamental (albeit unverified) propositions from the declaratory policy of the Blair era which sit comfortably with the continuity of British policy at least since Suez. These are:

- The UK is a great power and has transubstantiated this status economically and militarily since the early 1980s, following the post-Second World War decline and retreat from empire;

- The British public presume that their country has this status and will support policy that clearly reinforces it;
- This status is supported by a good reputation for 'values led' diplomacy, which is enhanced and modified by 'the pragmatic approach';
- The UK is particularly dependent on a secure world environment as a trading nation and because of its geostrategic position, its social associations and responsibilities;
- International influence born of the first two propositions is the primary way to a secure world (Chalmers, 2008);
- Influence can have its greatest effect through the US, which has the dominant capacity for good or bad;
- Influence over the US must be sustained and developed in major part through a consistent and reliable contribution of a discrete military capacity, which has the strategic significance to be genuinely influential;
- This discrete capability must still have operational autonomy if it is to claim strategic significance – UK forces must not be dependent on US capabilities to conduct operations assigned to them;
- This military capacity must be large enough, effective enough and agile enough to fulfil roles and missions in a US led coalition at the theatre level early in an intervention, when the need for the contribution is most urgent and the consequences on policy in shaping a campaign will be most evident (Codner, 1998);
- Expeditionary capability can always be brought home if the priorities became territorial defence or domestic security.

These propositions have not been stated in so many words in any government White Paper, including the 2008 National Security Strategy, or in other public policy outlets. There are obvious reasons why. One the one hand, there is a British sensitivity to the perspectives of other states. The UK cannot boast publicly about its international influence. On the other, the propositions have such a long history that they now have the status of axioms. Perhaps for some policy makers they are intuitive to the degree that they do not need cognitive treatment. They never really needed to think about things that way.

Of course, these premises cannot be treated as axioms. Indeed, Cornish and Dorman's view of the abject state of the British system of defence in 2009 lead to the conclusion there have been three possible failures. The first is that there has been insufficient review of policy and process since SDR. The second is that SDR's recommendations for structure and process were insufficiently visionary. The third is that the premises themselves were inaccurate. In any event, all require serious testing in some putative future defence review that is expected of whichever political party is in power after a General Election, which must be called by June 2010.

In particular, the effectiveness of British influence over the US must be questioned after the Iraq war. Britain's status as an economic great power may not be sustainable through economic downturn. The required military capacity in any evolved form that it might assume may not be affordable. And, Britain's military reputation as the world's most competent stabiliser, if not as a prompt and agile intervener, has certainly been challenged on the evidence of Iraq and Afghanistan. As analysis, they do, however, explain the UK's military behaviour since the end of the Cold War and through the Blair/Brown period, to the time of writing. They explain the 1990–91 Gulf War, Bosnia, Kosovo and Sierra Leone, as well as the early stages in Afghanistan and the Iraq war. They also explain the subsequent embroilments in Iraq and Afghanistan as strategic continuity rather than deviation or decay.

A Force for Honour

Colin Gray has reminded us in an essay – in which he takes his own arguments forward – of Thucydides' primitive motives for using the military instrument, namely fear, interest and honour, as the generators for British strategy in the future (Gray, 2008). The ten propositions listed earlier can all be derived from these motives and seven of the ten relate directly to honour. Gray sees honour specifically as reputation. However, there are four aspects to honour, of which military reputation is indeed one that bears heavily on influence. The second is moral, as expressed in Robin Cook's 'Force for Good' concept – which was eventually incorporated formally into defence policy (Ministry of Defence, 2008) – which might contribute to influence. The third is respect for international order, as mandated through treaties and international law. And the fourth is reflexive and is the nation's perception of itself as a world power. For these reasons, 'honour' is rather a neat descriptor of Britain's silent military strategic concept. 'A Force for Honour' is probably nearer the mark than 'Force for Good', labelling these ten propositions as the 'Force for Honour Propositions'.

The Joint Rapid Reaction Force

SDR envisaged a highly agile and responsive force on which the US could rely as a partner for early intervention. It concluded that the force should have the capacity for a major operation and that there would be concurrent minor operations. The land component for a major invasion would be of the scale of a division. Operational analysis, using a range of scenarios, would have influenced this decision, as would experience of the First Gulf War. However, bearing in mind that an intervention would be discretionary and as a partner of the US under the rules of SDR, the argument for this size of land force is not obvious. The author's conclusion at the time was that it was the size that would be generally necessary for a task in which the UK would have operational autonomy. A land force smaller than a division would not have the full range of capabilities to operate without the presumption of enabling support from other states. The UK would be merely contributing a selection of capabilities, not providing discrete operational effect. Without national effect at this level and on this scale, it would not have strategic influence over the conduct of the campaign, nor over the US in particular.

A second feature would be the ability to be the framework nation for a multinational operation – explicit in the UK's role as the framework nation of NATO's Allied Command Europe Rapid Reaction Corps (ARRC) and implicit in the command structures of 'coalitions of the willing', in which national command arrangements of a leading nation form the hub of the multinational force (Codner, 2003) – with the capacity for operational level command and control. A UK led multinational component with operational autonomy in a US led campaign would be another route to strategic influence. For both roles, the UK would require high levels of multinational interoperability. The ability to coordinate – and indeed integrate with US forces – would be a *sine qua non* and would set the standards for information systems and doctrinal development. However, interoperability with principal European partners and Australian and Canadian forces was also a requirement. The potential problem of choices to be made in developing interoperability with the US on the one hand and other friends and partners on the other could be resolved by encouraging allies to adopt standards of interoperability that had a similar US focus. The impediment to this approach was the lack of US interest in – and awareness of – the needs to take forward interoperability on a multinational basis.

Operational autonomy required that there would be naval and air components with comprehensive capabilities for sustained combat, in addition to the land component. Indeed, the ability to shape operations through early intervention emphasised the maritime leanings of SDR and bolstered the case for two large aircraft carriers. For the Royal Navy, an expeditionary strategy was synonymous with a maritime strategy. In SDR they won their case. Needless to say, the expected duration of a major operation was months rather than years, drawing on the First Gulf War model and the pattern of roulement arrangements for operations in the Former Yugoslavia. Smaller scale operations would be sustainable for longer periods.

The 2002 and 2003/4 White Papers broadly confirmed this scheme for force planning. However, both predated the return to Afghanistan in 2005 for which Britain's role as framework nation of the ARRC was invoked (Ministry of Defence, 2002, 2003, 2004). The UK was now engaged in two major operations in worsening circumstances, with no roulement options. The London bombings happened in the same year. These events raised serious questions about purpose, sustainment and national priorities (Cornish and Dorman, 2009). However, it is the issue of technology's relationship with this strategy that is the focus of this chapter.

Technology after SDR

Precision and Effect

There have been considerable advances in technology in the period. The use of precision weaponry, particularly air launched weapons, increased greatly between the 1990/1 Gulf War and the war in Iraq. Precision has allowed for the more subtle use of destructive weapons with reduced collateral injury and damage. However, it has also raised expectations. NATO military operations in Kosovo focused the spotlight on military coercion, in particular the ineffectiveness of air power to force the Bosnian Serb leader, Slobodan Milosevic, to withdraw Serbian forces from Kosovo within the timelines envisaged by NATO at the start of the campaign. This failure was the genesis of a discussion on both sides of the Atlantic into 'Effects Based Operations' (EBO) and the 'Effects Based Approach' (EBA).

While there was nothing new in the notion that military action should be planned and executed to deliver the required military and political effect, EBO emphasised the importance of accurate targeting in delivering military effect through coercion. In the development of EBO and EBA, there has been something of a presumption in the Western military community that a full understanding of a mechanical relationship between targeting and purpose will be the philosopher's stone for success. This hope has not been borne out. The US 'Shock and Awe' attacks on Baghdad in the Iraq war are a case study in misunderstanding the complexities of the cognitive domain (Codner, 2003). It would be fair to say that precision has not as yet had the expected significant influence on British military strategy.

Unmanned Systems

There has also been a steady growth in unmanned systems, particularly in the US. Unmanned ground and underwater systems arc important enablers in clearing unexploded ordnance such as mines. It is in Unmanned Airborne Vehicles (UAV), however, that the greatest expectations for strategic change have been invested. The US has advanced the use of UAVs into weapon delivery, where the loitering potential has advantages over cruise missiles if air defence is not a challenge. Both classes of system spare aircrew from risk. The UK is a burgeoning user of UAVs for information gathering. The small vehicle launched Phoenix UAV was in regular use by the Royal Artillery from Kosovo in 1999 to 2008, while the Army's larger Watchkeeper system will formally enter service in 2010, when it will replace the earlier Hermes 450 model, which has been in service for surveillance and target acquisition since 2007 as a UOR. The RAF's Reaper, which has twice the wingspan of Watchkeeper, is also a UOR deployed in Afghanistan. It is a version of the US Predator. Although the British Reapers are unarmed, they can carry bombs and missiles, in addition to optical and electronic sensors. Much is expected of UAVs in the next two decades, particularly in contributing to situational awareness. It is too early, however, for them to have influenced Britain's strategic options.

Information Led Revolution, Transformation and Evolution

With hindsight, the chief technological demands of SDR's strategic concept of intervention, agility and interoperability were in information and in the utility of land-air capability. The essential information demands for early interventions in complex emergencies are, firstly, good situational awareness that can be developed rapidly and, secondly, the ability to integrate national capabilities and those of other states through networking and friendly force identification.

The matter of information technology in this context exposes an important difference in approach between the US and UK. It is a crude but pertinent observation that the US expects technology to provide solutions to security problems, while the UK sees it as a contributor to the means of coping with these problems. A great deal of scholarship has been devoted to the identification and analysis of military technological revolutions in history. It is a feature of the US approach that these revolutions can be predicted and should b exploited. In the early 1990s, the Revolution in Military Affairs (RMA) was the revolution of the day, particularly in the US. Its champions were Andrew Marshall, Director of the Office of Net Assessment in the US Department of Defence and Admiral William Owens, Vice Chairman of the US Joint Chiefs of Staff from 1994 to 1996. As Jeremy Black has summarised the history of RMA succinctly (Black, 2009), there is no need to go into it in depth here. Suffice to say that, in the last decade, RMA has given way as the catalytic language of the day in the US to its more recent manifestation of 'transformation', an expression that lingers on with meanings that are progressively wider and more diffuse as its value in stimulating urgent reform has dwindled.

Information technology as exploited in Network Centric Warfare (NCW) was at the core of the RMA and transformation. NCW has been defined by advocates as follows:

> an approach to the conduct of warfare that derives its power from the effective linking or networking of the warfighting enterprise. It is characterised by the ability of geographically dispersed forces (consisting of entities) to create a high level of shared battlespace awareness. (Alberts et al., 1999)

NCW is an elaborate suite of strategic and operational concepts, all enabled by the future potential of information technology. NCW permits among other things a distributed battlespace composed of dispersed sensors and weapon systems. When integrated by networks, these elements constitute new capabilities. They can be very small and will place technological demands on miniaturised engineering, electronics and avionics. NCW was the great experiment for which the Transformation Force and Objective Force were formed (Department of Defense, 2001; US Army, 2003). These forces were developed to realise NCW and to test its effectiveness and to allow the US, in the rhetoric of the Department of Defense, to skip a technological generation. The rest of the US order of battle would then be reconstructed and equipped to deliver NCW concepts. Needless to say, only the US could afford the risk entailed in such an experiment. European powers, such as the UK, are obliged to take an evolutionary route and condemned therefore to lag behind. The Iraq War demonstrated that British forces could not have integrated fully with the US land-air operation technically and, as importantly, behaviourally, in the advance to Baghdad

In the same period, the UK tentatively embarked on what at that time was called battlespace digitisation, with a view to achieving and maintaining connectivity with the post-NCW US force. However, SDR skirted the matter (Cornish and Dorman, 2009). Information networking had actually been progressively exploited since the 1970s in the maritime domain, in which the US and UK achieved high levels of interoperability through the use of Link 11 and development of the Composite Warfare Concept in the 1980s. More recently, the US Navy's Cooperative Engagement Capability has been an objective for British maritime interoperability. Similar progress has been made in the air domain. However, the land environment is considerably more challenging, because of the complexity of the land operational picture and much higher levels of granularity that land force integration demands. It is a much simpler matter to integrate relatively large and discrete units such as ships and aircraft into a network to operate in the relatively barren environments of ocean and aerospace, compared with integrating land forces comprising small units of section size or even individual soldiers in very complex terrain, which includes mountains, forests and urban areas. The British approach was understandably incremental and conservative. In any event, the US grand experiment of NCW would have been unaffordable for Britain. It made sense to draw on the US experience as a proven way ahead was established.

The parallel UK concept of Network Enabled Capability (NEC) appeared in the public domain in 2002 (Ministry of Defence, 2002). In its early days, NEC differed from NCW in that the intention was – in the first place – to make existing doctrine and command and force structures more effective rather than to use information technology and the commercial experience to effect radical change in both. More recently the concepts of NCW and NEC have become closer in meaning. The theologians of NCW have had to confront reality. Vulnerability to cyber-attack demands redundancy in capability and non-networked fall-back options. Meanwhile, NEC approaches NCW in addressing doctrinal change in its later manifestations, in which the 'Third Epoch' of NEC is characterised by so comprehensive a network that it is expected to drive doctrinal development through 'synchronisation' (Ministry of Defence, 2005). The timelines are way behind those of the US and this poses the problem of worsening interoperability.

The problem is not only one of lack of connectivity and poor sharing of information. It is the consequent changes in behaviour, through new doctrines, tactics, techniques and procedures, that will hinder interoperability. The UK is, of course, not alone in this respect and can expect generally to have better interoperability with the US than most other allies and coalition partners. The challenge is greater for the UK, aspiring to be a framework nation, than for these other partners alongside the US. The solution is not a simple matter of prioritising connectivity with the US but of being a hub with adequate connectivity with the more serious European military partners and of having devices to share an adequate common operational picture with others.

The UK has not been alone in Europe in developing networking. NEC has been adopted by NATO as an Alliance concept. France has not seen US interoperability as an imperative to the same extent as the UK, but has interests in developing integration of European military capability. Of the smaller states, Sweden and the Netherlands in particular have taken networking of capabilities seriously. A problem for all medium and minor military powers is affordability in the context of shrinking defence budgets. Where choices have to be made, it has tended to be platforms and major systems that have been an investment priority because their military value is more apparent to the non-expert policy maker and they are more likely to have sponsorship from the individual armed services. Indeed, arguments that networking through information technology can in fact enhance the effectiveness of weapons and sensors have been challenged politically, as attempts to take a cheaper option and cut numbers of platforms

Friendly Force Identification

There were some high profile incidents during the Iraq war of mistaken US attacks on British forces and much discussion in the media of fratricide, friendly fire and 'blue on blue' attacks, as these incidents are variously called. Identification Friend or Foe (IFF) systems, such as Blue Force Tracker, typically employ technology in the form of sensors, communications and cryptography. The situation in the Iraq War was not, however, that UK forces did not have access to the relevant technologies but that small units were not generally equipped with discrete identifiers. Multinational interoperability among dispersed units was not a feature of previous high intensity campaigns involving UK forces, so the systems were not a priority in the contest for funds. Traditionally, multinational land formations might be integrated as large units, such as brigades, whose tasks would be separated geographically. As dispersion becomes a feature of networked forces, states whose land forces are not networked at smaller unit levels, such as sections and vehicles, cannot integrate with those networked at these levels. Of course, the problem of inadequate friendly force identification is exacerbated when one state, such as the US, which expects the ability to network at small unit levels, provides air support to another which does not. FFI systems are, needless to say, an essential part of a network enabled future and they have become an urgent priority for British land forces. The need is particularly pressing in intense combat, when there is not the time for systematic target identification and risks must be taken.

Armoured Vehicles

To serve an expeditionary strategy, ground forces must be highly strategically mobile, as well as operationally and tactically. The emphasis therefore has been on light to medium weight and this imposes demands on advanced protective armour to compensate for thickness and weight. SDR reinforced this need for agility and the ongoing Future Rapid Effect Systems (FRES) programme to replace UK's aging armoured vehicle fleet has attempted to address this focus on medium weight. The programme has had a poor history of indecision and delay. In its original conception, it was meant to be a comprehensive programme of systems and capabilities to replace armoured vehicles, with a range of roles including reconnaissance, fighting vehicles and personnel carriers, engineering and command. The range of capabilities and the integrating communications would all be part of this system and force protection was a major factor. The model was the all-embracing US Future Combat System (FCS). The problems of scoping the programme and its complexity resulted in significant delays. In the meantime, aging vehicles needed urgent replacement and there were operational needs in theatre for specific capabilities. As a result, FRES has been delayed in favour of a piecemeal vehicle replacement programme, which may be very useful in Afghanistan, for which it is being shaped, but which may create an armoured vehicle force that will be inefficient to sustain because of its diversity. As a consequence, it will not meet SDR's expectations for agility.

Assuming that an expeditionary strategy of sorts will continue to be the UK's choice for the future, the technological challenge will be in reducing weight while preserving firepower and protection using advance armour technology. In the debate, champions of the main battle-tank will fight the case for armoured protection and for the tank's symbolic role in escalation dominance. Physical size has also emerged as a consideration in Afghanistan. The use of small light vehicles has been criticised because they lack protection. However, they may be the only vehicles that can travel down narrow streets in built up areas, where a military presence may be essential.

Helicopters

The one capability that transcends all expeditionary scenarios, whether high intensity combat, counter-insurgency or strategic raiding, is rotary wing. In the land battlefield environment, these platforms have the versatility to deliver three broad missions. They can be used to gather information through surveillance and reconnaissance and target acquisition – the 'find' mission. They can 'fight' using a range of integral weapons – in particular air-ground missiles and guns. The 'lift' mission provides rapid mobility for personnel, vehicles and stores. And they can deliver these missions in very diverse environments, where ground access cannot be assured. The challenge of Afghanistan has been for adequate helicopter capability that can cope with high ambient seasonal temperatures on the one hand and high ground altitudes on the other. Both 'hot and high' factors require helicopters to operate in less dense air and limit the lift that engines and rotors can provide to an aircraft.

There is a misconception that helicopters are military workhorses that are not particularly sophisticated technologically. The truth is that the helicopter is an aerodynamically unstable platform that is highly dependent on advanced technology if it is to function operationally. Although inadequate numbers of helicopters for operations has been a political issue with regard to Iraq and Afghanistan, the problem is not so much the numbers in service but the numbers that are at the required readiness for these testing environments.

The challenge is both in the design and support aspects of helicopter acquisition and the problem is not helped by the large number of different systems employed by three separate services. The creation of the Joint Helicopter Force, which was one of a number of cross-service 'joint' initiatives launched by New Labour's SDR, goes a long way towards rationalising operational employment across the Services. However, the British system of acquisition does not at present give a User entity, such as a mere two star commander, much influence in defining operational requirements and affecting their delivery. This problem of availability is one that affects all European helicopter provision in Afghanistan. The wider issue of the further evolution of joint rationalisation should certainly be a key one for a future defence review.

Urban Operations

Versatile expeditionary forces must also be capable of operating in a wide range of complex environments. US forces fought in mountains and attacked cave hideouts in pursuit of Al Qaeda in Afghanistan. Jungles and forest are testing terrain for surveillance. During the Cold War, the Royal Marines needed to specialise in arctic warfare launched from the sea. The prospect of cold weather operations cannot be excluded from an expeditionary future. However, among the most likely and challenging complex environments are urban areas in which there are particular demands for surveillance and precision munitions.

During the Iraq War neither US nor British forces had the capability to prosecute an enemy effectively in urban areas without the prospect of high levels of civilian casualties and destruction of property and infrastructure. The Russian 'Grozny' model of urban counterinsurgency operations, involving wholesale destruction of property, would have been totally unacceptable during a discretionary war ostensibly of liberation in which moral considerations were paramount. The tactical solution in Iraq was one of siege or investment for as long a period as necessary for a 'tipping point' to arise, when intelligence and special forces reconnaissance indicate that entry might be relatively free of violence. The problem with 'tipping point' tactics in combat operations is that the intervening force loses control of timing of lines of operation. Events of this kind were manageable in the combat phase in Iraq, but generically will allow any opposition the option of prolongation, a classic asymmetric device.

Subsequent counter-insurgency operations in Iraq and Afghanistan have emphasised the problems of countering irregulars in towns and villages. The Maoist dictum of 'swimming in the people as fish swim in the sea' is a feature of insurgencies that has consistently been effective in recent history, particularly against Western opponents who are constrained by the *jus in bello* principle of proportionality. So, irregulars of the future will continue to develop their doctrines to exploit it. The particular challenges for proactive operations in urban environments are the need for surveillance inside and between buildings, for identification of hostiles and for munitions that can be sufficiently selective. There are also protective and reactive requirements for capabilities to deal with improvised explosive devices (IEDs) and other terrorist weapons. Domestic counter-terrorism has similar needs and there are clearly options for rationalisation among government departments in funding and developing the technologies, a concrete example of the putative 'comprehensive approach'. The difference between expeditionary and domestic capability is that the latter can be incorporated into physical and social domestic infrastructure. An expeditionary force must import generic capabilities and apply them to particular circumstances.

Missile Defence

Ballistic missile defence is an area of massive technological development in the US. The UK has attempted to maintain a close relationship with the US with regard to defence of homelands against missile attack. Successive British governments have not invested in capability, because the threat to the British islands is not obvious, as yet at least. There has also been the question of affordability. UK policy has been, on the one hand, to assist the US in developing its own capabilities by allowing the development of surveillance capabilities on the UK mainland. On the other hand, a close relationship with the US and some research activity in missile defence will allow the UK to be an intelligent customer and to integrate specific UK capabilities into a US system, should the need arise. A benefit of offering geography is of course some extended protection by US systems.

However, in the expeditionary context, it is the issue of theatre missile defence which exposes a weakness in British capabilities. The eighth of the 'Force for Honour' propositions presented earlier in the chapter states that UK forces need some level of operational autonomy for strategic influence. Dependence on US theatre missile defence capability would undermine this autonomy. If the UK were to have significant theatre capability, for example with a sea launched interceptor in its air defence destroyers, this would offset this perception of dependency and would provide British led medium scale and minor operations with some protection against short range ballistic systems. NATO has been engaged in a study of theatre missile defence, but it has not been an investment priority for the UK. At present, the UK is on the safer periphery of Europe compared with East European and Mediterranean countries but a malign power could, in the future, develop systems with the range to attack the UK mainland. It is possible that missile defence could become a priority for the UK in the future and there would be large cost implications. Any British capability, for instance missiles in the Type 45 destroyers, would be part of a bi- or multi-national system.

Exploitation of Technology

One of the principal lessons from Afghanistan in relation to technology has been the speed at which up to date technological solutions have been brought into theatre in the form of what are known in British acquisition practice as UORs, those additional capabilities that the government funds outside the defence budget specifically for the operation, whether it is force protection, communications or other needs. Capabilities which would have taken several years to bring into service through the normal acquisition system can be brought into theatre in weeks with the necessary funding.

If technology can be accessed so quickly by close cooperation between industry and the military when it is urgently needed for operations, why can it not always be done in this way? This question is important for reform of defence acquisition in the UK. Acquisition agility and adaptability in acquisition processes is needed to give prompt access to new technologies. There are a number of ways of doing this:

- *Modularity* – Building platforms that allow new capabilities to be inserted as roles evolve to meet changing strategic circumstances;
- *Incremental or spiral acquisition* – Although this is related to modularity, it is deliberately procuring cost effective but less than perfect systems in a timely way, which can be upgraded easily as new technologies mature;
- *Open information architectures* – Which allow the best available technological solutions to be used, not the ones that the prime contractor necessarily has to hand;
- *Dual use and Commercial Off The Shelf (COTS)* – Technology to make the best use of civil sector innovation, which, in many sectors, is more agile because it is developed to meet commercial demands;
- *Through Life Capability Management* – Long term partnering arrangements with industry which can allow industry to plan for cost-effective agility in the initial design of systems – as well as keeping big companies in the defence business when there is only occasional demand for new build platforms.

Future Strategy and Technology

New technology can modify present strategy. It can provide additional options in ways and means. However, its particular significance is in shaping strategy for the future, in enabling future strategic and operational concepts. New technologies are an important feature of the future strategic environment, as well as offering solutions for future military capability.

Military Strategy for the Future

A major challenge in designing the UK's military strategy is the conflict of short term and long term needs. This is a particular problem for the RAF and Royal Navy. At the time of writing, the immediate demands are for stabilisation and counter-insurgency operations. With no short term solution to Afghanistan, it is counter-insurgency that has dominated the present debate in which the predominant opinion is commitment to these stabilisation operations into the medium term. Indeed, the Defence section of the recently published Institute of Public Policy Research Report on the UK's security policy reinforces this focus on land stabilisation options (IPPR, 2009). There is a view that counter-insurgency should be at the heart of the UK's military strategy. This view maintains that there is a need for long term commitment to Rupert Smith's 'war amongst the peoples' rather than the capability for major interstate combat operations (Smith, 2005).

The problem with this thesis, however, is that there will be a reluctance in the electorate and among politicians to commit specifically to major land interventions in the future, certainly those involving regime change with the subsequent legal and moral responsibilities for governance. Continued stabilisation and counter-insurgency operations in Afghanistan are likely to be necessary in the short to medium term, but there will be political pressure to avoid them in the future. This is not to say that the UK would opt out of an expeditionary strategy once it had withdrawn from Afghanistan. There are other options which will be considered later. However, operational art and tactics, techniques and procedures for countering irregular operations will continue to be very important if a state is to commit to interventions of any sort. General Krulak's 'Three Block War' will continue to describe possible outcomes whenever troops are put into theatre, even for humanitarian operations and disaster relief. In any operation where combat is a possibility, troops must be prepared to exert military control of territory. In that situation, they must be capable, both in equipment and training, to change roles quickly from combat to constabulary to benign.

The Expeditionary Motivation

Of course, national territorial defence remains the absolute obligation for governments insofar as they have the capacity to do it alone. Yet, Western states who are medium and smaller military powers are likely to continue to take part in military interventions for three broad reasons. First, it remains part of the *strategic bargain* or deal with larger friends and allies – in particular, of course the US – to ensure collective security in the widest sense, whether in a NATO context or some other arrangement. This bargain is reminiscent of the Cold War but it certainly remains a major consideration in relation to Russia for new NATO members. For the UK, the strategic bargain with the US in this European context is no longer at the heart of defence policy. However, the UK's contribution to common defence and security in the context of NATO remains a consideration which has a quantitative element. Secondly, there is the matter discussed earlier in the chapter of *world influence* and influence over larger partners, such as the US, in relation to policy generally and conduct of specific operations. Whether this influence works or not is another matter. Finally, prosperous developed states may continue to have a *moral purpose* in liberal intervention, which was also discussed earlier in the chapter. For the UK, the relationship between moral purpose and influence – the 'Force for Honour' concept that seems to have been the unwritten basis for the SDR – is one that should be tested and evaluated systematically in any future defence review. The bargain with larger states and influence over them relates to an important additional factor – *inherent* (or existential) *military deterrent capability*. This is the need collectively to maintain sufficient levels of military capability – in particular combat capability – to deter any emerging or existing power in the future from developing or using the military instrument for bullying or blackmail. It is to exclude the use of military power as a cost-effective option. One does not need to identify a particular state – Russia, China, Iran or some other emergent power – although these countries may be useful benchmarks for military capability.

Strategic Choices for the UK

Of course, a worsening global economic situation could bring serious security challenges that would require military responses and which would raise the priority of defence in government spending. These challenges could be matters of obligation to government such as:

- state on state conflict invoking treaty obligations and the need to deter this possibility;
- interrupted access to economic resources;
- breakdown of law and order at home, terrorist attack or consequences of natural disaster beyond the capacity of civil authorities.

There are therefore two axes that must be considered in mapping a future national military strategy for the UK. The first is that of aspiration to deliver expeditionary capability beyond the UK homeland. The other is the possibility of a worsening global security situation that could enhance the priority on defence spending. There are – at the time of writing – huge economic uncertainties and, indeed, questions as to the longer term implications of political change in many key powers. The US, Russia, Iran, India, South Africa, Israel, and France are all going through or have recently gone through electoral processes of which the medium to long term outcomes are not certain. However, it is possible to speculate on some broad strategic options for the UK which bear comparison with the Expeditionary, Contributory (Muck In), and Gendarmerie Options[3] identified by the author in 1997, in advance of the General Election and the subsequent SDR (Codner, 1997a–b). First, it is likely in the short to medium term that the UK will continue

---

3 Little Britain and Iceland Strategies were included in the pre-Election article but were not mentioned in the pre-Review article because the Secretary of State's important 'boundaries to the scope of the Review' excluded them from consideration (Robertson, 1997).

with its commitment to stabilisation in Afghanistan. Any short term surge to take advantage of the withdrawal from Iraq and support the Obama Administration is unlikely, however, to be consolidated into an increase in medium term commitment. The broad strategic options for the longer term future are bluntly as follows.

Option 1 – the Continental Continuous COIN (Three Cs) Option This option focuses more specifically on a continuation of ground operations for stabilisation, which will provide continuity in Afghanistan for the foreseeable future and will allow governments to develop and sustain aspirations for global influence through regular and long term ground commitments and the ability to act as framework nation for ground operations. High intensity ground combat capability would be retained to provide effective escalation dominance and to contribute to trans-Atlantic inherent deterrent capability. Naval and air forces would have relatively minor supporting roles. The use of the word 'continental' broadens the 'continental' versus 'maritime' debate of Jonathan Swift and others from the European context of the seventeenth to twentieth centuries to an expeditionary meaning (Swift, 1713). Basil Liddell-Hart incorporated this meaning of 'continental' in a lecture at the RUSI (Liddell-Hart, 1931). However, the European sense of 'continental' is preserved in the notion that the UK should contribute substantial land forces for conventional deterrence in a Trans-Atlantic and European context.

Option 2 – the Maritime 'Strategic Raiding'[4] Option This option recognises that there is unlikely to be the political will in government or in the electorate for further embroilment in operations such as Iraq and Afghanistan in the foreseeable future, as can be seen in the 2009 commitment of additional troops in both the UK and US alongside greater emphasis on exit strategies. It limits this capacity for ground campaigns and refocuses on short term operations using agile specialist ground forces. It emphasises sea basing and very early presence and inducement operations. High intensity ground combat capability is retained but is very specialised strategically. Special Forces and agile infantry, such as the Paratroop Regiment, Royal Marines and other air mobile formations, would be supported by light to medium weight armour with a view to developing ground forces more widely as specialist forces, but with a ceiling on numbers in favour of quality. The premise is that a small (relative to other Western states of similar size) elite ground force would limit government choices very specifically to short term early interventions, which would be influential in shaping the pattern of subsequent operations. The UK would make a substantial contribution to maritime security,

---

4   Gwyn Prins uses the expression 'strategic raiding' in a specific sense 'the swift, surprising use of force, implicitly on the ground – against the strategic centre of the new-old insurgent threat' (Prins, 2002). However, its provenance is in the distant past and in this chapter means 'raiding to achieve strategic effect in response to diverse threats' where 'raid' is used literally to mean a 'sudden attack made by (a) military party, ship(s) or aircraft'.

which would permit a degree of international leadership in this respect. The UK's contribution to trans-Atlantic and European security and inherent deterrence should focus on proactive and maritime capability.

Option 3 – the 'Contributory' Option   Of the present capabilities of the UK's armed forces, a selection would be made that would specifically contribute to needs identified in some international context. The context could be a bilateral US–UK relationship, the European context – whether within a NATO or EU force planning construct – or some other multinational context. This option would sacrifice any possibility for national autonomy for intervention operations because the UK would be dependent on others for all the capabilities that it had surrendered.

Option 4 – the 'Gendarmerie' Option   This option accepts that aspirations to be a major expeditionary power are unaffordable and focuses ground forces on contributing to stabilisation options as the offer – albeit a weak offer – in a strategic bargain without aspiration to retain framework nation capacity or significant high intensity combat capability. This Option could also include some constabulary naval capability to contribute to maritime security.

Option 5 – the 'Little Britain' Option   This option focuses specifically on defence and internal security of the British islands, its air space and territorial seas, offering such capacity as is available as a contribution to overseas operations if and when the home situation permits. This option abandons any strategic bargain. There is also the question of the UK's Dependent Territories around the world to which there is a legal obligation for defence and security. A government taking this option would have concluded that these responsibilities are unaffordable and would need to relinquish them and transfer them formally to some other authority or, alternatively, insist that these territories assume their own independence in this respect, regardless of capacity and consequences.

Clearly Options 1 and 2 would reflect sustainment of comparable levels of defence funding to the present but with a rationalisation of capabilities. One could speculate that a reduction of the defence budget by 10 to 15 per cent might allow a degree of strategic specialisation under one of these options that could be compatible with great power status. However, Options 3, 4 and 5 would allow significant reductions in defence funding. Options 1 and 2 imply retention of specific high intensity combat capability and therefore, *inter alia*, the ability to take part in and provide conventional deterrent capability against major inter-state war. Under Option 3 the UK could develop high quality specialism in some niche capability areas which would confirm it as a military partner of choice and with some concomitant international influence. Options 4 and 5 rely on the relative security of an island nation in a benign geo-strategic situation – although economically vulnerable to world events. These latter options also imply a relinquishment of aspirations to sustain global influence. Retention of nuclear deterrent capability is not necessarily inconsistent with Options 4 and 5. There is an argument that the need for nuclear capability is more important, if conventional capability for high intensity combat is relinquished. Furthermore, the nuclear deterrent could preserve world power status and influence cost effectively. This notion would require validation (and has been discussed in more depth by Smith earlier in this volume).

A choice between Options 1 and 2 or some compromise between them, will clearly be the preferred policy situation for a future government, whether Labour or Conservative. The result could approximate to Option 3 and may meet strategic bargain criteria but is likely to sacrifice international influence. These options also address the possibility of a seriously worsening global security environment in which the obligation for military action increases. The premise that expeditionary forces can always be brought home extends the range of uncertainties that Options 1 and 2 can address to considerations of territorial defence and domestic security. Conversely Options 3, 4 and 5 do not provide robust options for intervention. Options 4 and 5 would indicate a profound reversal of policy and abandonment of international reputation that has been acquired through decades, indeed centuries, of expeditionary military activity.

Strategic Versatility

Options 1 and 2 will require the UK's armed forces to continue in the process of developing strategic versatility, the capacity to adapt both capabilities and behaviour (manifestation of doctrine, tactics, techniques and procedures) to the demands, threats and challenges of an uncertain and evolving security environment. Strategic versatility is less important for the UK in capability terms for Options 3 and 4 because the state will have the opportunity to select a range of capabilities of enduring utility to contribute. Adaptation of capabilities will be a problem for the organisation to which the UK formally makes these contributions – NATO, the EU or some other. British forces will need to be behaviourally versatile but it would be for the relevant international organisation to decide on the doctrinal choices and standards. Under Option 5, the demands of versatility would be specifically in addressing terrorist threats to domestic security and in making a military contribution to preventing illegal immigration, drug smuggling and contraband.

Autonomy

Only Option 2 would preserve any real strategic or operational autonomy to conduct national operations – for instance, to evacuate British civilian and non-combatants at short notice from a crisis or to protect the security of the UK's Dependent Territories. In the context of multinational operations, autonomy is only important insofar as Proposition 8 of the 'Force for Honour' propositions discussed earlier might be evaluated by a future government as relevant for the future.

Future Capability Demands

So what are the key capability demands likely to be in the future strategic environment? Much depends on the choice of Option. However, there are some broad capability demands that are common to all Options to a greater or less degree:

- The ability to achieve genuine *network enabled capability* providing a tailored common operational picture and full sensor to shooter connectivity. And network enabled capability must deliver multinational interoperability to the extent that allies can be fully integrated, not merely co-operate or have their actions co-ordinated. The notion that NEC is an attempt to compensate for inadequate scale of effort through technology or that it is only relevant to high intensity warfighting is mistaken. Armed forces who cannot exploit the information domain to advantage in this respect will be outwitted, pre-empted and defeated by enemies of all sorts, who have access to state of the art information technology whether military or commercial.
- *Precision* which requires a combination of effective C4ISTAR and precise weapons permitting destructive capability, for instance using small warheads or directed energy. Precision will be essential to addressing legal and moral demands as well as in managing the perceptions that armed forces are behaving well in theatre.
- The ability to operate effectively in *urban environments* (and other complex environments) – a huge problem in Iraq and subsequent operations. Once again, C4ISTAR and highly discrete and selective destructive power are key and autonomous systems will be an important enabler, both for surveillance and to deliver precise destructive effect when necessary.

Situational awareness is essential to Options 1, 2 and 5. Under Option 3, this could be a UK contribution but it could be provided by others. Under Option 4, UK forces would be dependent on other states for situational awareness above the tactical level. Access to situational awareness under all Options would be through NEC. Substantial *rotary wing* capability is essential to both Options 1 and 2, although specific needs will differ. Option 2 is the most heavily dependent on rotary wing capability. The UK's helicopter forces need to be rationalised to reduce the number of types and improve availability in theatre. There is probably scope for more integration of helicopter capability across the armed services. The full scale combat demands of *inherent deterrence* mentioned earlier apply to Options 1, 2 and 3. However, this scale of conventional deterrent capability only makes sense in a multinational alliance context. Under all three Options the matter of specific UK capability contribution is one for strategic bargaining. Under Options 1 and 2 the UK contributions would be fairly clear. Under Option 3 experience, legacy capability and negotiation will be important. Inherent deterrence implies competition at the high end of the spectrum of conflict – not an arms race perhaps but the need for some allies and friends at least to be able to operate at the leading edge of technology.

Other capability needs will be very specific to the Option taken. In particular, Option 1 supports a larger Army for which heavy armour could be a significant element. Option 2 would restrict the Army's size and would support aircraft carriers, amphibious shipping and development of special force capabilities. Both Options support fixed wing air attack capability, although Option 2 favours sea basing in this respect. It is not difficult to derive full notional capability suites to meet the needs of both Options. Options 3, 4 and 5 offer the prospect of surrendering large capabilities wholesale, in the case of Option 3 by way of strategic bargaining. Options 1 and 2 should address all the capability needs for security of the British islands of Option 5, on the basis that expeditionary forces can always be brought home. Under Options 3 and 4 this security would be provided by a formal alliance relationship, although the UK would contribute specific capabilities, which would be decided through negotiation.

Priorities for Advanced Technology

The technologies that are likely to contribute to the future strategic environment include: information technology; unmanned and autonomous systems; nano-technology; biotechnology; directed energy; 'non-lethal' technology; space technology; and nuclear technology. One general point is that these new technologies can be strategic enablers but there can also be constraints on their use which may not be obvious. Many of these constraints will be moral. In this respect, autonomous systems will create some particular legal and moral challenges of accountability which will be important, as much to the perception of good behaviour by the users as in their compliance with objective legal criteria (Quintana, 2008). There are similar issues with information technology with regard to networking. Non-lethal technology presents different but equally awkward legal and moral problems.

As for British strategic choices that must be made in the short term, Options 1 and 2 are most heavily dependent on the exploitation of advanced technology. The principal enablers and shapers of strategy in the short to medium terms will be information technology and unmanned and autonomous systems. All the advanced technologies listed above (except space and nuclear) are relevant to allowing British armed forces to exploit the urban environment effectively. And all five Options are dependent on progress ahead of potential enemies in this respect. One technological breakthrough which would fundamentally change the strategic environment at the highest level would be in underwater detection. If sensor technologies could be developed that would render the oceans transparent and reveal the positions of submarines, nuclear strategy based on continuous at-sea nuclear deterrence provided by submarine launched nuclear missiles would be invalidated. However, anti-submarine warfare has taken a low priority since the end of the Cold War and the potential for a breakthrough through techniques considered seriously in the 1980s, such as the detection of internal waves and use of blue-green lasers, has dwindled.

Conclusions

Both major political parties have confirmed that they will conduct a defence review after the General Election in 2010. The strategic choices that must be made in such a review must follow from an evaluation of the ten 'Force for Honour' propositions that, one can adduce, were unstated premises for the 1998 SDR. These propositions relate reputation, national self-perception, international influence, the relationship with the US, national autonomy and moral purpose to the national interest and obligations of government.

The expeditionary strategy set out in SDR required a force structure that is unaffordable. If the UK's defence budget is sustained at present levels or cut modestly, two options remain for robust expeditionary capability, a continental option or a maritime one. Only the maritime option will preserve vestiges of full national autonomy to serve purely national military obligations and interests abroad. Severe cuts in the budget would lead to options from contributing specific robust capabilities to an alliance force structure to providing no more than constabulary capabilities to interventions to withdrawing from interventions almost completely. These options must be evaluated against affordability.

Since SDR, information and communications technology and the evolution of weaponry and communications for terrorism and irregular operations have had primary influence in the evolution of the UK's military strategy. In the medium term, future information technology will continue to be an important influence whatever the strategic choices. If a defence review selects one of the two robust expeditionary options or some intermediate course, the technology of unmanned and autonomous systems will become an increasingly important influence, with legal and moral implications. Better military access to the urban environment will be a capability driver, which is also relevant for domestic security, as are technologies that will afford greater detection capabilities and protection against weapons of irregulars and terrorists.

There is the strong possibility that some compromise between the hard continental and maritime expeditionary choices will result in a contributory option that neither meets the robustness criteria of the tough options nor the financial economies that a rationally bargained contributory option would achieve. The 'Force for Good' was already doomed. A 'Force for Honour' may still have mileage but will require rebuilding a broad political consensus, strong and conscious electoral support and levels of funding that are at the top end of expectations in the recession.

Bibliography

Alberts, D, Gartstka, J and Stein, P (1999), *Network Centric Warfare -Co-operative Research Programme* (Washington, DC: Department of Defense)

Black, J (2009), 'The Revolution in Military Affairs: A Historian's Perspective', *RUSI Journal* 154/2, 98–102

Chalmers, M (2008), 'A Force for Influence?: Making British Defence Effective', *RUSI Journal* 153/6, 17–20

Chalmers, M (2009), 'The Myth of Defence Inflation', *RUSI Defence Systems* 12/1, 12–16

Clarke, M (2008), 'The Overdue Defence Review: Old Questions, New Answers', *RUSI Journal* 153/6, 4–10

Codner, M (1997a), 'Make do or Mend? What the British Electorate Ought to be Asking About the Defence of their Realm', *RUSI Newsbrief* 17/4, 26–32

Codner, M (1997b), 'The United Kingdom's Strategic Defence Review: Strategic Options', *RUSI Journal* 142/4, 44–51

Codner, M (1998), 'The Strategic Defence Review: How Much? How Far? How Joint is Enough?', *RUSI Journal* 143/4, 5–10

Codner, M (2003), 'An Initial Assessment of the Combat Phase', in Eyal, J (ed.), 'War in Iraq: Combat & Consequence', *Whitehall Paper* 59

Codner, M (2004), 'Hanging Together: Multinational Interoperability in an Era of Technological Innovation', *Whitehall Paper* 56

Coles, J (2000), *Making Foreign Policy: A Certain Idea of Britain* (London: John Murray)

Cornish, P and Dorman, A (2009), 'Blair's Wars and Brown's Budgets: From Strategic Defence Review to Strategic Decay in Less Than a Decade', *International Affairs* 85/2, 247–61

Department of Defense (2001), *Transformation Study Report: Transforming Military Operational Capabilities* (Washington, DC: Department of Defense)

Gray, C (2002), *Strategy for Chaos: Revolutions in Military Affairs and the Evidence of History* (London: Frank Cass)

Gray, C (2008), 'Britain's National Security: Compulsion and Discretion', *RUSI Journal* 153/6

Institute of Public Policy Research (2009), *Shared Responsibilities: A National Security Strategy for the UK. The Final Report of the IPPR Commission on National Security in the 21st Century* (London: IPPR)

Kirkpatrick, D (2008), 'Is Defence Inflation Really as High as Claimed?', *RUSI Defence Systems* 11/2, 66–71

Liddell-Hart, B (1931), 'Economic Pressure or Continental Victories', *RUSI Journal*

Ministry of Defence (1998), *The Strategic Defence Review: Modern Forces for a Modern World* (London: HMSO)

Ministry of Defence (2002), *The Strategic Defence Review: A New Chapter* (London: HMSO)

Ministry of Defence (2003), *Delivering Security in a Changing World: Defence White Paper* (London: HMSO)

Ministry of Defence (2004), *Future Capabilities: Defence White Paper* (London: HMSO)

Ministry of Defence (2005), *Defence Industrial Strategy: Defence White Paper* (London: HMSO)

Ministry of Defence (2008), *Defence Plan 2008–2012* (London: HMSO)

Prins, G (2002), *The Heart of War: On Power, Conflict and Obligation in the Twenty-first Century* (London, Routledge)

Quintana, E (2008), *Occasional Paper: The Ethics and Legal Implications of Military Unmanned Vehicles* (London: RUSI)

Robertson, G (1997), *Press Briefing by the Defence Secretary on 28 May 1997 and Oral Answers to Defence Parliamentary Questions on 16 June 1997* (London: HMSO)

Smith, R (2005), *The Utility of Force: The Art of War in the Modern World* (London: Allen Lane)

Swift, J (1713), *On the Conduct of the Allies* – http://www.ucc.ie/celt/published/ E700001-019/index.html

US Army (2003), *Posture Statement – The Objective Force* (Washington, DC: Department of Defense)

Weinberger, C (1986), *Annual Report to the Congress – Fiscal Year 1987* (Washington, DC: CPO)

Chapter 12

Striking a Balance? Labour's Legacy and the Next Chapter of British Defence Policy

David Brown[1]

As all three main political parties within the UK committed to holding some form of review in the aftermath of the 2010 General Election – and to continue the process on a more regularised basis than has thus far been the case – this seems a particularly timely moment to consider the progress of defence policy under New Labour. In effect, this was part of the rationale for this volume, to fill a glaring gap in the academic literature, which had not kept pace with developments in a comprehensive fashion. In addition, by considering what lessons have been at least identified – it may be too optimistic to say learned at this stage – from the Blair and Brown governments' handling of a whole spectrum of defence issues, some consideration could be given as to how defence policy should – and could – develop in the future, taking into account potential changes under a putative Conservative government. Having included an array of differing aspects of the wider defence debate – in order to provide as comprehensive an analysis as possible within the confines of one volume – it was necessary to provide some greater structure and thematic coherence. This was done by arranging the chapters in terms of four potential balances to be struck:

- Between the potentially competing demands of the US 'Special Relationship', both through NATO and in less formal coalitions, and the developing defence identity within the EU.
- Between the demands of defending the UK homeland and of projecting military power into the wider international arena – the so-called 'home and away' debate.
- Between treating the Armed Forces – notably the Army, which has been the focus of particular attention in the New Labour era – as a *sui generis* institution, different in ethos and approach to much of the wider public sector, and to considering it as part and parcel of a wider approach to management and governance.

---

1 The views contained within this chapter reflect solely those of the author, and are not representative of the views of the Royal Military Academy Sandhurst, the British Army, the Ministry of Defence or the British government more widely.

- Between the demands of manpower, both in terms of recruitment and
  retention, and in relation to the wider level of scale of treatment due to
  military personnel, and the need to ensure modern technology is being
  effectively harnessed to maximum effect. This issue is particularly important
  within the context of straitened economic circumstances and in terms of
  whether contemporary or future defence requirements are of greatest import
  in terms of shaping wider defence procurement and organisation.

Drawing on the analyses contained within the individual chapters, it is now time to
consider if and how balance was struck in each area, what lessons can be learned
from each process and what inheritance will be bestowed upon the 2010 SDR,
regardless of which party finds itself in charge.

The Atlantic Dimension – Rebuilding the Bridge?

The Blair era in particular has witnessed both the operationalising of the 'special
relationship', in Kosovo – as part of a wider NATO commitment – Afghanistan
and most controversially Iraq – and the institutionalisation of an EU defence
component, with its flurry of committees, capability conferences and limited
peace missions. At first glance, therefore, it would seem that balance has
indeed been struck here, with the Blair government meeting its commitment to
stand 'shoulder to shoulder' even with the almost universally unpopular Bush
administration, while still making progress within the EU arena, initially as part
of the 1998 Anglo-French initiative at St Malo and subsequently within the formal
auspices of the EU, a process that notably predates, but was arguably shaken
by, the fallout from the 'war on terror', notably the contested decision to target
Iraq. As has been detailed by both Sperling and Shepherd respectively, progress
has been made in both policy areas. In that sense, it should not automatically
be assumed that the Atlantic dimension is always a zero-sum game, particularly
given that the widening gulf forecast by Robert Kagan (Kagan, 2004) may have
been fuelled as much by specific personalities and circumstances (as well as the
erroneous supposition that there is always a united and consistently held to EU
line to measure against) than a perceived gulf in the power differentials of both
sides of the Atlantic – 'it will be difficult for the UK to play the role of convenor
between two essentially similar world views' (Niblett, 2007, 636).

The overall assumption with regard to the impact particularly of the Blair
administration on the Atlantic dimension is that he had ended up overly
strengthening the US side of the equation, at the expense of the EU (Wallace,
2005). There is plenty of initial evidence to reinforce this view, not least the crunch
decision to side with the Bush administration in its timetable for intervention
in Iraq, in the face of opposition from leading lights within the EU, notably
France and Germany. The influence of the US is clear throughout UK defence
policy, from the need to remain interoperable with US forces impacting on UK

procurement choices to the evolution and operational tempo of UK responses to the 'war on terror' (in and of itself a US invention). As one small example, a change in wording within the 2003 Defence White Paper accepts the political realities within Washington DC at the time, amending the initial agreed condition for EU defence co-operation from 'where NATO as a whole is not engaged' (a concept that caused some difficulty in the initial stages of the development of the ERRF – Interview, 2005) to the acceptance that the real criteria for determining the involvement of the ESDP is 'where *the US* is not participating' (emphasis added) (Ministry of Defence, 2003).

Yet, it is not quite as clear cut as this. As a result of what was considered the overt closeness of the Blair-Bush relationship particularly, there was a brief – but significant – backlash against the 'special relationship', which was hardly the legacy that Blair wished to leave. Fuelled by the popular, but misplaced, image of the British Prime Minister as loyal 'poodle', being dragged around by the unilateralist US administration, this backlash occurred firstly in terms of public opinion – with polling showing a dip in popular support for the US, from a high of 83 per cent approval at the end of the Clinton administration to barely a majority view, of 56 per cent, in 2006 (McNamara, 2008, 203). This was followed by what David Hastings Dunn has referred to as the period of the 'double interregnum', with the Brown government taking tactical, symbolic steps 'that were more presentational than substantial' away from the Bush administration (Dunn, 2008, 1137), such as the Foreign Secretary using the phrase 'our most important bilateral relationship' (Miliband, 2007) to describe the Anglo-American relationship. Such moves are all the more ironic, given the paroxysms of panic that seem to grip the British political and media classes if a US President fails to treat his UK counterpart with appropriate respect or fails to use the traditional, pre-ordained 'special' label to describe Anglo-American relations. Emphasising once again the role of personalities, as much as policies, in this arena, the tactical moves were relatively short-lived, with the Brown administration only too willing to scurry back in the direction of Washington DC, amongst a scrum of other political leaders, desperate to bask in the presence of the newly elected US President Barack Obama. Although short-lived – and suggestive more of an anti-Bush feeling than an anti-American one with hindsight – it needs to be borne in mind when assessing the overall impact of the Blair approach to the 'special relationship'. In fact, as Sperling has shown in some detail in his chapter, the 'special relationship' is far more robust than perhaps media and some academic commentary would suggest, reliant less on the changes of personality at the political level, important though they may be, than on the underlying levels of co-operation, of which defence is a central aspect. Defence co-operation, in terms of the identification of shared interests and enemies, the level of information exchange and shared planning and the wider defence industrial aspect, has provided a strong foundation for the 'special relationship' and ensured that it will remain a central focus of all aspects of the defence debate. While it may not be as explicit as during periods of the

Blair administration particularly, the serious work of the 'special relationship' will continue apace.

This is what Shepherd is hoping will be achieved in the related sphere of EU defence co-operation also, not least because – in the current Conservative front-bench – there is little but hostility towards both the underlying principles and practices of the EU defence element of British Defence Policy. In his conclusion, that there has been a 'European turn' in the UK's defence outlook that is ultimately 'irreversible', he draws attention to the scale and relative speed in developing both institutional processes and actual military and policing operations, including the UK led EU naval operation to combat piracy off the coast of Somalia. While noting the wider flaws and obstacles that still remain to be resolved if the EU is to have a truly credible military component (Menon, 2009; Witney, 2008), he believes that sufficient progress has already been made and credibility invested for such a component to survive the ravages of political change. In that sense, he is hoping that the European dimension of the wider transatlantic relationship will ultimately mirror the process of the US–UK relationship, propped up by committed practitioners, regardless of political changes. Yet, even he accepts – whether Euro-philes would wish to accept it or not – that the high-water mark of the UK's involvement in EU defence co-operation came during the Blair administration, with the latter part of Shepherd's assessment significantly emphasising the role played by the UK's partner at St Malo, the French, rather than the contribution made by the Brown government.

While it is unlikely that the policy will be formally reversed, in no sense should the supporters of further EU integration in this area underestimate the antipathy felt by the Conservative Party towards a process where 'every pound sterling or Euro spent on international institutions is a pound or Euro that cannot be spent equipping and supplying deployed front line troops' (Fox, 2008). Theoretically, some faint optimism may be found by focusing on the reference to 'international institutions' rather than the EU specifically, although this may say more about the antipathy of certain leading Conservative spokesmen towards the contribution made by the UN than anything else. It certainly does not apply to NATO – 'we are a NATO first party'(Cameron, 2008) – which is promoted as the central focus of any future co-operation, even with acceptance of the problems that NATO has found in the field both in Kosovo and Afghanistan. Trenchant criticism of the process begun at St Malo – where Blair 'opened Pandora's box', according to Fox, without thinking through the wider consequences of such a decision (Fox, 2008) – is one of the few consistent themes on defence to emerge from the speeches of major Conservative spokesmen. Nor can it be wholly dismissed as rhetoric, primarily to shore up the Euro-sceptic base of the wider Party in the run-up to a General Election, as the rhetoric is equally robust in private – when asked about progress in this area, one leading Conservative figure, in considering a whole range of developments, from Battlegroups to the European Defence Agency (both of which have been significantly lesser priorities under Brown than they were under Blair) summed up thus: 'the answer is no to all of this' (Interview, 2009).

As Fox himself has argued, 'there is nothing irreversible about this process at all' (Fox, 2006). Time will ultimately tell whether the Conservatives, if elected, are true to their word; if so, then the UK is likely to see a significant reorientation back towards the traditional embrace of the US, leaving the St Malo process as primarily a Blairite blip.

Home and Away – The Need to Intervene?

There is a similar theme with regard to the second relationship – the balance between external power projection and the defence of the homeland, with the Blair administration particularly – although maintained to some degree by his successor – believing that there was no choice to be made, with the former effectively guaranteeing the latter. The efficacy of military intervention has been a central theme of the era, with Blair considered the most interventionist Prime Minister since William Ewart Gladstone (Kampfner, 2004). The interventionist streak can be clearly identified in terms of the justificatory rhetoric, the operational tempo – with its wider implications for perceived overstretch within the Armed Forces, with a whole host of informed commentators queuing up to note the discrepancy between Blairite ambitions and the ultimate funding arrangements and force structures to sustain this interventionist impulse (Campbell, 2008; Cornish and Dorman, 2009a; House of Commons, 2009a) – and in terms of longer term procurement choices. Military intervention was seen not only as a means to advance the UK's wider credibility and status within the international community, but also as one of the primary instruments to meet a whole host of international challenges, be they security related – notably in the case of terrorism, as discussed earlier by this author in relation to the applicability of the roles contained within the 2002 New Chapter – and for wider humanitarian concerns. The self-branding of the UK as a 'force for good' in the world (a labelling challenged in Michael Codner's chapter) emphasised a belief in muscular humanitarian intervention that so epitomised military intervention in Kosovo in 1999 (and which some, including Steven Haines in this volume, believe was ultimately sacrificed on the road to Baghdad, as part of the post-11 September prioritising of more specific security concerns). As well as considering some of the wider consequences of this approach – in terms of its impact on the policy planning process and the management of the Armed Forces – this section will also consider the longer term future of such a policy, which has come under substantive academic – if not political – challenge.

In terms of the latter aspect, the key individual here is Paul Robinson, who views the emphasis on intervention as wholly the wrong approach, believing that it has been not only unnecessary, but ultimately counter-productive. One of the few analysts to remain involved in the wider debates surrounding British defence policy in recent years, he portrays the UK as having been involved in a policy not of defence, but offence, as 'military intervention is neither necessary for Britain's defence, nor even beneficial to it' (Robinson, 2005b, 15). He takes as his initial starting point the same baseline assumption of the SDR – that there is no immediate conventional threat to the UK homeland or its dependent territories, a position effectively reiterated in 2003, when the White Paper concluded that 'it is now clear that we no longer need to retain a capability against the re-emergence of a direct conventional strategic threat to the UK or its allies' (Ministry of Defence, 2003). Coupled with a much more reductionist position regarding the actual threat posed by international terrorism – which is not wholly shared by this author – Robinson effectively predates the more limited intervention of former Foreign Office Minister Kim Howells in the debate regarding Afghanistan by four years, proposing a far more narrow definition of what is actually in the UK's national interest. Arguing for a return to threat based planning – rather than looking at the effects that the projection of military power can initiate, as in the New Chapter – Robinson focused primarily on the defence of the territorial homeland as the most legitimate and necessary rationale for the use of military force in the post-Cold War security environment, arguing that the UK should be stripped of all but the bare essentials for territorial defence. All other potential motivations – whether it be alliance preservation, resource protection or humanitarian imperatives – are not considered essential to a genuine 'defence' policy.

The other explanations offered – that the capabilities already exist to assist in 'wars of choice', that military establishments have a vested interest in the projection of force to justify and protect budgets or the belief in the need for a precautionary principle or 'just in case scenario' in defence planning – were unacceptable, particularly as the costs of intervention, in terms of financing, manpower and reputation were too great (Robinson, 2005a). Robinson believed that far too great a price was being paid to attempt to maintain the UK's wider credibility and that it would ultimately be better for the UK to punch 'at its weight' rather than above it. Citing the Iraq war as a particular example, he went on to suggest that such interventions, in terms of the dubious legality, flawed planning assumptions and violent consequences, had not, in fact, advanced the UK's credibility, at home or within the wider international community. Finally, he argued that such a policy was equally counter-productive with regard to the UK's security, which he did not believe was threatened as the government had argued, from a combination of terrorists and their state sponsors. Rather than ensuring the security of the UK, Robinson argues that such a policy has ultimately made us less secure by increasing radicalising tendencies within aspects of the UK Muslim community and, on 7 July 2005, by bringing terrorism to the doors of the UK. In essence, he is arguing that the interventionist policy – even if it does have a longer term security rationale, in terms of the government's expressed belief that it is better to 'go to the crisis rather than have the crisis come to you' – is a good example of the 'security dilemma', with a perceived move aimed at securing the UK at a longer distance making it ultimately less secure as a consequence.

There is a need to respond directly to Robinson's arguments – for example, his overly narrow definition of the national interest, which effectively excludes wider alliance linkages, diplomatic prestige, the protection of trade and resource supplies, international legal obligations and a whole host of other potential factors that should at least warrant consideration when making such important decisions – rather than seek to side-step the arguments altogether. Just as the Blair characterisation of terrorism as a 'clash about civilisation' seems to err on the alarmist side, there is an equally valid argument to suggest that Robinson has, for example, overly minimised the nature of the continuing terrorist threat, as well as the 'fear of the unknown', to make his case for substantive cuts in the defence budget and wider capabilities. Yet, there is a problem, in presentational terms as much as anything else, in the repeated insistence of successive British politicians across the political spectrum that the motivating factor for both wider radicalisation and Islamist terrorist activity is based on the principle of 'who we are and what we believe' rather than what we have done, either historically or in more contemporary times. Such an insistence is in no small part due to a desire to portray the wider policy of military intervention – and particularly the intervention in Iraq – as effectively, at worst, cost neutral in terms of the wider security of the UK. Such a position is disputed both by those involved – see, for example, the video testimony of Mohamed Siddique Khan, one of the four suicide bombers on 7 July 2005, who branded himself a 'soldier' responding to the threat posed by the UK and its allies to the wider Muslim community (McGrory and Theodoulou, 2005) – and from within the wider political community. In fact, one political insider, considering the '4 P's' that make up the central element of the CONTEST programme – 'Prevent, Pursue, Protect, Prepare' – believed that the military could add a fifth 'P' – 'Provoke' (Interview, 2008).

Such a view needs to be delineated, rather than dismissed out of hand. To try and distract onto more insoluble factors – such as the nature of UK society, its underlying values and freedoms – at the expense of other considerations only succeeds in adding to the wider cynicism that seems ever present in contemporary political debate towards politicians generally, as it seems to be an argument driven by obvious political self-interest, trying to delink our actions as a potential cause of terrorist activity. This is not meant to suggest – as some have, such as Paul Robinson – that the UK should effectively close the door on future intervention, for fear of the consequences, in terms of potential future radicalisation and terrorist activity. It should always be remembered that the events of 11 September 2001 predate both the intervention in Afghanistan and Iraq, and stemmed, at least in part, from decisions taken by the previous Bush administration with regard to the protection of Saudi Arabia in the early 1990s.

Likewise, the underlying rationale of UK intervention more widely – that came to greater prominence in the post-11 September environment – is that it is better to 'go to the crisis, rather than have the crisis come to you'. This needs to be explored in a little more depth. While such an approach makes perfect sense in principle – who would argue with the underlying logic of protecting the UK by tackling the problem elsewhere? – the problem is that it assumes that there is some sort of choice involved, where, in an ideal world, the state gets to decide where the problem is tackled. As has been seen, you can go to the perceived crisis –

whether it be in Afghanistan or Iraq or elsewhere, as it is unlikely that the targeted terrorists will remain static – and it will ultimately come to you as well, whether as a consequence of the higher profile you have adopted or of the greater internal radicalisation initiated as a consequence of military intervention. Geoff Hoon, in 2003, explained the rationale with an interesting turn of phrase – 'we are likely to be much better off going to deal with the threat *at source*, rather than waiting for the threat to arrive at the UK' (emphasis added) (House of Commons, 2003, 42). In 2003, the UK Defence Secretary was still blissfully portraying terrorism solely as an external threat, something done to us from the outside, rather than something that can – and has – been born and bred in the UK, inculcated by a sense (however misplaced) of distance from the wider UK community, concocted by a confused sense of identity, a clash of possible loyalties and perceived slights and a growing sense of grievance, all of which can then be explained by a convenient narrative of victimhood or exploited by a more radical group. The events of 7 July 2005, coupled with the attempted attack on Glasgow Airport in 2007, led by Bilal Abdullah, who was born in Aylesbury, have led to a belated recognition that the source can equally be located at home. In fact, as Trevor C Salmon has demonstrated in his chapter – which in itself underscored the greater emphasis on external projection, by exploring the wider implications and lessons learned from the British Army's experience in Northern Ireland – there is always a need to bear the homeland dimension in mind. The resurgence of dissident Republican activity (with promises of more to come – see Rayment, 2009), coupled with greater radicalisation within sections of the UK Muslim community, serves a salutary warning that the home base and home-grown terrorism cannot be underestimated, even within the changed security calculus of the post-11 September world.

There is some recognition of this, both with the Brown administration – in terms of its handling of its Afghan commitments particularly, as well as the slow drawdown in Iraq- and the Conservative Opposition. However, before considering developments there, it is worth highlighting an aspect of the Blair administration's approach to such matters that has not perhaps had as sufficient an airing as it deserves. This relates to Blair's 1999 'Doctrine of the International Community', and Haines' conclusion that there is little evidence to suggest that the Blair approach was more widely inculcated either into defence doctrine or wider policy at the time or subsequently, in itself a useful corrective to the Robinson thesis, as well as a further indication of the division between policy-makers on one hand and those who implement and enact such policy statements on a daily basis. It is significant to note that, while both the UN and later Lord Malloch-Brown, both with revised versions of the five point model for legitimising force, continued to explore the themes, Blair himself made no serious attempt to revive the 'Doctrine' as part of his wider campaign to 'sell' the virtues of an Iraqi intervention, a position that Blair himself had considered for some time prior to the arrival of the Bush administration (D Brown, 2008). As with this author's critique of both the explanation and execution of the New Chapter framework – which seems to have limited utility for the future, particularly in relation to the targeting of state sponsors of terrorism- the 'Doctrine' seems to be a creature of its time, with even its author unprepared to return to it, even when it seemed of potential value. Additionally, having effectively widened the scope of UK operations as part of the 2002 New Chapter, from the original 'core regions' of the SDR, it was predicted as part of a wider consideration of 'the future land operational concept' that there would be a return to a more regionally specific strategic focus in the future (Joint Doctrine and Concept Board, 2008, 3)

In addition, there has been some more subtle rebalancing being carried out by both parties, as they seek to jettison some of the more controversial baggage from the Blair era. For example, although the Conservatives remain committed to military operations in Afghanistan, proposals have been floated for a separate National Home Command, to be there to support other homeland security agencies in times of emergency (Neville-Jones, 2007). It remains to be seen how this would work, alongside the existing CCRF structure and within the wider Armed Forces framework, given its current wholehearted commitment to Afghanistan. Additionally, it remains to be seen how such a development would be financed, given the stringent financial constraints that all government departments – with the exception notably of Health – will be operating under for the foreseeable future. However, when coupled with the main ideological prop of Cameron's Conservative Party in recent years – a belief in 'liberal conservatism' rather than neo-conservatism, with its greater scepticism over the utility or worthiness of bringing about democratic change by military force – this does suggest a slight change of emphasis, although within the wider context of a party signed up to supporting both current operations and the underlying security rationale that has provoked them, as was demonstrated by this author in his earlier chapter.

Likewise, the handling of announcements during 2009 by the Brown government on Afghanistan suggest a greater awareness of both public scepticism and tolerance towards the claims that have underpinned the Blair approach of preserving security at a distance. While Brown remained as invested in the defence of the Afghan operation as his predecessor, committing a further 500 troops in November 2009 – bringing the UK total to 10,000 – the delay in making the announcement and the caveated commitment suggests an incremental change in approach. Such an approach is worthy of brief consideration, as to what it suggests about the future of defence policy more generally, in terms of an even greater emphasis on burden-sharing (which is unlikely to be helped by the hostile tone adopted by the Conservative Party regarding the future of EU defence, given that part of the perceived *quid pro quo* for France's 2009 return to NATO was further progress on developing an EU defence component), military assistance and training missions – the so-called 'Afghanisation' strategy – and the sensitivity with which the issue of defence procurement is approached. His first caveat – that the troops being sent were fully and properly equipped – while meaning to be reassuring, may only have served to remind the wider public of past equipment failures. The third – relating to the need for an acceleration in the training and equipping of Afghan forces, to allow for a more rapid withdrawal of international troops – 'we will have succeeded when our troops are coming home because the Afghans are doing the job themselves' (G Brown, 2009a), also indicates a potential longer term trend highlighted in this author's earlier chapter, relating to the greater prioritisation being given to training and more military assistance, as a means to contribute towards the international efforts to counter terrorism.

While committing the additional troops before the third criteria in particular could, by definition, be demonstrated – although there were assurances from the military regarding equipment and further NATO commitments in the wake of the Obama administration's announcement of a time-limited 'surge' of 30,000 additional troops (Obama, 2009) – the Brown administration was, perhaps, signalling a more limited approach to military intervention. Account must also be taken regarding the unnecessary confusion over both the appropriateness of establishing a deadline for commencing the process of troop withdrawal (G Brown, 2009b; Sylvester et al., 2009) and the possible date for doing so, with different suggestions floated, regarding initiating the process in 2010 or 2011, before denials were issued regarding either specific deadline (G Brown, 2009b). Initially, this stood in contrast to the seemingly much clearer manner in which the Obama administration handled the same issue (Obama, 2009; Clinton, 2009), although its message was also subsequently – and relatively rapidly – muddied by contradictory signals being sent by other elements of the Obama administration (De Young, 2009; Gates, 2009). Not only is this suggestive of a somewhat chaotic policy process on both sides of the Atlantic, but also that the initial rationale – of presenting a more caveated, time limited commitment, signalling to the wider public that there are limits to the UK's interventionist approach – had to be balanced against military realities on the ground.

Making a Military Exception?

Balancing rhetoric with reality also seems to be a central consideration when considering part of the next balance – the treatment of military issues, notably the Army in this case – as separate to the wider processes and practices of domestic governance, processes that have continued regardless of the changing personalities or specific security circumstances. Before considering the 'Covenant' in more depth – although a similar criticism can be levelled, as the inflated media rhetoric during the Brown administration in particular at times obscured more than it revealed regarding the wider treatment of UK servicemen and women – the issue of the 'comprehensive approach' will be briefly highlighted. Another contemporary *cause celebre* (see House of Commons, 2009b), part of a wider cross-governmental initiative to produce more 'joined up' solutions to complex problems, the record of the Labour administration, both at home and in the field in Afghanistan, has been critically examined in this volume by Gordon, drawing on his own considerable experience of the nascent administrative arrangements underpinning such an approach, both within Whitehall and in Helmand. Significantly, having considered the initial motivations

– an ultimately unsuccessful desire to break down the stovepipes of departmentalism within Whitehall – and the nature of progress thus far, Gordon comes to the almost ironic conclusion that the problems most in need of a more 'comprehensive' solution are also those most resistant to such an approach.

Coordination needs to take place at a number of levels, at the political/strategic level, between departments and the institutions created to put further institutional flesh on the bones of the 'comprehensive approach', such as the Stabilisation Unit (SU – replacing the Post Conflict Reconstruction Unit – PCRU – in 2007), between government representatives and military personnel on the ground and between Whitehall and the operational-tactical level. Such a task would be difficult enough to achieve without considering additional political tensions, due to different administrative cultures, objectives – at times, particularly with DFID's narrowly defined and legislatively mandated focus specifically on poverty reduction, rather than as part of wider conflict prevention activities (Interview, 2009) – approaches and terminology – 'when DFID, the FCO and the MoD get into a room together, they barely understand the language they use together' (Farrell cited House of Commons, 2009b). Such tensions clearly have not been properly dissipated, even with greater levels of operational co-operation, institutional reworking and regular exhortations that everyone believes in the validity and importance of such a joint approach. In effect, part of the problem is that everyone believes in the principle, but have different ideas about how it should look in practice; as a consequence, as responsibility is effectively diffused between and across government, no-one is actually wholly responsible. One seasoned observer, commenting on the role of the SU thus far, seemed to underline this point, describing it as a 'rogue element' that had not really found its place within the potentially treacherous and territorial landscape of wider Whitehall (Interview, 2009).

There does seem to be a particular problem between the three government departments most heavily involved in foreign and defence policy. One experienced Whitehall commentator had nothing but praise for the level of co-ordination between the MoD and the Home Office during the concurrent reviews into aspects of UK counter-terrorist policy (although the fact that there were concurrent reviews suggests that the institutional response was not as comprehensive as it could have been (Interview, 2009)). In the same interview, the previously positive participant cited decisions taken by the FCO to cut its contribution to the overall budget for defence attaches by £10m, without consulting the MoD in advance of the decision. Given that the MoD, as part of the wider Defence Diplomacy role, held such posts in high esteem, giving the UK a 'more agile' approach, with valuable personal contacts maintained, the recommendation was later made to completely reverse this decision. An issue of differing priorities, exacerbated by tightening budgets – which may only get worse in the longer term – and a lack of formal (or even informal) consultation only succeeded in souring relations further.

The issue of budgets has impacted on the nature of the trilateral relationship, not least because, as a consequence of notable rates of increase in its overall budget, DFID has continued to grow, leaving the FCO looking remarkably like the poor relation as a consequence (the DFID budget sits at £9.1bn for 2010–11, exceeding the FCO's £1.7bn, although both are dwarfed by the MoD's budget totals of £36.89bn for the same period).[2] Additionally, if the Conservative Party are returned to government, DFID's budget will be protected from the wider impact of essential cuts (described as 'a purely political decision', made to avert any potential criticism from aid agencies and to protect the 'compassionate Conservative' image that has been essential to the rebranding of the modern Conservative Party (Interview, 2009)). However, there was also wider consideration of a more comprehensive use of budgets, with one political commentator noting that the commitment was to have 'ring-fenced the budget', without the same commitment to 'ring-fence the functions'. It is to be hoped that there will be a further change of culture – building on personnel changes from the Short era, when DFID was criticised for being 'particularly un-cooperative' in the immediate post-conflict situation in Iraq, allegedly because senior political personnel were unsure that the Iraqis were 'poor enough to deserve aid' (Boyce cited BBC, 2009). One suggestion made was that more of the MoD's activities, particularly in the areas of wider defence diplomacy and reconstruction, would be paid for from DFID's budget, even if the MoD and military personnel were actually undertaking the task (Interview, 2009).

This is one of a range of potential solutions that have been floated, and must be placed alongside Miliband's calls for thinking 'more radically' in terms of joint initial plans, for example single country outlooks, and more co-location of staff (Miliband, 2008), so that underlying bureaucratic cultures can be broken down (once again indicating an underlying theme regarding the wider area of defence policy, the distinction between the political level and the bureaucratic, administrative level). This idea has been given further consideration by former CGS General Sir Richard Dannatt, who is likely to take a prominent place in the national security apparatus of a future Conservative government. Dannatt suggested that it would be a good idea to place military officers in other government departments, so as to bring a more baseline level of experience sharing, thereby potentially breaking down persistent cultural barriers – 'Why not have a captain spending two years with DFID before returning to a deployment in Afghanistan?' (Dannatt, 2007). Engrained departmental cultures are not the only obstacle; the issue of personality and leadership also features as a central concern. One commentator noted that, during the brief tenure of John Reid as Defence Secretary, co-operation at least at the political level was better, with the so-called 'Reid Group' ensuring that senior members of all three departments and the security services came together on a regular basis to collectively monitor progress, particularly in Afghanistan (Interview, 2009). Without such leadership there is a danger of departmental drift, yet, with one department taking overall charge, there is equally a danger that the solution agreed will be skewed towards its own particular priorities – 'if only one actor dominates the Comprehensive Approach, they are likely to emphasise those tasks in which they have a comparative advantage' (Chalmers cited House

---

2   See each Department's own website for details of individual budgets.

of Commons, 2009b). Even with all of these problems, there seems to be a general determination to continue with the process.

The issue of privatisation – and the contribution and commitment that both PMCs and PSCs should play within wider British defence and foreign policy – has not been embraced quite as readily. As part of what Deakin refers to as a 'managerial' approach to wider government – with the MoD heavily involved in wider Private Finance Initiatives (PFIs), with 48 such projects committed to during 2008–09 (UK Defence Statistics, 2009) – greater prominence has been given to the roles and responsibilities of private companies across the military spectrum (Singer, 2005, 2007; Simons, 2004; Scahill, 2007). Stephen Deakin, in his chapter in this volume, as well as considering some of the more traditional concerns regarding the greater use of private entities within the sensitive area of defence – in terms of the balance of costs, the lingering image of mercenary behaviour, the issue of wider enforcement and regulation – also raises the wider issue of a clash of ethics between traditional militaries and the process of privatisation more generally. While the 'Values and Standards' of the British Army are particularly important in terms of developing not only esprit de corps but also a wider sense of professionalism – and therefore anything that threatens to tarnish such a reputation, even by association, is to be resisted – in a time of economic restriction it remains to be seen whether such arguments will carry as much sway as perhaps they might have done, given that 'the overall process may be brilliant from a business standpoint' (Singer, 2005, 510).

There is also a need to keep in perspective the nature of the debate within the UK. Many of the most egregious examples of law-breaking and unethical behaviour come from US based companies, where the size of the private military and security sector is significantly larger. In its 2009 assessment of the requirements for regulation – a useful step in reassuring wider concerns, as part of the regulation process would be greater scrutiny of training, personnel and ethical standards for such companies formally embraced by such a process – the FCO estimated that there were at most 30 small companies registered in or operating from the UK (Foreign and Commonwealth Office, 2009, 23). In addition, it is estimated that approximately 95 per cent of such activity is focused on the far less newsworthy and innocuous activities of risk analysis, consultancy, Security Sector Reform (SSR) and asset protection, which showed a brief growth in activity during the immediate post-Iraq invasion (Interview, 2009). The UK also used – as of mid-2009 – only five PMCs in Iraq for close protection work, static guarding and wider police work.

However, there have been complaints – from within the PMC/PCS industry and wider – that the government has not effectively grasped the nettle of regulation, which would be a useful step in providing the greater legitimacy and credibility that the industry requires, to separate themselves out from the excesses of wider elements of the PMC community particularly. One experienced commentator on such matters was sceptical about the very nature of governmental consultation, which he noted had been on-going for over 10 years. While everyone knew that effective regulation was required, the government did not seem to want to lead; in effect, he equated the process to being 'like walking through treacle' (Interview, 2009). Such hesitation was effectively 'inhibiting' the greater use of such private companies, with the government preferring to rely on a wider international process – with all the complications that has in terms of increasing the number of participants and legal codes – or a greater level of self-regulation and enforcement by the industry itself (Interview, 2009). In its impact assessment, which considered a range of issues – including licensing of either individual operations or specific activities – the government came down in favour of self-regulation, which had the 'advantage' of voluntary buy-in by the industry, which 'therefore empowers the industry' (Foreign and Commonwealth Office, 2009, 16). It was also significantly less expensive and burdensome than the other two options explored. While the government has at last produced its view of the main options, which the industry itself has been lobbying for, a hands-off approach may not provide sufficient reassurance to the wider public. It may be a matter that has to be returned to again in the future.

There is one final aspect of the applicability debate that needs to be highlighted. It concerns the use of Public Service Agreements (PSA), effectively a wider governmental process of target setting, which, while appropriate within aspects of domestic policy, seems more difficult to justify within the wider sphere of defence and particularly its contribution to foreign policy, in part because it is far more difficult to determine cause and effect between specific UK actions and 'results' on the ground. The two tranches of reviewing – from 2004 to 2008, and subsequently – are worth considering in a little more depth to illustrate the point. In addition, they serve as the public 'scorecard' for measuring progress across a whole range of issues, from equipment provision to force readiness, from conflict prevention to the wider contribution of the UK to the development of the ESDP (in itself an example of joined up government, as it is a shared assessment with the FCO). Three overall targets were established – 'to achieve success in the military tasks we undertake at home and abroad' (Objective 1), 'to be ready to respond to the tasks that might arise' (Objective 2) and to 'build for the future' (Objective 3) – which are then subdivided into six separate target areas, which are self-evaluated by the MoD (and somewhat scathingly critiqued by the Defence Select Committee) (Ministry of Defence, 2008a–b; House of Commons, 2009a). In essence they also demonstrate a further balance to be maintained, as far as it is possible, between current operations – presentism – and preparations for the future and potentially the unknown.

Considering the review of the MoD's performance during the 2004–08 period first of all – the most complete analysis in terms of both assessing a full PSA period and accompanied by more independent assessment from the Defence Select Committee available at the time of writing – the MoD concluded that it had met one target from six, partly met four targets and completely failed to meet the final target area, in terms of force generation for future tasks, given the ever greater concentration on Afghanistan (although, interestingly, in 2006, at the first interim assessment stage, the MoD was confident that it was 'on course' to meet all of the targets, a situation dismissed with customary understatement by the MoD Permanent Secretary, Sir Bill Jeffrey as a 'bit of institutional over-optimism' (House of Commons, 2009a, 21).

On the face of it, this seems a useful process of accountability – even if there is some confusion as to when the assessment 'partly met' is utilised. This was particularly the case with regard to the somewhat vague and amorphous 'improved effectiveness of UK and international support for conflict prevention', which was considered 'partly met' when only two of the 12 sub-areas were considered to have been achieved, leading the Defence Committee to complain that it was 'not clear what the relative weight and subjectivity of these sub targets is nor is it clear to what extent each of the 12 sub targets were only partially met' (House of Commons, 2009a, 22). Yet, in his defence of this performance, then Defence Secretary John Hutton actually indicated the wider problem with this process, protesting that 'I hope people can cut us some slack on failing in the time of this annual report to actually deliver peace in the Middle East' (Hutton cited House of Commons, 2009a). This point is well made, given the intractable nature of the problem, the wider international context in which it operates and the fact that 'the MoD's own direct influence in relation to some of its objectives will be necessarily limited' (House of Commons, 2009a, 23). While there were areas that were both statistically measurable and directly controlled by the MoD or the wider British government – in terms of force readiness levels, trained strength or Key User requirements for equipment provision and procurement – the wider aspects of foreign policy delivery on the ground seemed wholly inappropriate as a means of assessing the MoD's wider performance. Interestingly, the MoD was subsequently – as part of the 2008–09 assessment and beyond – subsumed within wider PSAs, controlled by the FCO and the Home Office, the former relating to conflict prevention, the latter in relation to counter-terrorism (Ministry of Defence, 2009b), a further example of the institutionalisation of the 'comprehensive approach'. Such assessments will help, however, in consideration of the final balance to be considered, namely the relationship between manpower and technology.

Assuring Assets – Manpower and Technology

The issue of balance seems assured here, as the popular and political narrative is that, as a direct consequence of the Labour government's inability to square a relatively restrained resources base (with differing statistics and statements depending on the nature of the relative comparison being made) and a more intervention minded political leadership, both manpower – in terms of both the rate and scale of tasks that the military, notably the Army, has been asked to undertake – and equipment provision has suffered as a consequence. Although a central concern of both Forster, in terms of the wider management of the Armed Forces and the impact that an increased operational tempo has had on the quality of life for the Armed Forces, and Codner, with a particular focus on procurement, it is a theme that runs throughout the volume as a whole.

In an earlier section, the issue of limits – either formal or informal – on the scope of additional troop commitments to Afghanistan in 2009 was highlighted. Of course, such limits have existed in policy since the 1998 SDR, in the form of 'scales of effort' and subsequently 'harmony guidelines'. Yet, it remains the case that the level of commitment, particularly for the Army, is running significantly higher than that which was either initially expressed or amended – 'the current operations we are running is about three times above the levels at which the assumptions place us' (House of Commons, 2009c). The Armed Forces have effectively continued to operate for the past seven years above the overall level of concurrent operations for which they are resourced and structured to manage within. There are a number of consequences to this sustained tempo – even considering the drawdown of UK troops in Iraq – both for future preparedness and in terms of its wider impact on manpower more generally (or at least the popular perception thereof). In its 2009 assessment, the Defence Select Committee warned that 'the current level of sustained operational commitments puts at risk the … ability to prepare for potential future missions' (House of Commons, 2009a, 16). Certainly the MoD's own assessment with regard to this issue remains relatively pessimistic, although showing some small signs of improvement during 2009. In its 2008 assessment, it reached the blunt conclusion that objectives over the four year period of assessment had not been met, taking into account the level of physical deployability and 'serious or critical weaknesses' incurred by each service. In the second quarter of 2009, the percentage of force elements not showing a serious or critical weakness had risen slightly, from 39 to 42 per cent, although the wider outlook remained a matter for concern (Ministry of Defence, 2009b, 6). Given the stated priority of the government and the Armed Forces is to ensure success in Afghanistan – however that is being defined – such an outcome is not surprising, although care needs to be taken to ensure that future preparedness is not ultimately sacrificed for current operations. The MoD noted in 2008 that 'we simply do not know how long it will take to restore a generic contingent capacity in line with Defence Planning Assumptions' (House of Commons, 2009a). Equally, the potential impact on current operations in Afghanistan in terms of the UK's wider credibility, morale and the image of both government and Armed Forces has to be borne in mind when considering any attempt to rebalance in order to meet wider readiness targets. There is also a wider political issue here and it refers to the value of such 'Harmony Guidelines' in the first place, given that experience has shown that 'standardised scales of effort … rarely match the demands of military campaigns and the imperatives for success on operations' (Dannatt, 2007). Their value must ultimately be called into question as a tool of wider policy if they are continually broken on a year by year basis. This is a matter that the next SDR will have to consider.

Interestingly, given the wider publicity surrounding the impact of operations on the treatment and quality of life of military personnel – which crystallised into a highly visible political campaign to uphold the 'Military Covenant' – the evidence from service personnel themselves does not fully seem to back up this point. This is only one aspect of a much wider consideration, taking into account standards of accommodation, health care, provision of sufficient equipment in a timely manner, veterans care, visibility of Armed Forces personnel, legal restrictions and the adoption of wider societal standards to name but a few. These were examined in more depth in Forster's chapter, the cumulative effect of which led him to argue that 'the current challenges faced by the armed forces are the greatest since the ending of conscription in 1962'. However, there is a need for greater contextualisation, both on the specific issue of operational impact, in terms of the regularity of tours particularly, and the wider issue of the 'Military Covenant', which became a touchstone issue in the press and popular discourse regarding the Brown government's handling of matters military more generally. In terms of operational impact, the Armed Forces Continuous Attitude Surveys for both 2007 and 2008 – while highlighting a range of issues which caused greater dissatisfaction within the military – told a slightly different story. In 2007, while 38 per cent of those surveyed felt that the frequency of tours was too great, 51 per cent thought that the pace was 'about right', with a further 11 per cent arguing that it was not high enough. Similarly, when asked about the impact of the frequency of operations, 59 per cent declared themselves either to be unaffected or encouraged to stay by the frequency of operations, compared to 41 per cent, who stated that it would increase their likelihood of leaving the Armed Forces (Ministry of Defence, 2008c, 24–32). In 2008, the last full survey material available at the time of writing, the situation seemed to have improved even further, with 55 per cent (a 4 per cent rise) believing that the pace of tours was 'about right', compared to 34 per cent believing they were too high (a corresponding 4 per cent drop) (Ministry of Defence, 2009a, Annex 1). In part, the differences may reflect different experiences depending on what part of the Armed Forces the individual was based in, as there has clearly not been a uniform impact across or within the three services. In the 2009 Ministry of Defence assessment, the Army registered 28 so-called pinch points, where the situation regarding potential overstretch is more keenly felt (Ministry of Defence, 2009b, 10–11). Such statistics need to be borne in mind in terms of wider context in what became a very politically charged debate (Harvey, 2008; Forsyth, 2008).

Additionally, it should also be remembered that – perhaps contrary to wider public belief – the 'Military Covenant' is not a legally binding document, although it clearly embodies the wider moral obligations to be carried out by all sides, not simply the government. It is also at present Army specific rather than tri-service, having been drawn up as part of the wider Army 'Values and Standards' in 2000. It should also be remembered that some of the wider problems highlighted in a series of campaigns, both by relevant charities, former senior military personnel and others, were not solely the responsibility either of Gordon Brown or even the Labour government, having longer term roots than that, as was the case for military accommodation, for example. Equally, this should not wholly diminish the part that decisions, financial and otherwise, taken by the Labour government have played, as part of a much wider context, as discussed by Forster. While a proliferation of different proposals have been put forward, both by the government and the leading opposition parties, it is interesting to note that – in the Forsyth Commission established by David Cameron to examine the state of play in this area – all of the proposals made would have to be met within the current defence budget (Forsyth, 2008, 40). Given such potentially stringent financial constraints – outlined in some depth by Chalmers (Chalmers, 2009) – there will be a need to prioritise, with a particular focus of a potential Conservative government being on creating a mental health care service for military personnel and 'through life' care for veterans (Interview, 2009). As yet, no party – while accepting the need to broaden the Covenant to cover all three services – has committed itself to the idea of a more legally binding commitment, despite the Labour government's greater interest in setting legally binding commitments in other aspects of the wider public service, such as in terms of delivery of health care. Given the potential complexities of such a move, this may be one area where the preference is to treat the military as separate from wider public sector and governmental processes.

The other aspect of this relationship refers to equipment provision, another matter that has been given significant public airing, in terms of a litany of delayed projects, delayed delivery and procurement over-runs that are 'so endemic' that they have 'almost lost their power to shock' (Gray, 2009, 15). As such, this is not the place to go into such details, many of which are examined as part of Codner's assessment of how procurement fits within the wider deliberations regarding future strategy. It will serve to indicate the growing gulf between a range of assessments, carried out both by the MoD internally and external bodies, most significantly the 2009 Gray report into the wider processes of procurement. In 2008, the MoD's self-assessment was that the objective of 'delivering the equipment programme to cost and time' was 'partly met'; a National Audit Office report of the same year, examining the 20 largest procurement projects, found that the 'aggregate forecast cost of these projects increased by £205 million and the aggregate in-service date slippage increased by eight years' (cited House of Commons, 2009a 28). The following year, a similar discrepancy emerged, with the MoD's interim assessment highlighting at least one sub-category where it was 'exceeding target', with an average In Service Date (ISD) slippage of 1.4 months, compared to an average of 4.3 months in the previous report (although over a longer time-frame) (Ministry of Defence, 2008, 24; Ministry of Defence, 2009, 14).

However, such slight optimism must be placed within the wider context of the Gray report's findings, which make for troubling reading whoever ultimately ends up with the problem of generating genuinely 'smart' procurement (a problem for governments of all colours, not simply the Blair and Brown administrations). Its overall assessment was that there was 'average programme overruns by 80 per cent or over five years from the time specified at initial approval through to in service dates', with an average increase in costs of approximately 40 per cent (Gray, 2009, 7). His report estimated that 'between £1bn and £2.2bn is being lost each year as a result of the failure to control the overheated programme' (Gray, 2009, 38), although this figure was disputed by the government (Davies, 2009). One of the more controversial aspects of his assessment was that 'many participants in the procurement system have a vested interest in optimistically mis-estimating the outcome' (Gray, 2009, 19), due in part to inter-service competition and insufficient supervision. This may in part explain his recommendation of greater private involvement (Gray, 2009, 198), as part of a wider series of proposals, including fully costed reviews at the outset.

Finally, there is one specific aspect of wider defence equipment that deserves individual consideration, hence why it was given a chapter on its own – the maintenance and continuation of the UK's independent nuclear deterrent. Smith, in his detailed assessment, demonstrated the essential continuity in the Blair and Brown approach towards this question, even within the changing security environment of the post-11 September world (notwithstanding Blair's efforts to link the continued nuclear deterrent to the existence of state sponsors of terrorism, as part of the wider perceived nexus between international terrorists, rogue states and WMD – this should be considered in the context of this author's conclusions regarding the paucity of state sponsors to consider conventional military operations against, let alone a potential nuclear response). As with their predecessors, the Labour governments have essentially held firm to the concept of 'existential deterrence', a situation that Smith does not believe is likely to change, arguing that it is 'unlikely that the next change of government will usher in any significant re-evaluation of nuclear policy and doctrine'. This position has been criticised by the likes of Nick Ritchie, who has argued that the debate needs to move beyond 'simplistic arguments' regarding existential deterrence (Ritchie, 2009, 82), offering instead a slightly different position appraising the normative value of nuclear weapons in a changed security and political environment, considering the greater emphasis on nuclear disarmament as a central aspiration of the Obama foreign policy, rather than a critique of the Blair and Brown view of nuclear weapons. The US dimension is clear here, although interestingly, even within a potentially more stringent financial environment and with the possibility of sending a signal to the wider international community that the linkage between nuclear weapons and national security can be broken (McGwire, 2006, 643), the UK debate avoids even the slightest suggestion that it could shelter under a wider US nuclear guarantee, despite the continued existence of the 'special relationship' and unofficial suggestions that the US should consider extending its nuclear umbrella to the wider Middle East, to counter the possibility of Iranian nuclear proliferation (Lakshmanan, 2009). Such a move would be exceptionally controversial, although it might square the circle between a diminished budget and undiminished protection. Independence and credibility are still viewed as a price worth paying by Blair, Brown and Cameron, in much the same way as they were by Ernest Bevin, who insisted that 'we've got to have the bloody Union Jack on it' (cited in Newsinger, 2008). In an otherwise changing world, in terms of both security and politics, the nuclear dimension remains stubbornly constant.

Conclusion – The SDR Next Steps

This volume has produced the first comprehensive study of New Labour's defence policy. This has been done in two ways. Firstly, in terms of the time-period covered, taking into account both the Blair and Brown governments and, where appropriate, looking forward to consider how a Conservative government would act if confronted with the same issues. Secondly, it has considered a wide range of key defence and security issues, from the projection of force, both to counter terrorism and to provide humanitarian assistance, to the sustenance of key alliances and relationships, from the provision of an independent nuclear deterrent to the management of defence policy and its location across government, within the wider confines of private agencies and within society as a whole. Yet, even in producing the first extended contemporary analysis of New Labour's defence policy, the analysis raises as many questions as it has answered.

- What is the long-term vision of the UK's role within wider international affairs? What are the likely changes in the international security environment and how will this impact on the UK generally and the UK Armed Forces specifically?
- How can credibility be maintained and measured with regard to defence and the wider aspects of foreign policy? What price tag should be placed on it, particularly within straitened economic circumstances?
- What is the underlying purpose of an interventionist defence policy, in terms of both British and international security? Who should it be targeted at, particularly in relation to the current contemporary focus on international Islamist terrorism?
- Where does an independent nuclear deterrent fit within this framework? Can the UK continue to afford a policy predicated on the principle of 'existential deterrence'?
- How should such a policy be organised, in terms of potential alliance partners both in the US and with the EU, particularly in light of the perceived hostility of the Conservative Party particularly towards the European dimension? Is the perceived 'European turn' genuinely irreversible?
- In addition, what is the longer term role for private military or security companies? Should the government seek to initiate a more tightly structured regulatory framework for PMC/PSCs, so as to increase confidence in their wider usage within defence policy? What emphasis should be placed on issues of ethos in this debate?
- How does such an approach fit within the so-called 'comprehensive approach', in terms of its relationship with wider security actors within government and beyond, given the greater interest of organisations such as the EU and NATO with regard to organising a wider comprehensive approach? Can such an approach ever actually be achieved?
- Should the Military Covenant be made more binding? How would this look, both for the Army and as a wider tri-service document?
- Where should the government's financial priorities lie, with a burgeoning equipment programme or the provision of adequate working conditions for the Armed Forces? Can genuinely 'smart' procurement be achieved, in light of the devastating conclusions of the Gray Report?

These are just some of the wide-ranging questions that remain to be properly answered as the UK prepares for its first Strategic Defence Review in twelve years. In talking about the possibility of organising such a review, should the Conservatives be returned to government in 2010, William Hague, the Shadow Foreign Secretary, argued that the focus should be 'not on whether Britain should be able to project military force elsewhere in the world but how it will do so' (Hague, 2009). In this, he has some academic support from the likes of Cornish and Dorman, who, in speculating about the form of a future defence review, considered that 'the forthcoming defence review might be able to spend less time on the high politics of Britain's place in the world and more time ensuring that the defence mission can be met' (Cornish and Dorman, 2009a, 742). In part, this is because they believe the political and security environment is 'hardly likely to be conducive to a carefully considered full scale review' (Cornish and Dorman, 2009b, 261). While remaining aware of the various constraints a future review will be working under – the legacy inherited from 12 years of Labour government, which has been the primary focus of this volume, as well as the deteriorating financial situation – which will place even greater stress on the choices that are to be made (Chalmers, 2009) – and the continuing UK military commitment to Afghanistan – the approach advocated by both practitioner and academics seems somewhat limited.

Given that the original plan was for a second review five years into the SDR process – a position claimed by Cornish and Dorman, supported in the Gray report (Cornish and Dorman, 2009a, 252; Gray, 2009, 22) – before the events of 11 September allegedly got in the way, their reluctance to advocate a more wide ranging review after 12 years seems difficult to sustain. Also, it is difficult to envisage when would be a good time to hold it; while the situation is not ideal, the legacy of experience gained over the past 12 years and the imperative of financial restrictions – which will provoke cuts with or without a wider consideration of the strategic environment in which the UK will have to operate – seems to point in the direction of the political consensus regarding a 2010 review. This will become an even greater imperative should the government change. However, Hague's approach seems equally limiting. A focus on the mechanics of defence policy, notably in the area of procurement, while important, are surely a second order question, as Michael Codner has demonstrated in this volume, to be influenced and adapted once decisions have been taken regarding the wider structure and strategic outlook of defence and foreign policy more generally, whether it be a 'force for good', 'a force for honour' – as Codner advocates – or some further formulation. Asking such questions and scrutinising both the underlying assumptions and policy outcomes – of *all* aspects of defence policy – is not a distraction from the 'defence mission', but the essential completion of it. What is surely required is a more 'comprehensive' review, taking into account precisely the 'high politics' that Cornish and Dorman seem so opposed to – placing defence within a wider framework of security (and therefore ensuring that more than the voices of the MoD and the defence establishment are heard in the process of the review), considering the UK's role in the world, what it wishes to achieve and where military instruments, in a range of formats, can contribute effectively to such goals. To do anything other than this, both in these specific areas, and in the overall strategic thrust of defence policy more generally, would be an opportunity missed.

Bibliography

BBC (2009), 'Clare Short's post Iraq staff 'told to do nothing'' 3 December – http://news.bbc.co.uk/1/hi/uk_politics/8393358.stm

Blair, T (2007), 'What I've learned', *The Economist* 2 June

Brown, D (2008), 'Britain: Cheerleader for the US in the "War on Terror"?' in Eder, F and Senn, M (eds) *Europe and Transatlantic Terrorism: Assessing Threats and Counter-measures* (Berlin: Nomos)

Brown, G (2009a), *Statement by the Prime Minister to the House of Commons on Afghanistan and Pakistan on 14 October 2009* (London: Hansard)

Brown, G (2009b), *Statement by the Prime Minister to the House of Commons on Afghanistan and Pakistan on 30 November 2009* (London: Hansard)

Cameron, D (2008), *The Crossroads for NATO: How the Atlantic Alliance Should Work in the Twenty-First Century – Speech by the Leader of the Opposition to Chatham House on 1 April 2008* (London: Conservative Party)

Campbell, M (2008), *No Choice but Change: The Military Covenant in its Strategic Context* (London: Liberal Democrats)

Chalmers, M (2008), *British Security Policy in Transition: Paper for RUSI's British Security Policy Programme* (London: RUSI)

Chalmers, M (2009), 'Preparing for the lean years', *RUSI Future Defence Review Working Paper* 1

Clinton, H (2009), *Statement of Secretary of State Hilary Clinton to the Senate Foreign Relations Committee on 3 December 2009* (Washington, DC: US Senate)

Codner, M (2007), 'British Defence Policy: Rebuilding national consensus', *RUSI Journal* 152/2, 18–23

Cornish, P and Dorman, A (2009a), 'Blair's wars and brown's budgets: From strategic defence review to strategic decay in less than a decade', *International Affairs* 85/2, 247–61

Cornish, P and Dorman, A (2009b), 'National Defence in the age of austerity', *International Affairs* 85/4, 733–53

Daddow, O (2009), 'Tony's war? Blair, Kosovo and the interventionist impulse in British Foreign Policy', *International Affairs* 85/3, 547–60

Dannatt, R (2007), *Speech by the Chief of the General Staff, General Sir Richard Dannatt to the International Institute for Strategic Studies on 21 September 2007* (London: IISS)

Dannatt, R (2009), *Speech by the Chief of the General Staff, General Sir Richard Dannatt to the Institute for Public Policy Research on 19 January 2009* (London: IPPR)

Davies, Q (2009), *Oral questions to the Ministry of Defence in the House of Commons on 2 November 2009* (London: Hansard)

De Young, K (2009), 'Gates: "No deadline" on Afghanistan troop withdrawals', *The Washington Post* 4 December

Dunn, DH (2008), 'The "double interregnum": US-UK relations beyond Blair and Bush', *International Affairs* 84/6

Foreign and Commonwealth Office (2009), *Private Military and Security Companies: Impact Assessment* (London: HMSO)

Fox, L (2006), *The Europeanisation of Defence – Speech by the Shadow Defence Secretary on 19 June 2006* (London: Conservative Party)

Fox, L (2008), *Britain, Europe and NATO: Heading in the Wrong Direction – Speech by the Shadow Defence Secretary on 31 January 2008* (London: Conservative Party)

Gates, R (2009), *Statement of Secretary of Defense Robert Gates to the Senate Foreign Relations Committee on 3 December 2009* (Washington, DC: US Senate)

Hague, W (2009), *The Future of British Foreign Policy with a Conservative Government – Speech by the Shadow Foreign Secretary to the International Institute of Strategic Studies on 21 July 2009* (London: Conservative Party)

Home Office (2006), *The United Kingdom's Strategy for Countering International Terrorism* (London: HMSO)

Home Office (2009), *The United Kingdom's Strategy for Countering International Terrorism* (London: HMSO)

House of Commons (2003), *A New Chapter to the Strategic Defence Review: Sixth Report of the Defence Select Committee in May 2003* (London: HMSO)

House of Commons (2008), *Recruiting and Retaining Armed Forces Personnel: Fourteenth Report by the Defence Select Committee on 15 July 2008* (London: HMSO)

House of Commons (2009a), *Ministry of Defence Annual Report and Accounts 2007–08 – Fifth Report by the Defence Select Committee on 18 March 2009* (London: HMSO)

House of Commons (2009b), *Oral Contributions on the Comprehensive Approach to the Defence Select Committee during June–July 2009* (London: HMSO)

House of Commons (2009c), *Readiness and Recuperation for the Contingent Tasks of Today – Testimony by Lieutenant General Sir Graham Lamb to the Defence Select Committee on 3 February 2009* (London: HMSO)

House of Commons (2009d), *Readiness and Recuperation for the Contingent Tasks of today – Testimony by Defence Secretary John Hutton to the Defence Select Committee on 28 April 2009* (London: HMSO)

House of Lords (2007), *Debate on Defence on 27 November* (London: HMSO)

Howells, K (2009), 'It's time to pull out of Afghanistan and take the fight to Bin Laden in Britain', *The Guardian* 3 November

Hutton, J (2009), *Ministerial Statement by the Defence Secretary to the House of Commons on 11 February 2009* (London: Hansard)

Joint Doctrine and Concept Board (2008), *The Future Land Operational Concept 2008* (London: Joint Doctrine and Concept Board)

Kagan, R (2004), *Of paradise and power: America and Europe in the new world order* (London: Atlantic Books)

Kampnfer, J (2004), *Blair's Wars* (London: Free Press)

Lakshmanan, I (2009), 'Iran might be deterred by US nuclear umbrella, Gulf ally says', *Bloomberg News* 9 April – http://www.bloomberg.com/apps/news?pid=20601070&sid=aOSbraDk5bvI

Lunn, J, Miller, V and Smith, B (2008), *British Foreign Policy Since 1997: House of Commons Research Paper 08/56* (London: HMSO)

McGrory, D and Theodoulou, M (2005), 'Suicide bomber's confession blames Iraq war', *The Times* 2 September

McNamara, S (2008), 'Is the 'Special Relationship' still 'special'?', *Journal of International Security Affairs* Spring

Menon, A (2009), 'Empowering paradise? The ESDP at Ten', *International Affairs* 85/2

Meyer, C (2005), *DC Confidential* (London: Weidenfeld and Nicolson)

Miliband, D (2007), *New Diplomacy: Challenges for Foreign Policy – Speech by the Foreign Secretary to Chatham House on 19 July 2007* (London: HMSO)

Miliband, D (2008), *Speech by the Foreign Secretary to the FCO Leadership Conference on 4 March 2007* (London: HMSO)

Ministry of Defence (1998), *The Strategic Defence Review: Modern Forces for a Modern World* (London: HMSO)

Ministry of Defence (2007), *Ministry of Defence Plan 2007* (London: HMSO)

Ministry of Defence (2008a), *Annual Report and Accounts for 2006–07* (London: HMSO)

Ministry of Defence (2008b), *Annual Report and Accounts for 2007–08: Volume One* (London: HMSO)

Ministry of Defence (2008c), *Armed Forces Continuous Attitude Survey Results 2007* (London: HMSO)

Ministry of Defence (2008d), *The Future Land Operational Concept 2008: Report by the Joint Doctrine and Concept Board* (London: HMSO)

Ministry of Defence (2009a), *Armed Forces Continuous Attitude Survey Results 2008* (London: HMSO)

Ministry of Defence (2009b), *MOD Public Sector Agreement – Autumn Performance Report 2008–09* (London: HMSO)

Mullen, M (2009), *Statement of Chairman of the Joint Chiefs of Staff Admiral Michael G Millen before the Senate Foreign Relations Committee on 3 December 2009* (Washington, DC: US Senate)

Newsinger, J (2008), 'America right or wrong: Anglo-American relations since 1945', *Monthly Review* December

Niblett, R (2007), 'Choosing between America and Europe: A new context for British Foreign Policy', *International Affairs* 83/4

Obama, B (2009), *Address to the nation by the President of the United States on the way forward in Afghanistan and Pakistan on 1 December 2009* (Washington, DC: Office of the White House)

Rayment, S (2009), 'Real IRA plans "Christmas spectacular"', *The Sunday Telegraph* 6 December

Ritchie, N (2009), 'Deterrence dogma? Challenging the relevance of British nuclear weapons', *International Affairs* 85/1

Robinson, P (2005a), 'Are we wasting money on defence?', *The Spectator* 9 July

Robinson, P (2005b), *Doing Less with Less: Making Britain More Secure* (London: Imprint Academic)

Scahill, J (2007), *Blackwater: The Rise of the World's Most Powerful Mercenary Army* (London: Serpent's Tail)

Seldon, A, Snowdon, P and Collings, D (2007), *Blair Unbound* (London: Simon and Schuster)

Simons, D (2004), Occupation for hire: Private military companies and their role in Iraq', *RUSI Journal* 149/3

Singer, PW (2005), 'Outsourcing war', *Foreign Affairs* March/April

Singer, PW (2007), *Corporate Warriors: The Rise of the Privatized Military Industry* (Cornell: Cornell University Press)

Sylvester, R, Thomson, A and Elliott, F (2009), 'Bob Ainsworth: UK can't back Obama pledge on Afghan pullout', *The Times* 5 December

Taylor, C and Waldeman, T (2008), *British Defence Policy since 1997: House of Commons Research Paper 08/57* (London: HMSO)

UK Defence Statistics (2009), 'MoD Payments on Private Finance Initiative Projects 2008–09' – http://www.dasa.mod.uk/modintranet/UKDS/UKDS2009/c1/table112.html

Wallace, W (2005), 'The collapse of British Foreign Policy', *International Affairs* 82/1

Witney, N (2008), *Re-energising Europe's Security and Defence Policy* (London: European Council on Foreign Relations)

Index